DATE			

Jean Hewitt's
INTERNATIONAL
MEATLESS
COOKBOOK

Jean Hewitt's
INTERNATIONAL
MEATLESS
COOKBOOK

Over 300 Delicious Recipes, Including Many for Fish and Chicken

Times
BOOKS

Published by TIMES BOOKS, a division of
Quadrangle/The New York Times Book Co., Inc.,
Three Park Avenue, New York, N.Y. 10016

Published simultaneously in Canada by
Fitzhenry & Whiteside, Ltd., Toronto

Library of Congress Cataloging in Publication Data

Hewitt, Jean.
  Jean Hewitt's International meatless cookbook.

  Bibliography: p. 291
  Includes index.
    1. Vegetarian cookery. 2. Cookery, International.
I. Title. II. Title: International meatless cookbook.
TX837.H48 1980   641.5   79-56895
ISBN 0-8129-0918-6

Manufactured in the United States of America

Contents

Introduction

For reasons of diet, philosophy, or economy more and more people are becoming interested in lessening their consumption of red, cured, and processed meats and in increasing the quantities of complex carbohydrates, especially whole grains, fruits, and vegetables they consume. They are looking to alternate sources of protein such as peas, beans, fish, poultry, cheese, eggs, milk, and milk products.

This book was written to offer the greatest variety of good-tasting, good-looking dishes that fit into such a modified eating regime. I like to think that eating patterns have changed enough to allow a meal of a hearty soup, substantial salad, or vegetarian main dish and bread with fruit and cheese for dessert. You can stay with one cuisine or, for excitement, you can mix and match. There are no hard and fast rules, but you should try to avoid duplicating the main ingredients in more than one course and arrange combinations of flavors that go together and are pleasant to the eye and the palate.

Many will enjoy a completely vegetarian meal and will find intriguing and satisfying vegetable recipes in this book. Then it will be time to think of surprising guests with a vegetarian buffet which is a logical extension of the popular salad bar. No one is going to suffer if he or she eats all vegetarian meals (with eggs, milk, and cheese) several times a week and it could be a boon to the budget. Followers of such a regime will be eligible to join the estimated half-million part-time vegetarians.

Volumes have been written on the best ways to combine various food elements to deliver necessary protein, such as serving beans and grains (as in bread, pasta, rice, etc.) in the same meal. One general rule often quoted is that if half your daily protein comes from animal sources the other half will take care of itself. Small amounts of meat, cheese, eggs, milk, fish, or poultry can complement a vegetarian diet. Simple examples are macaroni and cheese, and cereal with milk. Details of complementary protein cooking are spelled out accurately in *Diet for a Small Planet* by Francis Moore Lappé (see bibliography) and in *Laurel's Kitchen* by Robertson, Flinders, and Godfrey (see bibliography). The special needs of pregnant and lactating women and children of different ages should be carefully noted.

Through recipes from cuisines around the world, this book illustrates how many cultures and sects have been sufficiently concerned for moral, religious, ecological, economic, or health reasons to develop meatless eating patterns. The recipes here are modern adaptations of the classics and are not intended to be completely authentic. In general, only ingredients available in most supermarkets are called for. Techniques have been simplified and shortened for contemporary North American kitchens and seasonings modified to appeal to North American tastes, which happily have become increasingly sophisticated and adventuresome in recent years as the result of travel, cooking schools, and media coverage of food. Alternatives to fats high in saturated fatty acids are given where practical and deep frying in oil has been used sparingly (because of resulting high caloric content and the inconvenience of the method) and only when essential to the texture and appearance of the finished dish. A diet high in whole grains, vegetables, and fruits and low in red, cured, and processed meats tends to be lower in calories and cholesterol. Sugar is used in few recipes and an attempt has been made to keep the salt levels on the low end of a range that promotes optimum flavor. To complete the diet, dried fruits (for iron) and fresh fruits of the season are suggested for desserts and snacks. If you are concerned that there is too little protein in an all-vegetarian meal serve a custard for dessert and milk as a beverage. Other excellent sources of protein, which the western world is discovering, include bean curd (tofu), soy beans, nuts, and seeds.

This book offers vegetable appetizers, soups, main and side dishes, and salads, as well as fish and poultry appetizers and main dishes for a varied diet that is the surest way to obtain all the nutrients the body needs for good health. Given the numerous excellent bread books (see bibliography) already on the market and the increasing availability of good whole-wheat breads with wheat germ, cracked wheat, nuts, seeds, and sprouts added, it seemed unnecessary to duplicate them here.

The full fresh flavor of quality ingredients is another bonus of part-time vegetarian eating. Some nutritionists and physicians claim extensive and specific health benefits from this kind of modified eating pattern but the evidence is not conclusive. Recently released U.S. Government Dietary Guidelines advocate lowering the total fat, salt, and sugar intakes and increasing the consumption of whole grains, fresh fruits, and vegetables.

Followed sensibly, with as wide a variety of elements as possible, I believe the part-time vegetarian diet is here to stay. Vegetarians who eat eggs, milk, and cheese are called lactoovarians; those who favor fish have been dubbed pescovegetarians, and those eating chicken pollovegetarians. Plan to rate a three-part name and enjoy good healthy eating.

Jean D. Hewitt
Westerly, R. I.

Appetizers

QUICHE PROVENCALE
(French)

Serve with a spinach and mushroom salad and top off the meal with a rich dessert.

Bake pie shell at 425° for 5 to 8 minutes, and quiche at 350° for 30 minutes.

Makes 6 appetizer or 4 main-dish servings.

1 unbaked 9-inch pie shell, homemade, frozen, or made from mix (see note)
1 small eggplant (about 1 pound)
¼ cup olive or vegetable oil
1 medium-size onion, peeled and diced (½ cup)
1 can (8 ounces) whole, peeled tomatoes, drained and diced
1 teaspoon leaf basil, crumbled
¾ teaspoon salt
¼ teaspoon freshly ground black pepper
3 extra large or jumbo eggs
1 cup light cream
1 cup (4 ounces) coarsely grated Gruyère or Swiss
¼ cup (1 ounce) freshly grated Parmesan

1.   Heat oven to 425°. Prick bottom of pie shell with a fork and bake 5 to 8 minutes, or until lightly browned. Remove from oven and set aside.
2.   Wipe eggplant with a damp paper towel and remove and discard cap. Cut eggplant crosswise into ½-inch-thick rounds. Stack a few rounds at a time and cut into ½-inch dice.
3.   Heat 3 tablespoons of the oil in a large skillet. Add eggplant and cook over moderate heat 5 minutes, or until the oil is absorbed and eggplant is beginning to brown.
4.   Add remaining oil, onion, tomato, basil, salt, and pepper and toss to blend. Cover skillet and cook 10 minutes, stirring often, or until eggplant is tender. Remove from heat.
5.   In a bowl beat eggs with cream. Stir in eggplant mixture. Pour into prepared pie shell and sprinkle with the cheeses.
6.   Reduce oven temperature to 350° and bake quiche 30 to 35 minutes, or until custard is golden and a knife inserted one inch from edge comes out clean. Remove from oven and let stand 10 minutes before serving.

Note: If using a frozen crust, purchase the large, deep-dish style if available. Any frozen ready-made crust should be thawed slightly and transferred to a standard 9-inch pie pan before baking.

EGG ROLLS
(Chinese)

Now that supermarkets are carrying more Oriental ingredients, fixing a Chinese dinner is no longer a major project.
Makes 10 appetizer servings.

10 wrappers available in many supermarkets or
1 egg, lightly beaten
1 cup lukewarm water
1 cup plus 2 tablespoons flour
¼ cup cornstarch
½ teaspoon salt
½ teaspoon sugar

Filling

1 cup chopped cooked chicken or shrimp
½ cup chopped bean sprouts
½ cup chopped water chestnuts
½ cup chopped bamboo shoots
¼ cup chopped green onions, including the green part
¼ cup chopped green pepper
2 teaspoons chopped fresh ginger root, or ½ teaspoon ground
1 teaspoon sugar
1 tablespoon soy sauce
1 egg, lightly beaten
Vegetable oil for frying

1. To make the wrappers combine the egg and water in a medium-size bowl and gradually beat in the flour, cornstarch, salt, and sugar to make a smooth mixture.
2. Heat a 10-inch skillet and brush lightly with oil. Pour in enough batter to spread and make a 5-inch square of paper-thin dough. Cook until underside is set, remove, and repeat to make 10 or more wrappers, or until all batter is used.
3. For the filling combine the chicken or shrimp, bean sprouts, water chestnuts, bamboo shoots, green onions, green pepper, ginger, sugar, and soy sauce.
4. Divide the filling among the wrappers, placing it down the center of each pancake. Fold in the sides and roll like a jelly roll. Seal edges with the beaten egg. Let sit 30 to 60 minutes.
5. Heat oil in a deep fryer to 360° and fry the egg rolls, two at a time, until golden on all sides, about 8 minutes. Drain on paper towels. Serve immediately or keep warm in a very low oven (200°).

SAMOSAS
(Indian Filled Turnovers)

Samosas make a pleasant addition to a picnic basket.
Makes 12 turnovers.

1 cup unsifted all-purpose flour
2 tablespoons butter or margarine,
  melted
1 tablespoon ground coriander
  (seeds can be ground in a blender
  or coffee mill)
½ teaspoon salt
½ cup warm water, approximately
1 pound potatoes, peeled and
  cubed
1 cup fresh or frozen peas
1 tablespoon vegetable oil
1 medium-size onion, finely
  chopped (½ cup)

1 clove garlic, finely chopped
1 teaspoon curry powder
Pinch of cayenne, optional
2 tablespoons chopped fresh
  cilantro leaves (Chinese parsley)
  or flat Italian parsley
1 tablespoon cider vinegar
½ teaspoon salt
2 teaspoons flour
Water
Vegetable oil for frying

1. Place the flour in a medium-size bowl and stir in the butter, coriander, salt, and enough water to make a soft dough. On a lightly floured
   board knead the dough until smooth and elastic, about 3 minutes.
   Cover with a damp cloth and set aside while making and cooling
   filling.
2. Place potatoes in a medium-size saucepan with hot water to a depth of
   1 inch. Cover and cook 10 minutes. Add fresh peas and cook until
   vegetables are barely tender. If frozen peas are used, cook the potato
   15 minutes, add peas, and cook 3 minutes. Drain.
3. Meanwhile heat the oil in a small skillet and sauté the onion until
   tender. Add the garlic, curry powder, and cayenne and cook, stirring,
   2 minutes.
4. Stir in the parsley, vinegar, and salt and let cool.
5. Divide the dough into 12 pieces and roll out each piece on a lightly
   floured board to a 4-inch circle. Place a heaping dessert spoonful of
   the potato filling on one side of each circle. Mix the flour with enough
   water to make a smooth brushable mixture.
6. Brush the edges of the circles with flour-water mixture. Fold over to
   make a half-moon turnover and seal with fork tines.
7. Heat 2 inches of oil in a heavy straight-sided saucepan until it registers 365° on a deep-fat thermometer. Fry the turnovers, a few at a
   time, until lightly browned, turning often. Drain on paper towels and

keep them warm while frying remainder. Alternately the turnovers can be brushed with beaten egg and baked on a greased cookie sheet in a preheated oven (425°) for about 25 minutes, or until lightly golden.

STUFFED VINE LEAVES
(Greek)

You may have to trek to a specialty food store for the vine leaves but this appetizer is worth it.
Makes about 36.

¾ cup olive or vegetable oil
1 large onion, finely chopped (1 cup)
2 cloves garlic, finely chopped
2 bunches green onions, finely chopped
¾ cup raw rice
2 tablespoons snipped fresh dillweed
2 tablespoons chopped fresh parsley

½ cup plus 2 tablespoons lemon juice
¾ teaspoon salt
¼ teaspoon freshly ground black pepper
1 cup hot water
1 jar (12 ounces) grape leaves in brine
1 cup boiling water, approximately

1. Heat ½ cup oil in a heavy skillet and sauté the onion until tender but not browned. Add the garlic and cook 1 minute.
2. Add the green onions and rice and cook, stirring, 3 minutes. Add dill, parsley, ½ cup of the lemon juice, salt, pepper, and hot water. Bring to a boil, cover, and simmer 15 minutes, or until liquid has been absorbed.
3. Rinse the grape leaves well to remove brine. Place 1 teaspoon of the rice mixture on the dull side of each leaf (if leaves are small use two). Roll up, tucking in the sides to make a neat bundle.
4. Arrange stuffed leaves in a large skillet, separating rows with sprigs of parsley. Add remaining oil, lemon juice, and boiling water to barely cover leaves in skillet. Weight the leaves down with a plate, cover, and simmer 45 minutes, adding water to skillet if needed. Cool and chill. Serve with lemon wedges.

PIROSHKI
(Russian Vegetable-filled Turnovers)

Traditionally served with borscht, piroshki are delicious
enough to stand on their own or to go into a picnic hamper.
Bake at 400° for 15 minutes.
Makes 36 turnovers.

Pastry

3 cups sifted all-purpose flour
1 teaspoon salt
1 cup (2 sticks) butter or margarine
Cold water

Filling I

2 tablespoons butter or margarine
1 medium-size onion, finely
    chopped (½ cup)
3 cups finely shredded cabbage
½ cup cottage cheese
1 hard-cooked egg, sieved
½ teaspoon salt
¼ teaspoon freshly ground black
    pepper
2 tablespoons snipped fresh
    dillweed

Filling II

2 tablespoons butter or margarine
1 medium-size onion, finely
    chopped (½ cup)
3 cups finely shredded cabbage
1½ cups cooked shrimp, coarsely
    chopped
¼ teaspoon salt
⅛ teaspoon freshly ground black
    pepper
2 tablespoons snipped fresh
    dillweed

Filling III

3 tablespoons butter or margarine
1 medium-size onion, finely
    chopped (½ cup)
1 pound mushrooms, sliced
1 cup (2 slices) fresh bread crumbs
½ teaspoon salt
¼ teaspoon freshly ground black
    pepper

1 egg lightly beaten with 1
    tablespoon water

1. To make the pastry: Place the flour and salt in a medium-size bowl.
    With a pastry blender or the fingertips blend in the butter until
    mixture resembles coarse oatmeal.
2. Using a fork stir in enough cold water, about 5 tablespoons, to make a
    stiff dough. Knead dough lightly 5 times. Chill while making one of
    the fillings.
3. To make Filling I: Melt the butter in a medium-size heavy skillet and
    sauté the onion until tender but not browned. Add the cabbage and
    cook, stirring, 6 minutes. Cover and cook until wilted and tender.
    Stir in the cheese, egg, salt, pepper, and dill. Cool.

4. To make Filling II: Melt the butter in a medium-size heavy skillet and sauté the onion until tender but not browned. Add the cabbage and cook, stirring, 6 minutes. Cover and cook until wilted. Stir in the shrimp, salt, pepper, and dill. Cool.

5. To make Filling III: Melt the butter in a medium-size skillet and sauté the onion until tender but not browned. Add the mushrooms and cook until mushrooms give up their liquid. Add crumbs, salt, and pepper. Cool.

6. On a lightly floured board roll out the pastry into an 18-inch square. Cut into 36 squares each 3 × 3 inches.

7. Preheat oven to 400°. Place 1 to 2 tablespoons of filling in the middle of each square. Brush edges with egg-water mixture and fold over into a triangle shape and seal, or fold in half to make a rectangle turnover. Place piroshki on a baking sheet, brush with remaining egg mixture, and bake at 400° for 15 minutes, or until golden.

ARTICHOKES VINAIGRETTE
(French)

Spectacular first course that can be prepared ahead.
Makes 4 appetizer servings.

4 medium-size artichokes
1 lemon, halved
  Boiling salted water
6 tablespoons olive or vegetable oil
2 tablespoons red wine vinegar
⅛ teaspoon salt
⅛ teaspoon freshly ground black pepper

1 tablespoon chopped fresh chives, or 1 teaspoon freeze-dried
1 tablespoon chopped fresh parsley
1 small onion, finely chopped (¼ cup)
2 tablespoons drained capers
2 small sour pickles, finely chopped

1. Trim the bottoms of the artichokes, rubbing all cut surfaces with half a lemon. With scissors trim the leaves and cut off the top ½ inch.

2. Place in a single layer in a saucepan that they just fit. Squeeze lemon juice from the second half lemon over, cover with boiling water, and cook, covered, 40 minutes, or until bottom stalk is tender.

3. Remove with a slotted spoon and drain upside down. Cool and when they can be handled push down to open up the leaves. Remove the choke. Cover and chill.

4. Meanwhile to make vinaigrette dressing combine remaining ingredients and whisk or shake to blend. Serve artichokes filled with vinaigrette dressing inside for dipping.

GUACAMOLE
(Mexican)

A chunky version of an old favorite.
Makes about 3 cups.

2 ripe medium-size avocados, peeled and pitted

2 tablespoons red wine vinegar or lime juice

1 tablespoon olive or vegetable oil, optional

1 teaspoon salt

1 teaspoon finely chopped garlic

8 drops liquid red pepper seasoning, or 1 to 2 jalapeño peppers, seeded and chopped

¼ cup diced red onion

1 medium size ripe tomato, diced (½ cup)

1 small green pepper, diced (½ cup)

1. Mash the avocado to a lumpy purée with the vinegar, oil, salt, garlic, and red pepper seasoning. Fold in remaining ingredients.
2. To prevent guacamole from darkening, cover surface with a square of plastic wrap. To prevent leaks, place another piece of plastic wrap across top of bowl. Chill 2 hours or longer before serving. Taste for seasoning, adding more salt, pepper seasoning, vinegar, or garlic if needed. Serve with raw vegetable or taco chip dippers or on shredded salad greens.

AVOCADO AND ARTICHOKE HEARTS VINAIGRETTE
(American)

Two popular California products combined with a simple dressing.
Makes 6 to 8 appetizer servings.

½ teaspoon finely chopped garlic

1 teaspoon salt

½ cup lemon juice

½ cup olive or vegetable oil

¼ teaspoon freshly ground pepper

¼ cup snipped fresh dillweed

2 ripe avocados

2 cans (14 ounces each) artichoke hearts, drained and halved

1. In a bowl mash the garlic with the salt until smooth. Blend in the lemon juice, oil, pepper, and dill.
2. Peel avocados, cut into ½-inch chunks, and quickly add to dressing to prevent discoloration.
3. Add the artichoke hearts and toss gently to coat with dressing. Serve at once in small parfait glasses, ramekins, or on lettuce-lined plates, or chill 1 hour or longer before serving.

NACHOS
(Mexican)

No Mexican feast is complete without these little nibbles to start.
Makes 12 appetizer servings.

1 dozen thawed frozen, refrigerated, or canned corn tortillas
Vegetable oil for frying

2 cups refried beans (see page 238)
1 can (3 to 4 ounces) jalapeño peppers
2 cups (8 ounces) Monterey Jack

1. Cut each tortilla into 6 wedges. Heat 1 inch oil in a heavy skillet and fry the pieces of tortilla, a few at a time, until golden. Drain on paper towels.
2. Spread refried beans over triangles. Top with piece of seeded and diced jalapeño pepper and a small thin slice of cheese.
3. Broil 30 seconds or until cheese melts and bubbles.

REFRIED BEAN DIP
(Mexican)

Popular enough for food companies to put in a can but easy and economical to make at home for a crowd.
Makes 2½ cups.

1 cup (½ pound) dried pinto, pink, or red kidney beans
2½ cups water
2 medium-size onions

½ cup lard or margarine
2 canned jalapeño peppers, seeded and chopped, or to taste
Salt to taste

1. Wash and pick over the beans and place in a medium-size saucepan with the water and onions. Bring to a boil and boil 2 minutes. Remove from heat, cover, and let stand 2 hours.
2. Return to heat, bring to a boil, and simmer until beans are very tender, about 1½ to 2 hours. Adjust cover during cooking so that there is not too much liquid with beans at end of cooking.
3. Drain and reserve cooking liquid. Mash beans with a potato masher, adding just enough reserved liquid to make the task easier.
4. Heat the lard in a medium-size skillet. Add mashed beans and cook, stirring, until fat has been absorbed. Stir in peppers and salt. Serve with fried tortilla chips.

HUMMUS BI TAHINI
(Middle Eastern Chick-pea Spread)

Chick-peas are the basis for this well-known and popular appetizer.
Makes about 2 cups.

2 very large cloves garlic
¼ cup water
2 tablespoons lemon juice
1 tablespoon olive or vegetable oil
½ teaspoon salt
1 can (20 ounces) chick-peas or garbanzos, drained

¼ cup tahini (sesame paste)*
Paprika
Chopped fresh flat leaf parsley or mint

1. In a blender place the garlic, water, lemon juice, oil, and salt and blend on high speed until garlic is puréed.
2. Add beans and blend again until smooth. Add the tahini and blend until mixture has the consistency of a thick mayonnaise. Add a little more water to thin if necessary.
3. To serve, mound hummus in a serving bowl and sprinkle with paprika and parsley. Serve with raw vegetables, Melba toast and/or toasted pita bread.

*If sesame paste is not available from a store carrying Middle Eastern ingredients, grind sesame seeds in an electric blender with an equal amount of vegetable oil.

CAPONATA
(Italian Eggplant Appetizer)

Serve with crusty bread, raw vegetables, including fennel, or thin toast triangles.
Makes 6 appetizer servings.

1 large eggplant (about 2 pounds), unpeeled and cut into ½-inch cubes
Salt
½ cup olive or vegetable oil
1½ cups diced celery
1 large onion, finely chopped (1 cup)

⅓ cup red wine vinegar
2 tablespoons tomato paste
1 cup water or vegetable broth (see page 59)
⅓ cup sliced pitted black olives
1 tablespoon drained capers
1 tablespoon chopped fresh parsley
½ teaspoon salt

1. Sprinkle the eggplant with salt and let stand 20 minutes. Rinse well and pat dry.
2. Meanwhile heat the oil in a heavy skillet and sauté the celery 3 minutes. With a slotted spoon transfer celery to a medium-size bowl. Add the eggplant cubes to the skillet and cook, stirring often, until lightly brown and soft. Add the onion and cook until onion is tender but not browned. With a slotted spoon transfer eggplant and onion to bowl with celery. Discard any oil in skillet.
3. Add the vinegar, tomato paste, and water and bring to a boil, stirring. Simmer 5 minutes. Return celery-eggplant mixture to skillet. Add olives, capers, parsley, and salt and simmer, uncovered, 10 to 15 minutes. Cool and serve at room temperature.

BABA GHANOUJ
(Armenian Eggplant Spread)

An inexpensive, but delicious, spread.
Makes about 2 cups.

1 medium-size eggplant (about 1½ pounds)	1 teaspoon finely chopped garlic
2 tablespoons lemon juice	¾ teaspoon salt
2 tablespoons tahini (sesame paste)*	¼ cup diced onion
	2 tablespoons chopped fresh flat-leaf Italian parsley

1. Heat broiler. Rinse eggplant, dry, and prick in several places with a fork. Place on a baking sheet and broil about 6 inches from heat for 30 to 40 minutes, turning every 10 minutes, until eggplant is tender. Remove from broiler and let stand until cool enough to handle.
2. Scrape eggplant flesh into a bowl and discard skin and cap.
3. Mash the eggplant with the remaining ingredients, blending until fairly smooth. Serve at once or cover and chill 2 hours or longer until serving time.
4. To serve, mound on a plate or in a bowl and surround with toasted pita bread, cut into triangles, and crisp raw vegetables.

*Available in stores carrying Middle Eastern ingredients, or grind sesame seeds in an electric blender with an equal amount of vegetable oil.

EGGPLANT-WALNUT CAVIAR
(Turkish)

Makes about 2 cups.

1 large eggplant (about 2 pounds)
½ cup shelled walnuts
2 tablespoons olive or vegetable oil
⅓ cup thinly sliced green onions or
minced onion

½ teaspoon salt
¼ teaspoon freshly ground black
pepper

1. Heat broiler. Rinse eggplant and dry and prick in several places with a fork. Place on a baking sheet and broil about 6 inches from heat for 30 to 40 minutes, turning every 10 minutes, until eggplant is tender. Remove from broiler and let stand until cool enough to handle.
2. Toast walnuts in oven or toaster oven at 350° for about 7 minutes. Remove and allow to cool before chopping finely.
3. In a skillet heat oil over moderate heat. Add onions and cook for a minute or so until just beginning to brown.
4. Halve the eggplant, scoop out pulp, and add to skillet. Cook about 5 minutes, stirring and mashing eggplant with the side of a spoon until fairly smooth. Add the salt, pepper, and walnuts and spoon into a serving bowl.
5. Serve warm or cover and chill. Return to room temperature before serving. Serve with crackers, breadsticks, toasted pita bread, sweet red pepper wedges, cucumber rounds, and celery sticks.

MUSHROOMS À LA GRECQUE

Make-ahead appetizer that only needs toothpicks at a cocktail party. Leftovers can be tossed into a mixed salad.
Makes 6 to 8 appetizer servings.

½ cup olive or vegetable oil
½ cup dry white vermouth
½ cup red or white wine vinegar
1 teaspoon finely chopped garlic
1 teaspoon salt
½ teaspoon freshly ground black
pepper

¼ teaspoon ground coriander
1 teaspoon leaf basil, crumbled
1 teaspoon leaf thyme, crumbled
Few sprigs fresh parsley
1 pound small fresh whole
mushrooms

1. In a 3-quart saucepan combine all ingredients except mushrooms and bring to a boil. Simmer 5 minutes.
2. Meanwhile trim mushroom stems and wipe caps. Add mushrooms to simmering liquid and return to boiling. Reduce heat and simmer 1 minute, stirring to make sure that liquid coats all of the mushrooms.
3. Remove from heat and transfer mushrooms and liquid to a glass or ceramic bowl. Cover and chill several hours or overnight.
4. To serve, remove mushrooms to a serving dish with a slotted spoon. If desired, sprinkle with chopped fresh parsley. Strained poaching liquid can be refrigerated and used again to cook more mushrooms or other vegetables.

BAKED STUFFED MUSHROOMS
(American)

If you prefer, the stuffed mushrooms can be sautéed in a heavy skillet using the remaining three tablespoons of butter. Spoon pan drippings over each cap before serving.
Bake at 400° for 20 to 25 minutes.
Makes 6 appetizer servings.

1 pound large fresh mushrooms
1½ cups (3 slices) fresh bread crumbs
¼ cup finely chopped green onions
1 teaspoon finely chopped garlic
¼ cup chopped fresh parsley
¾ teaspoon salt
¼ teaspoon freshly ground black pepper
½ teaspoon leaf thyme, crumbled
6 tablespoons (¾ stick) butter or margarine, melted
¼ cup packaged bread crumbs, approximately

1. Wipe mushrooms with a damp paper towel. Trim off and discard a thin slice from the bottom of each stem. Remove stems and finely chop.
2. In a bowl combine chopped stems, onions, garlic, parsley, salt, pepper, and thyme. Toss thoroughly, add half the butter, and toss again.
3. Preheat oven to 400°. Lightly pack stuffing into each mushroom cap. Sprinkle tops with bread crumbs and drizzle with remaining butter.
4. Arrange on a lightly greased baking sheet and bake in the upper level of the oven at 400° 20 to 25 minutes, or until stuffing is lightly browned and crisp.
5. Remove mushrooms from oven and let stand several minutes before serving.

ROASTED PEPPERS
(Italian)

Makes 6 appetizer servings.

6 sweet peppers, green, yellow, or
  red
⅓ cup lemon juice
½ cup olive or vegetable oil

¼ teaspoon salt
6 flat anchovy fillets, finely
  chopped

1. Spear each of the peppers in turn and char them over a gas flame,
    turning frequently to cook evenly. Or place on a broiler pan and broil
    until they are charred, turning often.
2. Put hot charred peppers into a brown paper bag and leave until cool
    enough to handle. Peel off skins, halve, seed, and cut into ½-inch
    strips. Place in a serving bowl.
3. In a small bowl or screw-top cap jar combine the lemon juice, oil,
    salt, and anchovies. Mix well and pour over pepper strips. Allow to
    stand at room temperature 1 hour, stirring occasionally.

PLAKI
(Armenian Cold Vegetable Salad)

A delightful way to begin a Middle Eastern dinner.
Makes 6 appetizer servings.

¼ cup olive or vegetable oil
1 medium-size onion, finely
  chopped (½ cup)
2 cloves garlic, finely chopped
2 carrots, diced
2 stalks celery, sliced
4 medium-size potatoes, cubed
1 green pepper, seeded and diced
1 can (1 pound) plum tomatoes
2 tablespoons snipped fresh
  dillweed

2 tablespoons chopped fresh
  parsley
¾ teaspoon salt
¼ teaspoon freshly ground black
  pepper
1 cup vegetable broth (see page 59)
  or water
Lettuce leaves
Lemon wedges

1. In a large heavy casserole heat the oil and sauté the onion until tender
    but not browned. Add the garlic, carrots, celery, potatoes, and green
    pepper and cook, stirring often, 8 minutes.
2. Add the tomatoes, dill, parsley, salt, pepper, and broth. Cover and
    cook over low heat, stirring occasionally, until vegetables are tender
    but not mushy, about 20 minutes. Cool and chill and serve on lettuce
    leaves with lemon wedges.

VEGETABLE PATE I
(French)

Fashions in foods go in cycles, and this is the year of the vegetable pâté both hot and cold.
Makes 8 appetizer servings.

1 medium-size eggplant (about 1½ pounds)
Salt
1 large carrot, cut into 4- × ¼-inch sticks
¼ pound tiny green beans
3 small zucchini, cut into 4- × ½-inch sticks
2 red peppers
4 tablespoons vegetable oil, approximately
1 large Spanish or Bermuda onion, sliced

1 clove garlic, finely chopped
1¼ cups sliced celery
1 envelope unflavored gelatin
¼ cup cold water
1 can (13¾ ounces) chicken broth
¼ teaspoon salt
¼ teaspoon freshly ground black pepper
½ teaspoon leaf thyme, crumbled
Pinch of cayenne

1. Peel the eggplant and cut into ¼-inch slices. Sprinkle lightly with salt and let stand 20 minutes. Rinse and pat dry. Cut into 2-inch pieces.
2. Steam the carrot sticks 5 minutes, plunge into ice water, drain, and pat dry. Steam the green beans 5 minutes, plunge into ice water, drain, and pat dry. Steam the zucchini 3 minutes, plunge into ice water, drain, and pat dry.
3. Char the red peppers over a gas flame or under the broiler, turning frequently. Put in a brown paper bag until cool enough to handle. Peel, seed, and cut into ½-inch strips.
4. Heat the oil in a large heavy skillet and sauté the onion slices until barely wilted. Remove with a slotted spoon and reserve. Add the garlic and celery and cook 2 minutes. Remove with a slotted spoon and reserve.
5. In the oil remaining in the skillet sauté the eggplant pieces until barely tender and lightly browned. Add more oil only if absolutely necessary.
6. Soften the gelatin in the cold water for 10 minutes. Heat until gelatin dissolves. Stir in the broth, salt, pepper, thyme, and cayenne.
7. In a lightly oiled 9- × 5-inch loaf pan pour a ½-inch layer of the gelatin mixture. Chill until set.

8. On top of set gelatin mixture arrange a layer of carrot sticks, a layer of green beans, a layer of red pepper strips, a layer of eggplant, a layer of zucchini, a layer of onion, and a layer of celery. Repeat if some vegetables remain.

9. Pour over the remaining gelatin mixture, poking down with the point of a knife to get rid of air pockets and allow gelatin mixture to penetrate all the corners. Cover with wax paper and chill overnight. Unmold onto a bed of watercress or Boston lettuce. Slice and serve with a mustard mayonnaise, if you wish.

VEGETABLE PATE II
(French)

The three different-colored layers make this an attractive appetizer.
Bake at 350° for 2 hours.
Makes 10 appetizer servings.

Squash layer

1 butternut squash (about 1½ to 2 pounds)
2 tablespoons butter or margarine
2 tablespoons flour
¼ cup half-and-half
½ teaspoon salt
¼ teaspoon ground cinnamon
¼ teaspoon ground ginger
2 eggs, lightly beaten

Mushroom layer

¼ cup (½ stick) butter or margarine
1 pound mushrooms, finely chopped (4 cups)
1 large onion, finely chopped (1 cup)
1 teaspoon salt
¼ teaspoon freshly ground black pepper
2 eggs, lightly beaten
¼ cup packaged bread crumbs

Broccoli layer

2 packages (10 ounces each) frozen chopped broccoli
2 tablespoons butter or margarine
1 medium-size onion, finely chopped (½ cup)
1 clove garlic, finely chopped
½ cup half-and-half
3 eggs
¼ cup packaged bread crumbs
¼ cup (1 ounce) freshly grated Parmesan
⅛ teaspoon ground nutmeg
½ teaspoon salt

1. Peel and cut the squash into cubes and place in a large saucepan. Cover with boiling salted water and return to a boil. Cover and simmer until very tender, about 30 minutes. Drain and purée in the container of an electric blender or a food processor.
2. In a medium-size saucepan melt the butter, stir in the flour, half-and-half, salt, squash, cinnamon, and ginger. Cook, stirring, until mixture thickens and bubbles. Remove from the heat and stir in the eggs. Turn into a greased 9- × 5- × 3-inch loaf pan lined on the bottom and sides with foil.
3. Heat the butter and sauté the mushrooms and onion until tender and most of the moisture has evaporated. Off the heat stir in salt, pepper, eggs, and bread crumbs. Place on top of squash mixture.
4. Cook the broccoli according to package directions. Drain and chop finely. Place in bowl.
5. Meanwhile heat the butter in a small saucepan and sauté the onion until tender but not browned. Add garlic and cook 1 minute. Add to broccoli.
6. Preheat oven to 350°. Add half-and-half, eggs, bread crumbs, cheese, nutmeg, and salt to broccoli. Mix well and place on top of mushroom mixture. Place loaf pan in a 13- × 9- × 2-inch baking pan in the middle of the oven. Pour boiling water into outer pan to a depth of about 2 inches. Bake at 350° for 2 hours or until pâté is set. Remove loaf pan to a wire rack to cool. Chill several hours or overnight.
7. Unmold onto a platter and garnish with watercress, if you wish.

ZUCCHINI IN BEER BATTER
(Italian)

This popular restaurant dish is not difficult provided you don't mind deep-fat frying.

Makes 6 appetizer servings or 4 side-dish servings.

2 medium-size zucchini, cut into ¼- × 2-inch sticks
Salt
2 eggs
¾ cup beer
2 tablespoons butter or margarine, melted

¼ cup (1 ounce) freshly grated Parmesan
¼ teaspoon salt
⅛ teaspoon freshly ground black pepper
1 cup sifted all-purpose flour
Vegetable oil

1. Sprinkle zucchini with salt and let stand 15 minutes. Rinse well, drain, and dry the zucchini sticks very well on paper towels.
2. Place the eggs, beer, butter, cheese, salt, pepper, and flour in the container of an electric blender. Blend until smooth. Let stand at least 1 hour.
3. Check the consistency of the batter; it should coat the zucchini lightly. If it is too thick add a little more beer and whirl or if it is too thin add a tablespoon or two of flour and whirl.
4. Pour vegetable oil into a deep heavy saucepan or deep fryer to a depth of 1 inch. Heat to 365° on a deep-fat thermometer. Coat zucchini sticks with batter and fry, a few at a time, until golden and crisp. Drain on paper towels and keep hot while frying the rest of the sticks.

SAUCES FOR CRUDITES
(French)

Two flavorful sauces for dipping raw vegetables (broccoli, cauliflower, green peppers, cherry tomatoes, celery, carrots).

Sour Cream Dill Sauce (Makes about 1 cup)

¾ cup sour cream
¼ cup mayonnaise
1 tablespoon Dijon mustard
3 tablespoons thinly sliced green onions

3 tablespoons snipped fresh dillweed, or 1 teaspoon dried
¼ teaspoon salt
¼ teaspoon freshly ground black pepper

Combine all ingredients and blend thoroughly. Cover and chill 1 hour or longer before serving. Also delicious on cold meats, fish, and seafood.

Aïoli (Makes about 1½ cups)

3 very large cloves garlic	1½ cups olive or vegetable oil
2 large egg yolks	2 teaspoons lemon juice
1 teaspoon salt	

Place garlic, egg yolks, and salt in a blender and blend on high speed until garlic is puréed. Start adding oil by droplets until sauce begins to thicken. Continue adding oil in a thin stream until sauce is thick and blended. Pour into a bowl and stir in lemon juice. Taste sauce and add more salt and lemon juice if needed. Cover and chill 1 hour or longer until needed. Sauce will keep several days tightly covered in the refrigerator.

YOGURT DIP FOR CRUDITES
(American)

There's the tangy flavor of sour cream but without the added calories. However, no one would claim this is a low-cal dip. Makes about 1½ cups.

1 container (8 ounces) plain yogurt	½ teaspoon salt
1 cup mayonnaise	1 clove garlic, finely chopped
1 tablespoon chopped fresh parsley	⅛ teaspoon freshly ground black pepper
1 tablespoon snipped fresh dillweed	⅛ teaspoon celery seeds
1 tablespoon chopped fresh chives, or 1 teaspoon freeze-dried	

Combine all the ingredients in a small bowl, cover, and chill several hours before serving with raw vegetable dippers.

HERBED CHEESE
(French)

Some would dub this crème fraîche, but by whatever name you call it, it is delicious.
Makes about 1 cup.

2 cups half-and-half
2 tablespoons buttermilk
¾ teaspoon salt
¼ teaspoon freshly ground black pepper
¼ teaspoon garlic powder

¼ teaspoon celery salt
⅛ teaspoon onion powder
¼ teaspoon leaf thyme, crumbled
¼ teaspoon leaf savory, crumbled
¼ teaspoon leaf marjoram, crumbled

1. The day before you wish to serve the homemade cheese, mix the half-and-half with the buttermilk in a clean jar with a cover. Place the jar in a pan with very hot water extending to the level of the cream and set in a warm place for about 12 hours or until mixture thickens.
2. Chill several hours. Stir in remaining ingredients and chill again to allow flavors to mellow. Serve with crudités or Melba toast.

HERB-CHEESE DIP
(Italian)

This dip has more character than most and it does appeal to the diet group who can overlook the cream cheese for once.
Makes about 1¼ cups.

1 container (8 ounces) cottage cheese
1 package (3 ounces) cream cheese, softened
1 tablespoon chopped fresh chives, or 1 teaspoon freeze-dried
1 clove garlic, finely chopped
1 tablespoon finely chopped fresh parsley (Italian flat variety, if available)

¼ teaspoon salt
⅛ teaspoon freshly ground black pepper
¼ teaspoon leaf basil, crumbled
¼ teaspoon leaf oregano, crumbled
¼ teaspoon crushed hot red pepper flakes

Press the cottage cheese through a food mill or large strainer into a medium-size bowl. Beat in the cream cheese until smooth. Stir in remaining ingredients. Chill several hours. Serve with raw vegetable dippers.

FETA POCKETS
(Greek)

These cheese-filled pockets are substantial enough for a luncheon sandwich.
Makes 8 appetizer servings.

4 small loaves pita bread
8 small slices feta cheese
¼ cup (½ stick) butter or margarine
1 cup diced peeled cucumber

1 cup diced tomato
1 cup shredded lettuce
1 container (8 ounces) plain yogurt
2 cloves garlic, finely chopped

1. Wrap the bread in foil and heat 10 minutes at 250° in oven or toaster oven. Meanwhile sauté the cheese slices in the butter in a large skillet until warmed through.
2. Split each pita into two halves. Put 2 tablespoons each of cucumber, tomato, and lettuce into each pocket. Top with cheese.
3. Combine the yogurt and garlic and spoon over the filling. Garnish with Greek olives, if you wish.

ANTOJITOS
(Mexican Stuffed Tidbits)

Antojitos means tidbits or appetizers, so the filling can be changed as you wish.
Bake at 400° for 10 minutes.
Makes 6 appetizer servings.

6 eight-inch flour tortillas
2 packages (3 ounces each) cream cheese, softened
¼ cup diced green chilies

¼ cup chopped pitted black olives
2 tablespoons butter or margarine, melted

1. Spread the tortillas with about 2 tablespoons cream cheese. Sprinkle with chilies and olives. Stack tortillas in twos, one on top of the other.
2. Preheat oven to 400°. Roll each stack tightly like a jelly roll. Cut into 1-inch-thick slices and place apart on a cookie sheet. Brush with butter and bake at 400° for 10 minutes, or until lightly browned.

SPINACH-CHEESE TRIANGLES
(Greek)

One of the classics that never goes out of style and is always
"new" to someone.
Bake at 425° for 15 to 20 minutes.
Makes about 8 dozen.

2 packages (10 ounces each) frozen
chopped spinach, thawed
1 cup (2 sticks) sweet butter or
unsalted margarine, melted
¾ cup thinly sliced green onions
1 cup creamed cottage cheese
½ pound (about 8 ounces) feta
cheese, crumbled*
¼ cup (1 ounce) freshly grated
Parmesan

3 eggs
½ teaspoon salt
¼ teaspoon freshly ground black
pepper
¼ teaspoon ground nutmeg
4 tablespoons snipped fresh
dillweed, or 1 teaspoon dried
½ pound phyllo (strudel) pastry
leaves

1. With your hands squeeze spinach to remove all excess liquid.
2. In a large skillet heat 4 tablespoons of the butter over moderate heat.
   Add green onions and cook until soft. Add spinach and cook about 5
   minutes, or until most of the moisture has evaporated. Remove skillet
   from heat and stir in the cheeses, eggs, salt, pepper, nutmeg, and
   dill.
3. Cut the phyllo lengthwise into 3-inch-wide strips and keep them
   neatly stacked beneath a damp dish towel while you work.
4. Take 1 strip of pastry, lay it flat, and brush lightly with some of the
   butter. Place 1 teaspoon of filling in the right hand corner of one end
   of the strip. Bring the left hand corner over the filling to make a
   triangle flush with the right side. Fold triangle over and over until the
   entire strip of dough is wrapped in a triangle.
5. Preheat oven to 425°. Place triangles on a baking sheet and repeat
   with remaining filling and pastry. Brush triangles with more melted
   butter and bake at 425° for 15 to 20 minutes, or until golden brown.
   Serve immediately or slide onto racks to cool.

Note: Baked, cooled triangles may be put in plastic bags and frozen. To reheat,
place frozen triangles on buttered baking sheets, brush with melted butter, and
bake in a preheated oven (425°) for 20 minutes. To freeze unbaked, freeze triangles on baking sheets. When hard, remove, place in plastic bags, and return to
freezer. Bake as above, adding a few minutes extra time.

*If feta cheese is unavailable, substitute 2 cups freshly grated Parmesan.

CHEESE LOAF
(Greek)

Serve with toasted pita bread cut into triangles or Melba toast.
Makes 6 appetizer servings.

6 hard-cooked eggs, finely chopped
4 ounces feta cheese, crumbled
  (about 1 cup)
1 cup (4 ounces) shredded mild
  Cheddar
10 Greek olives, pitted and chopped
8 small gherkins, finely chopped

1 teaspoon Dijon mustard
2 tablespoons heavy cream
2 tablespoons mayonnaise,
  approximately
Salt and freshly ground black
  pepper
Watercress

In a large bowl combine the eggs, feta, Cheddar, olives, gherkins, mustard, cream, enough mayonnaise to bind together, and salt and pepper to taste. Pack into a small loaf pan or terrine lined with foil extending over edges of pan. Chill several hours. Lift out with foil, place on platter, remove foil, and garnish with watercress.

TEA EGGS
(Chinese)

A conversation piece at any cocktail party.
Makes 6 appetizer servings.

2 cups boiling water
1 tablespoon loose tea or 3 tea bags
2 teaspoons salt

2 tablespoons soy sauce
6 hard-cooked eggs, shells cracked
  by rolling gently on counter

1. In a skillet that will hold the 6 eggs in a single layer combine the boiling water, tea, salt, and soy sauce. Add eggs and more boiling water, if necessary, to cover eggs.
2. Cover and simmer very gently 2 hours. Remove from heat and leave overnight at room temperature. Carefully remove shells and cut into halves or quarters to serve.

HARD-COOKED EGGS
WITH YOGURT SAUCE
(Indian)

The gastric juices are encouraged to flow by this tangy, spicy appetizer.
Makes 6 appetizer servings.

1 container (8 ounces) plain yogurt
1 tablespoon butter
1½ teaspoons curry powder
⅛ teaspoon ground cumin
½ clove garlic, finely chopped
1 tablespoon lemon juice

½ teaspoon salt
1 tablespoon chopped fresh cilantro (Chinese parsley) or parsley
6 hard-cooked eggs, halved lengthwise

1. Beat the yogurt and place in a muslin bag. Tie to tap and allow to drain over the sink an hour or two.
2. Heat the butter in a small pan. Add the curry powder, cumin, and garlic. Cook, stirring, 1 minute. Allow to cool.
3. Empty the yogurt into a medium-size bowl and mix in the curry mixture, lemon juice, salt, and cilantro. Arrange egg halves on serving dish and spoon sauce over.

BAGNA CAUDA
(Italian Anchovy-Garlic Dip)

A delicious dish that combines two of my favorite flavors, garlic and anchovies.
Makes 8 appetizer servings.

¼ cup (½ stick) butter or margarine
¼ cup olive or vegetable oil
2 cans (2 ounces each) flat anchovy fillets
4 cloves garlic, finely chopped

6 cups raw vegetable dippers, including green bean pieces, cauliflower and broccoli flowerets, cherry tomatoes, celery, peppers, zucchini slices
Thin slices crusty bread

1. In a small deep saucepan heat the butter, oil, and oil drained from the anchovies.
2. Chop the anchovies finely and add to pan with garlic. Cook very slowly and keep warm while dipping raw vegetables and bread into the mixture for a piquant appetizer.

BAKED STUFFED CLAMS
(Italian)

Bake at 350° for 15 minutes.
Makes 4 to 6 appetizer servings.

12 large cherrystone clams, opened, juice and shells reserved, and clams chopped, or 1 can (7 ounces) chopped clams
2 eggs
½ cup mayonnaise
3 tablespoons chopped fresh parsley
1 teaspoon leaf oregano, crumbled

2 cloves garlic, finely chopped
½ teaspoon salt
3 drops liquid red pepper seasoning
¾ loaf Italian bread (12 ounces), with crusts removed, made into coarse crumbs
¼ cup (1 ounce) freshly grated Parmesan

1. Wash the clam shells and set aside on a baking sheet. In a medium-size bowl combine 1 egg, ¼ cup mayonnaise, parsley, oregano, garlic, salt, and liquid red pepper seasoning.
2. Preheat over to 350°. Stir reserved clam juice and chopped clams into mayonnaise mixture, and add bread crumbs. Mix well. Use mixture to fill the shells, about 1 tablespoon per shell.
3. Bake at 350° for 15 minutes or until heated through. Beat remaining egg, mayonnaise, and cheese together. Spoon over stuffed clams and place under a preheated broiler for 2 to 3 minutes or until browned and bubbly.

HERRING SPREAD
(Swedish)

Great way to stretch the silvery snacks.
Makes about 2 cups.

1 jar (8 ounces) herring snacks in wine sauce, drained and chopped
1 crisp apple, quartered, cored, and finely chopped
½ medium-size red onion, peeled and finely chopped

1 tablespoon Düsseldorf mustard
½ cup dairy sour cream or plain yogurt
1 tablespoon snipped fresh dillweed

Combine all ingredients in a medium-size bowl. Chill several hours before serving with pumpernickel triangles.

MARINATED MUSSELS
(Mexican)

Makes 6 appetizer servings.

24 very large fresh mussels
½ cup olive or vegetable oil
¼ cup fresh lime juice
¼ teaspoon finely chopped garlic
½ teaspoon salt
¼ teaspoon freshly ground black
  pepper
 8 or more drops liquid red peppe
  seasoning

½ cup diced red onion
1 small red pepper, seeded and
  diced (½ cup)
1 small green pepper, seeded and
  diced (½ cup)
2 tablespoons chopped fresh
  parsley
Lime wedges

1. With a short-bladed knife, clean mussels by scraping off barnacles and pulling out beards. Scrub shells with a stiff brush and rinse well under cold running water.
2. Pour water into a large skillet to a depth of about ½ inch. Place the mussels in the skillet, cover, and bring to a boil over high heat. Watch skillet carefully and remove mussels as soon as they open.
3. In a glass or ceramic bowl blend all ingredients except mussels, parsley, and lime wedges. Remove mussels from shells and add to dressing. Cover and chill several hours or overnight.
4. Rinse and dry half the mussel shells and reserve.
5. To serve, arrange clean shells on serving platter and fill each with a mussel and some of the dressing. Sprinkle with parsley and serve with lime wedges.

MUSSELS PROVENCALE
(French)

Pretty to look at and good eating.
Bake at 400° for 10 minutes.
Makes 6 appetizer servings.

36 mussels, well scrubbed and
  beards removed
1½ cups (3 sticks) butter or
  margarine
 3 cloves garlic, finely chopped
 2 green onions, finely chopped

2 tablespoons chopped fresh
  parsley, Italian flat variety, if
  available
1 bunch watercress, trimmed and
  leaves finely chopped
½ teaspoon freshly ground black
  pepper

1. Place mussels in a large kettle with ¼ cup water. Cover tightly and cook 5 minutes, or until mussels open. Drain and reserve broth for fish soup or sauce. Discard half of each shell and leave the mussels on the half-shell set in a jelly roll pan.
2. Preheat oven to 400°. Meanwhile, melt the butter in a small saucepan and cook the garlic and green onions over low heat until tender but not browned. Add the parsley, watercress, and pepper. Spoon butter mixture over mussels and bake at 400° for 10 minutes, or until piping hot.

FETTUCINE WITH SMOKED SALMON
(Italian)

Wonderful way to stretch precious smoked salmon.
Makes 4 appetizer or 2 main dish servings.

½ pound fettucine noodles
2 tablespoons sweet butter or unsalted margarine
½ cup heavy cream
⅓ cup freshly grated Parmesan

Salt
Pepper
2 to 4 ounces smoked salmon, finely chopped

1. Cook noodles in boiling salted water according to package directions. Drain.
2. Return empty pot to low heat and add butter and cream. When butter has melted, add noodles, cheese, salt, and pepper, and toss gently until well mixed.
3. Add smoked salmon and toss again. Taste for seasoning, adding more salt and pepper, if needed. Serve on heated plates with more grated cheese on the side.

GRAVAD LAX
(Swedish Dill-cured Fresh Salmon)

One way to fix really fresh salmon and produce an ethereal dish.
Makes 8 to 12 appetizer servings.

⅓ cup sugar
3 tablespoons coarse kosher salt
2 teaspoons crushed peppercorns, preferably white
2 pounds center-cut fresh salmon, halved lengthwise, bones removed

Large bunch fresh dillweed
Sweet Mustard Sauce (recipe follows)

1. Mix sugar, salt, and peppercorns in a small bowl. Rub mixture into flesh side of salmon.
2. Put a layer of dill in the bottom of a flat glass baking dish and place one slab of fish, skin side down, on the dill. Put a layer of dill on the fish and top with the second piece of salmon, skin side up.
3. Top with remaining dill and cover with plastic wrap. Weight with a plate topped with something heavy like large cans, clean bricks, or tiles. Chill 3 days.
4. To serve, rinse salt off salmon and pat dry with paper towels. Place fish on a wooden board and garnish with capers, snipped dill, parsley, and lemon slices. Slice very thin and serve with Sweet Mustard Sauce and tiny pumpernickel and sweet butter sandwiches.

SWEET MUSTARD SAUCE

Makes about ½ cup.

5 tablespoons Dijon mustard
1 teaspoon dry mustard
3 tablespoons sugar
2 tablespoons distilled white vinegar

⅓ cup vegetable oil
3 tablespoons snipped fresh dillweed

In a small bowl blend both mustards to a paste. Add sugar and vinegar. Beat in oil in a thin stream until mixture is thick and smooth. Stir in dill, cover, and chill until serving time. Prepare sauce on the day salmon is to be served.

SEVICHE
(Mexican)

This method of "cooking" fish has become an integral part of the much-touted nouvelle cuisine. It is fantastic in any language.
Makes 6 appetizer servings.

1 pound fresh bay or sea scallops
½ cup lime juice
½ teaspoon salt
1 small onion, thinly sliced and separated into rings
2 canned serrano or jalapeño peppers, seeded and chopped

2 small ripe tomatoes, peeled, seeded, and chopped
3 tablespoons olive or vegetable oil
½ teaspoon leaf oregano, crumbled
1 tablespoon chopped fresh cilantro (Chinese parsley) or flat Italian parsley

1. If the bay scallops are big, cut in half and place in a bowl. Cut the sea scallops into pieces the size of small bay scallops.
2. Add the remaining ingredients and toss to mix well. Cover and chill from 4 to 24 hours. The lime juice "cooks" the fish.

DILLED SHRIMP SPREAD
(American)

In England the dill is omitted and the spread is called potted shrimp.
Makes about 1 cup.

1 package (12 ounces) frozen shelled and deveined shrimp, cooked according to directions, drained, and cooled
½ cup (1 stick) butter or margarine, softened
½ teaspoon paprika
2 tablespoons snipped fresh dillweed

2 tablespoons chopped fresh parsley
1 tablespoon finely chopped green onion
1 teaspoon grated lemon rind
½ teaspoon salt
⅛ teaspoon freshly ground black pepper

1. Chop the shrimp finely. Add the remaining ingredients and beat with a wooden spoon to blend.
2. Spoon into a crock or bowl and chill well before serving with tiny triangles of thin pumpernickel bread.

SHRIMP TOAST
(Chinese)

I have experimented with baking and sautéeing shrimp toast
instead of deep-fat frying but neither is satisfactory.
Makes 8 appetizer servings.

1 pound raw shelled and deveined
shrimp
¼ cup (½ stick) butter or margarine,
melted
2 tablespoons finely chopped green
onion
4 water chestnuts, finely chopped

1 teaspoon salt
1 tablespoon cornstarch
1 egg, lightly beaten
Packaged bread crumbs
8 slices firm day-old white bread
Vegetable oil for frying

1. Whirl the shrimp in a food processor, put through a meat grinder, or
    chop finely. Place in a bowl and add the butter, green onion, water
    chestnuts, salt, cornstarch, and egg. Mix well. If necessary, add a few
    crumbs to make the mixture of spreadable consistency.
2. Remove crusts from bread and cut into 4 triangles or squares. Spread
    shrimp mixture on each piece of bread. Sprinkle with bread crumbs.
3. Heat 2 inches of oil in a heavy straight-sided saucepan until it regis-
    ters 375° on a deep-fat thermometer. Fry the shrimp toast, shrimp
    side down, a few at a time until golden. Turn and brown other side.
    Drain on paper towels. Serve hot.

SCAMPI WITH GARLIC
(Italian)

Expensive, but oh, so good. Think of it as quarter the cost of
eating the same dish in a first-class restaurant.
Makes 6 to 8 appetizer servings or 3 to 4 main dish servings.

1½ pounds large shrimp, shelled and
deveined
2 tablespoons olive or vegetable oil
2 tablespoons butter
2 cloves garlic, finely chopped
2 tablespoons chopped fresh flat
Italian parsley

¼ teaspoon salt
⅛ teaspoon freshly ground black
pepper
Lemon wedges

1. In a large heavy skillet heat the oil. Add the shrimp and stir-fry 3
    minutes, or until they turn pink.
2. Add the butter, garlic, parsley, salt, and pepper and cook, stirring, 3
    to 5 minutes. Serve at once with lemon wedges.

FISH PATE
(Chinese)

This recipe can be prepared in one batch in a food processor, or in two or three batches in a blender, depending on the machine's horsepower.

Bake at 325° for 1 hour.

Makes 8 to 10 appetizer servings.

1 pound fresh or frozen fillets of firm white fish, such as sole, flounder, scrod, or cod
2 eggs
2 tablespoons vegetable oil
2 tablespoons sesame oil, optional
1 tablespoon soy sauce
2 tablespoons dry sherry
1 teaspoon finely chopped ginger root, or ½ teaspoon ground
¼ teaspoon finely chopped garlic
½ teaspoon sugar
½ teaspoon salt
2 tablespoons thinly sliced green onions

1. If using frozen fish, thaw completely and dry thoroughly on paper towels. Cut fillets into quarters.
2. Place the fish and eggs in food processor bowl. Process 5 to 10 seconds, or until mixture is smooth. Transfer ground fish to mixing bowl and blend in remaining ingredients.
3. Preheat oven to 325°. Grease the inside of an 8- × 4- × 2-inch loaf pan with vegetable oil. Pack fish mixture into pan and smooth top with a wet knife.
4. Cover tightly with aluminum foil and place pan in larger pan filled with hot water to a depth of 1 inch. Bake at 325° for 1 hour, or until pâté is firm and a knife inserted in center comes out moist but clean. Run a knife between pan and pâté to loosen. Re-cover and chill several hours or overnight.
5. Just before serving, turn pâté out onto a serving plate and if desired garnish with more green onions or watercress. Cut into ¼-inch-thick slices to serve.

SUSHI
(Japanese)

Next time you pass an Oriental food store stock up on seaweed; it keeps forever, and you'll be ready to try this delicious Japanese specialty.

Makes 8 appetizer servings.

Filling I

2 eggs, lightly beaten
4 teaspoons sake (rice wine) or dry sherry
1 tablespoon sugar
½ teaspoon salt
¼ cup vegetable oil
1 three-once flounder fillet, cut lengthwise into ¼-inch strips
Flour
½ cup well-drained cooked spinach or ½ package (10 ounces) chopped frozen spinach, thawed and squeezed dry

Filling II

6 large shrimp, shelled and deveined
2 eggs
2 tablespoons sake (rice wine) or dry sherry
1 tablespoon sugar
¼ teaspoon salt
2 tablespoons vegetable oil

Rice

2½ cups water
½ cup white vinegar
1 tablespoon sugar
1 teaspoon salt
2 cups raw long-grain rice

Seaweed

2 sheets seaweed (available in Oriental stores and by mail order)

Sauce

Soy sauce
Slices fresh ginger root

1. To make Filling I: Mix the eggs, sake, sugar, and salt together. Heat 2 tablespoons of the oil in a small skillet and scramble the eggs. Set aside.
2. Heat remaining oil in a second small skillet. Dust the fish pieces lightly with flour and sauté in the oil until fish flakes, about 3 minutes. Set aside with spinach.
3. To make Filling II: Chop shrimp very fine and combine with the eggs, sake, sugar, and salt. Heat the oil in a small skillet and cook the shrimp mixture until it turns pink, about 4 minutes.

4. To prepare the rice: Combine the water, vinegar, sugar, and salt in a medium-size saucepan and bring to a boil. Add the rice, cover, and simmer 15 minutes. Turn off heat but do not remove cover for 10 minutes.

5. Soften the sheets of seaweed in a bowl of warm water for 3 minutes. Place 1 sheet on a bamboo mat or clean guest hand towel. Spread half the rice over the surface, leaving a 1¼-inch border of seaweed. Place half of either of the fillings down the center of the rice. In Filling I, place the egg first, spinach on top of egg, fish on top of spinach. Using the mat or towel as a guide, roll the seaweed like a jelly roll. Cut into slices ¾ inch thick and serve with a dipping sauce of soy sauce and ginger slices. Repeat with remaining seaweed, rice, and filling.

Note: If making both fillings, make twice the recipe of rice and soak 4 sheets of seaweed.

CANNELLINI AND TUNA ANTIPASTO SALAD
(Italian)

Serve in lettuce cups as a first course for dinner or arrange garnished with halved cherry tomatoes as part of an hors d'oeuvre selection.
Makes 4 appetizer servings.

1 can (20 ounces) cannellini beans, drained, rinsed, and drained again
1 can (7 ounces) solid white tuna, drained and flaked
2 large roasted sweet red peppers, diced (about ½ cup)
1 small onion, finely chopped (¼ cup)

1 tablespoon olive or vegetable oil
4 teaspoons red wine vinegar
¼ teaspoon freshly ground black pepper
¼ cup chopped fresh parsley
¼ teaspoon salt, optional

In a medium-size bowl combine all ingredients except salt and toss gently to blend. Taste salad and add salt if needed.

SALADE NICOISE
WITH TUNA DRESSING
(French)

The tuna is in the dressing for this salade Niçoise, an unusual twist.
Makes 4 to 6 appetizer servings.

½ cup mayonnaise
¼ cup milk
1 tablespoon olive or vegetable oil
4 teaspoons lemon juice
1 tablespoon drained capers
½ small onion, halved
⅛ teaspoon leaf basil, crumbled
⅛ teaspoon leaf thyme, crumbled
¼ teaspoon freshly ground black pepper
1 can (7 ounces) solid white tuna, drained and flaked

1 head romaine lettuce, washed, dried, and thoroughly chilled
1 pound fresh green beans, steamed until firm-tender and chilled
1 pound new potatoes, steamed until tender, chilled, and sliced
2 large ripe tomatoes, cut in eighths
1 red onion, peeled and sliced into rings
1 green or red pepper, seeded, cored, and thinly sliced
Black olives and anchovies

1. In a blender or food processor place the mayonnaise, milk, oil, lemon juice, capers, onion, basil, thyme, and pepper. Blend until smooth. Add tuna and blend again until smooth and creamy.
2. Line a large serving platter or bowl with the lettuce. Arrange remaining ingredients over lettuce and garnish with olives and anchovies. To serve, spoon some of each vegetable onto serving plates and pass dressing separately.

YAKITORI
(Japanese Broiled Chicken)

It's fun to let guests cook their own yakitori over a hibachi or barbecue grill.
Makes 6 to 8 appetizer servings.

3 whole chicken breasts, skinned, boned, and cut into 1-inch cubes
1 bunch green onions, cut into ¾-inch lengths
½ pound chicken livers, trimmed and halved, optional
⅔ cup soy sauce

⅓ cup dry sherry
2 teaspoons finely chopped fresh ginger root, or ¼ teaspoon ground
¼ cup water
1 teaspoon sugar

1. Alternate the chicken cubes, scallions, and chicken livers on individual skewers (soaked in water, if bamboo).
2. In a flat shallow glass or ceramic dish combine the remaining ingredients. Set the skewers in the soy mixture. Turn to coat all sides and let marinate 20 minutes, turning often or basting with the marinade.
3. Grill the skewers 4 to 5 inches from hot coals or preheated broiler 8 minutes, turning often, until lightly brown and cooked through. Brush with marinade at least twice during cooking. Dip in toasted sesame seeds, if you wish.

POLYNESIAN HOT OR COLD GLAZED CHICKEN WINGS

Sweet-sour dishes are winners on any occasion.
Bake at 400° for 1 hour.
Makes 6 to 8 appetizer servings.

3 pounds chicken wings
¼ cup light or dark brown sugar
¼ cup soy sauce
¼ cup red wine vinegar
3 tablespoons peanut or vegetable oil
3 tablespoons frozen pineapple juice concentrate
1 tablespoon finely chopped fresh ginger root, or 1½ teaspoons ground
1 teaspoon finely chopped garlic

1. Rinse chicken wings and pat dry. Remove wing tips and save for soup or discard. With a sharp knife, poultry shears, or cleaver separate wings at the joint.
2. Combine remaining ingredients in a large shallow bowl or glass baking pan and blend thoroughly. Add chicken and coat with marinade. Cover and chill overnight, turning pieces often while they marinate. Several hours before serving (if wings are to be served cold) heat oven to 400°.
3. Line a large baking sheet with foil and arrange wings, skin side down, on sheet. Bake 1 hour, turning wings after 30 minutes. If desired, wings can be put under the broiler for the final 5 minutes.
4. Let stand a few minutes until touchable. To serve cold, cover pan and chill 2 or 3 hours before serving.

SHREDDED CHICKEN
WITH WALNUT SAUCE
(Turkish)

Everyone will want the recipe for this Turkish specialty.
Makes 6 appetizer servings.

1 chicken (3½ pounds), cut into
  eighths
3 cups water
½ teaspoon salt
1½ cups shelled walnuts
1 medium-size onion, diced (½
  cup)
3 slices stale white bread, torn in
  pieces

1 teaspoon paprika
¼ teaspoon freshly ground black
  pepper
1 teaspoon salt
  Italian parsley
  Canned roasted sweet red
  peppers or pimientos

1. Place chicken in a Dutch oven with water and ½ teaspoon salt and
   bring to a boil over high heat. Reduce heat to moderate, cover pot,
   leaving lid slightly ajar, and simmer chicken 35 minutes or just until
   tender.
2. Remove chicken from pot and cool. Meanwhile increase heat under
   broth in pot and boil, uncovered, until broth reduces to 1½ cups and
   tastes rich, 20 to 30 minutes.
3. Pour half the broth into blender. Add half the walnuts and onion.
   Blend at high speed until smooth. Add half the bread and blend
   again, stopping blender when necessary to scrape sides and push
   down contents.
4. Transfer purée to a bowl and repeat with remaining broth, walnuts,
   and onion. Add the paprika, pepper, and the 1 teaspoon salt with the
   remaining bread. Mix both purée mixtures in the bowl.
5. Remove and discard chicken skin and bones. Shred chicken. Set
   aside ½ cup of the walnut sauce and add chicken to remainder. Toss
   well. Arrange chicken in a mound or pyramid on a serving plate,
   cover tightly, and chill several hours or overnight. Coat mound of
   chicken with remaining sauce and decorate with parsley and pepper
   strips or a simple sprinkling of paprika.

COLD ANISE CHICKEN
(Chinese)

Attractively glazed and spicy-tasting, the wings are always a hit
at an Oriental or Occidental gathering.
Makes 8 appetizer servings.

16 chicken wings, tips removed and
   used for soup
3 green onions, including green
   part, cut into 1-inch lengths
½ cup soy sauce
1 cup water

½ cup dry sherry
1 teaspoon anise seeds or 2 pieces
   star anise
4 whole cloves
¼ cup light brown sugar

1. Cut wings in half and place in a large saucepan with remaining ingredients. Bring to a boil, cover, and simmer 30 minutes. Remove cover and simmer 15 minutes longer, basting wings as they cook.
2. Chill until ready to serve.

CHOPPED CHICKEN LIVERS
(American)

Everyone has a favorite version of this popular appetizer, and
here is mine.
Makes 6 to 8 appetizer servings.

¼ cup (½ stick) butter or margarine
1 small onion, finely chopped
   (¼ cup)
1 pound chicken livers, trimmed
   and halved
2 tablespoons brandy, optional
¾ teaspoon salt

¼ teaspoon freshly ground black
   pepper
¼ teaspoon leaf thyme, crumbled
1 hard-cooked egg, chopped
2 tablespoons chopped fresh
   parsley

1. In a medium-size skillet heat the butter and sauté the onion until tender but not browned.
2. Add the chicken livers and cook, stirring, until livers are browned on the outside and still slightly pink inside.
3. Warm the brandy and pour it over livers. Stand back and ignite. When the flame subsides add the salt, pepper, and thyme.
4. Turn the liver mixture out onto a board and chop until fine. Place in a bowl with the egg and parsley, mix well, and chill. Serve with toast triangles or Melba toast.

Soups

ALMOND SOUP
(Spanish)

Makes 4 servings.

2 tablespoons olive or vegetable oil
1 small onion, finely chopped
(¼ cup)
½ cup blanched almonds
1 small green pepper, seeded and
finely chopped
2 cloves garlic, finely chopped

¼ cup chopped fresh parsley
1 quart vegetable broth (see page
59) or water
1 teaspoon salt
¼ teaspoon freshly ground black
pepper
2 slices pumpernickel bread

1. In a large heavy saucepan heat the oil and sauté the onion and almonds until onion is tender and almonds are barely brown.
2. Add green pepper and garlic and cook 1 minute. Add parsley, broth, salt, and pepper, bring to a boil, and simmer 10 minutes.
3. Place half the bread, torn into pieces, in an electric blender. Ladle in the hot soup and whirl until smooth. Repeat with second slice of bread and remaining soup. Reheat and serve very hot.

PASTA FAGIOLI
(Italian Pasta and Bean Soup)

Here the grain (or pasta) and beans are in the same dish to provide better quality protein than either alone.
Makes 6 servings.

1 cup (½ pound) dried white beans
5 cups water
1 teaspoon salt
¼ cup olive or vegetable oil
1 medium-size onion, finely
chopped (½ cup)
2 cloves garlic, finely chopped
2 stalks celery, finely chopped
1 can (1 pound) tomatoes

½ teaspoon leaf rosemary,
crumbled
½ teaspoon freshly ground black
pepper
1½ cups small elbow macaroni or
small shells
¼ cup chopped fresh parsley
Freshly grated Parmesan

1. Pick over and wash beans, drain, and place in a bowl with water to cover. Let stand at room temperature overnight.
2. Drain the beans and place in a kettle with the water. Bring to a boil, cover, and simmer 1 hour. Add salt.
3. Meanwhile in a medium-size skillet heat the oil and sauté the onion, garlic, and celery until tender.
4. Add cooked vegetables to bean mixture along with the tomatoes, rosemary, and pepper. Bring to a boil, add pasta, and cook 8 minutes or until al dente. Add parsley, check seasoning, and add more salt and pepper, if needed. Serve with grated Parmesan.

BLACK BEAN SOUP
(Cuban)

Lots of chopped raw onion on every serving is a must.
Makes 6 servings.

1 pound dried black or turtle beans (2 cups)	1 teaspoon leaf oregano, crumbled
6 cups water	1½ teaspoons salt
3 tablespoons vegetable oil	½ teaspoon freshly ground black pepper
1 large onion, finely chopped (1 cup)	Pinch of cayenne
2 cloves garlic, finely chopped	¼ cup lemon juice
1 stalk celery, finely chopped	⅓ cup chopped onion
	1 hard-cooked egg, chopped

1. Pick over and wash the beans and place in a bowl. Cover with cold water to a depth 3 inches above beans and soak at room temperature overnight.
2. Drain beans and place in a kettle with 6 cups fresh water. Bring to a boil, cover, and simmer 2 hours, or until tender.
3. Meanwhile heat the oil in a medium-size skillet and sauté the onion until tender but not brown. Add the garlic and celery and cook 3 minutes. Add the oregano, salt, pepper, and cayenne.
4. Remove 2 cups of the bean mixture and purée in an electric blender or food processor. Return to the bulk of the soup along with sautéed vegetable mixture. Reheat and taste for seasoning. Add more salt and pepper, if you wish. Add lemon juice. This should be a heavy thick mixture. Serve topped with the onion mixed with the egg.

BEAN AND SPINACH SOUP
(Italian)

It's worth a trip to an Italian produce market to experience the special flavor of fava beans.
Makes 6 servings.

2 tablespoons vegetable oil
1 medium-size onion, finely chopped (½ cup)
1 clove garlic, finely chopped
3 cans (13¾ ounces each) chicken broth, or 6 cups vegetable broth (see page 59)
2 cups fresh shelled fava beans, or 1 package (10 ounces) frozen baby lima beans

1 package (10 ounces) frozen chopped spinach, or 1 pound fresh spinach, chopped
½ teaspoon salt
¼ teaspoon freshly ground black pepper
½ teaspoon leaf oregano, crumbled
½ teaspoon leaf basil, crumbled
⅓ cup small elbow macaroni
3 medium-size ripe tomatoes, peeled, seeded, and chopped, or 1 can (1 pound) tomatoes

1. In a heavy saucepan or Dutch oven heat the oil and sauté the onion until tender but not browned. Add the garlic and cook 1 minute.
2. Add the broth and fresh fava beans and cook 5 minutes. Add frozen limas and spinach and cook until vegetables have thawed.
3. If using fresh spinach add with salt, pepper, oregano, basil, and macaroni. Cook, stirring occasionally, 8 minutes, or until macaroni is tender.
4. Add tomatoes, breaking up large pieces, and reheat.

BEER SOUP
(German)

Heady and hearty soup for cold winter days.
Makes 4 servings.

¼ cup (½ stick) butter or margarine
1 small onion, finely chopped (¼ cup)
1 small head cabbage, shredded (about 4 cups)
2 tablespoons flour

1 can (13¾ ounces) chicken broth, or 2 cups vegetable broth (see page 59)
2 cups strong ale
1 teaspoon salt
½ teaspoon freshly ground black pepper
1 cup hot milk

1. In a heavy kettle or Dutch oven heat the butter and sauté the onion until tender but not browned. Add the cabbage and cook, stirring, 4 minutes.
2. Sprinkle with the flour and stir to mix. Stir in the broth, ale, salt, and pepper. Bring to a boil, cover, and simmer 30 minutes.
3. In an electric blender or food processor purée the soup and put back in a clean kettle. Reheat and add hot milk but do not boil. Serve at once.

BORSCHT
(Russian Beet Soup)

Serve piroshki (see page 6) with this soup for Sunday supper.
Makes 8 servings.

8 small beets with tops	4 cups water
1 medium-size onion, finely chopped (½ cup)	1 teaspoon salt
1 carrot, cut into julienne strips	½ teaspoon freshly ground black pepper
1 tomato, peeled and diced	Sour salt or lemon juice
1 stalk celery, diced	1 tablespoon flour
2 cups shredded cabbage	½ cup sour cream
6 cups vegetable broth (see page 59) or chicken broth	1 tablespoon snipped fresh dillweed

1. Wash the beets very well. Cut off tops and chop. Cut the unpeeled beets into julienne strips. Peel if the beets are not young.
2. Place beets, tops, onion, carrot, tomato, celery, cabbage, broth, water, salt, and pepper in a heavy kettle. Bring to a boil, cover, and simmer until vegetables are tender, about 30 minutes.
3. Add enough sour salt or lemon juice to give a tart flavor. Blend the flour into the sour cream in a small bowl. Blend in some of the hot soup and then gradually whisk the sour cream mixture into the kettle. Reheat but do not boil.
4. Taste and add salt and pepper if necessary. Add dill.

BROCCOLI SOUP
(American)

Terrific way to use broccoli stalks.
Makes 4 servings.

3 tablespoons vegetable oil
1 large onion, finely chopped
  (1 cup)
1 clove garlic, finely chopped
1 small carrot, finely chopped
  Stalks from 1 bunch broccoli,
  peeled, if tough, and diced
½ cup broccoli flowerets, optional

1 can (13¾ ounces) chicken broth,
  or 2 cups vegetable broth
  (see page 59)
1½ cups water
½ teaspoon salt
¼ teaspoon freshly ground black
  pepper
½ teaspoon leaf rosemary,
  crumbled

1. Heat the oil in a heavy Dutch oven or casserole and sauté the onion until wilted and tender, about 8 minutes. Add the garlic, carrot, and broccoli stalks. Cook over low heat, stirring occasionally, until vegetables are golden, about 10 minutes.
2. Add broccoli flowerets, broth, water, salt, pepper, and rosemary. Bring to a boil, cover, and simmer 10 minutes. Remove flowerets with slotted spoon.
3. Purée the soup in batches in an electric blender until smooth and return to Dutch oven. Reheat, check seasonings, and garnish with flowerets.

CREAM OF CARROT SOUP
(French)

If you leave out the turnip you probably have all the other ingredients on hand.
Makes 4 servings.

3 tablespoons butter or margarine
1 medium-size onion, finely
  chopped (½ cup)
1½ pounds carrots (about 8 medium),
  scraped and diced
1 stalk celery with leaves, sliced
1 small white turnip, diced,
  optional

½ teaspoon salt
¼ teaspoon freshly ground black
  pepper
¼ teaspoon leaf thyme, crumbled
3 cups chicken broth or vegetable
  broth (see page 59)
½ cup heavy or light cream

1. In a heavy kettle or Dutch oven heat the butter and sauté the onion until tender but not browned.
2. Add the carrots, celery, and turnip and cook, stirring, 5 to 8 minutes. Sprinkle with the salt, pepper, and thyme. Add the broth and bring to a boil. Cover and simmer until the vegetables are tender, about 15 minutes.
3. Purée the mixture in batches in an electric blender or food processor and return to the kettle. Stir in the cream. Reheat but do not boil.

CAULIFLOWER SOUP
(Danish)

Serve with open-face sandwiches to provide color and texture to the meal.
Makes 6 servings.

3 tablespoons butter or margarine
1 medium-size onion, finely chopped (½ cup)
3 cups sliced cauliflowerets (1 medium head)
2 tablespoons flour
1 can (13¾ ounces) chicken broth, or 2 cups vegetable broth (see page 59)

2 cups half-and-half, light cream, or milk
2 cups (8 ounces) shredded Swiss or Gruyère
2 tablespoons chopped fresh parsley
¼ teaspoon freshly ground white pepper

1. In a large heavy saucepan or Dutch oven heat the butter and sauté the onion until tender but not browned. Add the cauliflower and sauté over low heat until crisp-tender but not browned. Cover for 2 to 3 minutes if necessary.
2. Sprinkle with flour and stir in the chicken broth. Cook, stirring, until mixture thickens, then simmer 2 minutes. Stir in the cream and cheese and cook, stirring, over medium-high heat until cheese melts, but do not boil. Add the parsley and pepper.

HARIRA
(Moroccan Chick-pea and Lentil Soup)

The combination of sweet spices, cilantro, and lemon juice is strange the first time but it grows on you with successive tastings.
Makes 6 servings.

½ cup dried chick-peas
2 tablespoons vegetable oil
1 large onion, finely chopped (1 cup)
1 pound chicken wings
1 stalk celery with leaves, chopped
½ teaspoon turmeric
½ teaspoon ground ginger
½ teaspoon ground cinnamon
¾ cup lentils, picked over, washed, and drained
1 can (2 pounds, 3 ounces) Italian plum tomatoes

½ cup chopped fresh cilantro (Chinese parsley) or flat Italian parsley
6 cups water
2 teaspoons salt
½ teaspoon freshly ground black pepper
½ cup very fine noodles (vermicelli), broken up
2 eggs
2 tablespoons lemon juice

1. Pick over and wash the chick-peas. Cover with water and let soak overnight at room temperature.
2. Heat the oil in a heavy kettle or Dutch oven and sauté the onion until tender but not brown. Cut the wings into three pieces and brown with the onion.
3. Add the celery, turmeric, ginger, cinnamon, lentils, drained chick-peas, tomatoes, cilantro, water, salt, and pepper. Bring to a boil, cover, and simmer 1½ hours.
4. Add the fine noodles and cook 5 minutes. In a small bowl combine the eggs and lemon juice. Remove kettle from heat and stir in the egg mixture. Serve immediately.

CORN CHOWDER
(American)

I make this soup only during the local corn season, a time when we eat fresh corn at least every other day.
Makes 6 servings.

¼ cup (½ stick) butter or margarine
1 large onion, finely chopped (1 cup)
2 medium-size potatoes, peeled and diced (2 cups)
3 cups vegetable broth (see page 59) or chicken broth

2 cups corn kernels cut from the cob (about 6 ears)
1 teaspoon salt
½ teaspoon freshly ground black pepper
2 cups half-and-half

1. In a large heavy saucepan heat the butter and sauté the onion until tender but not browned. Add potatoes and cook, stirring, 2 minutes.
2. Add the broth, bring to a boil, cover, and simmer until potatoes are tender, about 15 minutes.
3. Add corn kernels, salt, and pepper and cook 2 minutes. Stir in the half-and-half and reheat but do not boil.

CHILLED CUCUMBER SOUP
(Turkish)

Perfect for a hot summer day.
Makes 4 servings.

2 cucumbers, peeled, seeded, and chopped
2 cloves garlic, crushed
2 containers (8 ounces each) plain yogurt
1 container (8 ounces) sour cream
2 tablespoons snipped fresh dillweed

½ teaspoon salt
¼ teaspoon freshly ground black pepper
¼ cup finely chopped walnuts
Dill sprigs

1. Put the cucumber, garlic, yogurt, sour cream, and dill in the container of an electric blender or food processor. Whirl until smooth.
2. Add salt and pepper and whirl to mix. Chill.
3. To serve, place a tablespoon of walnuts in each of 4 serving bowls and pour soup over. Garnish with dill.

ESCAROLE SOUP
(Italian)

Makes 4 servings.

2 tablespoons butter or margarine
1 large onion, finely chopped
  (1 cup)
1 carrot, diced
1 stalk celery, sliced
1 head escarole (about 1 pound),
  washed, drained, and shredded
¼ cup raw rice or small elbow
  macaroni

2 cans (13¾ ounces each) chicken
  broth, or 4 cups vegetable broth
  (see page 59)
½ teaspoon salt
¼ teaspoon freshly ground black
  pepper
¼ teaspoon leaf thyme, crumbled
1 cup water
Freshly grated Parmesan

1. In a large saucepan or a kettle melt the butter and sauté the onion until tender but not browned.
2. Add the carrot and celery and cook 3 minutes longer, stirring occasionally. Add the escarole and cook, stirring, 2 minutes.
3. Add rice or macaroni, broth, salt, pepper, thyme, and water. Bring to a boil, cover, and cook until rice or macaroni is just cooked. Serve with grated Parmesan.

GARLIC SOUP
(Spanish)

Depression-proof soup that is surprisingly good.
Bake at 450° for 5 minutes.
Makes 4 servings.

2 tablespoons olive or vegetable oil
2 cloves garlic, crushed
8 thin slices stale French bread
½ teaspoon paprika

1 quart boiling water
½ teaspoon salt
¼ cup milk
4 eggs

1. In a heavy skillet heat the oil and sauté the garlic until browned. Remove and discard garlic. Fry the bread slices in the garlic oil until golden and crisp. Transfer to an ovenproof baking dish or 4 individual soup crocks. Stir paprika into oil remaining in skillet and cook 1 minute.
2. Pour water and salt into skillet. Bring to a boil, add milk, and pour over bread slices. Break eggs into hot mixture. Bake at 450° for 5 minutes, or until eggs are set and bread is crusty on top.

LEEK AND POTATO SOUP
(French)

Served cold it becomes vichyssoise.
Makes 6 servings.

3 tablespoons butter or margarine
3 medium-size leeks, cleaned and thinly sliced
1 medium-size onion, finely chopped (½ cup)
3 medium-size potatoes, peeled and sliced
1 quart chicken broth or vegetable broth (see page 59)
Salt and freshly ground black pepper to taste
1 cup heavy or light cream
2 tablespoons chopped fresh chives, or 2 teaspoons freeze-dried

1. In a heavy kettle or Dutch oven heat the butter and sauté the leeks and onion until tender but not browned.
2. Add the potato and broth. Bring to a boil, cover, and simmer until vegetables are tender, about 20 minutes.
3. Purée the mixture in an electric blender or food processor and return to the kettle. Season to taste with salt and pepper. Bring to a boil, stir in the cream, and reheat but do not boil. Sprinkle with chives.

Note: To serve cold, chill the mixture after it is puréed. Stir in the heavy cream just before serving. If it is too thick add milk or broth.

LENTIL SOUP
(French)

All the advantages of dried pulses without the need to soak.
Makes 4 to 6 servings.

1 cup lentils
2 cans (13¾ ounces each) chicken broth, or 4 cups vegetable broth (see page 59)
2 cups water
2 tablespoons vegetable oil
1 large onion, finely chopped (1 cup)
3 medium-size carrots, diced (1½ cups)

1 stalk celery with leaves, diced (½ cup)
1 clove garlic, finely chopped
1 teaspoon salt
¼ teaspoon freshly ground black pepper
½ teaspoon leaf rosemary, crumbled

1. Pick over and wash the lentils and place in a heavy kettle or Dutch oven. Add the broth and water, bring to a boil, cover, and simmer 50 minutes, or until lentils are tender.
2. Meanwhile heat the oil in a heavy skillet and sauté the onion until tender. Add the carrots, celery, and garlic and cook, stirring, 5 minutes.
3. Add vegetable mixture to lentils with salt, pepper, and rosemary and cook, covered, 10 minutes, or until vegetables are tender.

LENTIL SOUP
(Turkish)

Thick enough to be called a stew.
Makes 4 servings.

2 tablespoons vegetable oil
1 large onion, finely chopped (1 cup)
1 clove garlic, finely chopped
1 cup lentils, picked over, washed, and drained
2 cups vegetable broth (see page 59) or water
6 tomatoes, peeled and chopped, or 1 can (2 pounds, 3 ounces) Italian plum tomatoes

1 teaspoon ground coriander
1 teaspoon salt
¼ teaspoon freshly ground black pepper
4 ounces very fine noodles (vermicelli), broken up
¼ cup chopped fresh parsley

1. In a heavy saucepan heat the oil and sauté the onion until tender but not browned. Add the garlic and cook 1 minute.
2. Add lentils, broth, tomatoes, coriander, salt, and pepper. Bring to a boil, cover, and simmer 45 minutes. Add the noodles and cook 5 minutes.
3. Sprinkle with parsley.

MUSHROOM-BARLEY SOUP
(Swedish)

After the barley is cooked the soup can be puréed in an electric blender or food processor before adding mushrooms and cream, if desired.
Makes 6 servings.

¼ pound (½ cup) coarse pearl barley

4 tablespoons (½ stick) butter or margarine

1 large onion, finely chopped (1 cup)

1 large carrot, finely diced (1 cup)

1 stalk celery, finely diced

6 cups vegetable broth (see page 59) or chicken broth

1 teaspoon salt

¼ teaspoon freshly ground black pepper

1 pound mushrooms, sliced (4 cups)

1 cup heavy or light cream

1. Rinse the barley with warm water and place in a large heavy saucepan.
2. Heat 2 tablespoons of the butter in a skillet and sauté the onion until tender but not browned. Add the carrot and celery and cook 2 minutes. Add to barley.
3. Add broth, salt, and pepper to saucepan. Bring to a boil, cover, and simmer until barley is tender, about 1 hour.
4. Meanwhile heat remaining butter in skillet and sauté the mushrooms until wilted. Add mushrooms to soup and stir in cream. Taste and season with salt and pepper, if needed.

CREAM OF MUSHROOM SOUP
(French)

The number of servings can be stretched to 8 if it is served as the first course of a formal dinner.
Makes 6 servings.

½ cup (1 stick) butter or margarine
2 large well-trimmed leeks, washed and thinly sliced
1 clove garlic, finely chopped
1 pound mushrooms, sliced (4 cups)
¼ cup flour
1 teaspoon salt

¼ teaspoon freshly ground black pepper
1 tablespoon snipped fresh dillweed
3 cans (13¾ ounces each) chicken broth, or 6 cups vegetable broth (see page 59)
1 cup heavy or light cream

1. Heat the butter in a heavy saucepan or Dutch oven and sauté the leeks until tender. Add the garlic and mushrooms and cook 8 to 10 minutes, or until mushrooms are wilted.
2. Sprinkle flour over vegetables and cook, stirring, 3 minutes. Add salt, pepper, dill, and broth. Bring to a boil, cover, and simmer 20 minutes. Cool slightly.
3. Purée the mixture in batches in an electric blender or a food processor until smooth. Pour back into saucepan. Bring to a boil, stir in the cream, and reheat but do not boil. Serve immediately.

MUSHROOM SOUP
(American)

Because of new methods of growing mushrooms they have become a standard prepackaged product in every supermarket and can be enjoyed in many ways.
Makes 6 servings.

¼ cup (½ stick) butter or margarine
1 large onion, finely chopped (1 cup)
1 stalk celery with leaves, chopped
2 medium-size carrots, diced (1 cup)
1 pound mushrooms, sliced (4 cups)
1 can (1 pound) tomatoes

1 quart vegetable broth (see page 59)
1 teaspoon leaf rosemary, crumbled
1 teaspoon salt
½ teaspoon freshly ground black pepper
2 tablespoons chopped fresh parsley

1. In a heavy kettle or Dutch oven melt the butter and cook the onion until tender but not browned. Add the celery and carrot and cook 5 minutes longer, stirring often.
2. Add the mushrooms and cook, stirring, 3 minutes. Add tomatoes, broth, rosemary, salt, and pepper. Bring to a boil, cover, and simmer gently about 10 minutes. Sprinkle with parsley.

ONION SOUP
(American)

A quick version of the French masterpiece with an added Middle Eastern twist.
Makes 4 servings.

3 tablespoons butter or margarine
1 large sweet Bermuda or Spanish onion, thinly sliced and separated into rings
2 cans (13¾ ounces each) beef broth, or 4 cups vegetable broth (see page 59)
¼ teaspoon leaf thyme, crumbled
¼ teaspoon freshly ground black pepper

1 cup water
2 tablespoons freshly grated Parmesan
2 large loaves pita bread, split and cut into quarters
2 tablespoons butter or margarine
2 tablespoons sesame seeds
2 tablespoons freshly grated Parmesan

1. Melt the butter in a heavy Dutch oven or casserole. Add the onion rings and cook, stirring occasionally, over low heat until onions wilt and are golden, about 10 to 15 minutes.
2. Add the broth, thyme, pepper, and water. Bring to a boil, cover, and simmer 20 minutes or until onions are tender.
3. Stir in cheese and serve with toasted pita. Spread the pieces of pita bread with butter and sprinkle with sesame seeds. Toast in a toaster oven or under the broiler for 1 minute. Sprinkle with Parmesan and broil until bubbly and crisp.

POTATO SOUP
(Finnish)

Makes 6 servings.

3 tablespoons butter or margarine
1 large onion, finely chopped
  (1 cup)
1 stalk celery, finely chopped
6 medium-size potatoes, peeled
  and diced
6 cups vegetable broth (see page
  59) or chicken broth

2 tablespoons snipped fresh
  dillweed
1 teaspoon salt
¼ teaspoon freshly ground black
  pepper
2 tablespoons flour
1 container (8 ounces) plain yogurt
  or sour cream

1. In a large heavy saucepan heat the butter and sauté the onion and celery until tender but not browned. Add the potato and cook, stirring, 4 minutes.
2. Add the broth, dill, salt, and pepper. Bring to a boil, cover, and simmer until the potatoes are tender, about 25 minutes.
3. Whirl the mixture in batches in an electric blender or food processor until smooth. Return to pan. Mix the flour with the yogurt and gradually whisk into the blended soup. Heat, stirring, until mixture thickens but do not boil. Serve hot, or cool and chill. Check consistency and add milk, broth, or water to thin if necessary and garnish with dill sprigs, if you wish.

CREAM OF PEA SOUP
(French)

I often serve this soup before a main course of roast leg of lamb, oven-browned potatoes, and broccoli.
Makes 6 servings.

2 tablespoons butter or margarine
1 medium-size onion, finely
  chopped (½ cup)
1 stalk celery, finely chopped
1 carrot, diced
1 clove garlic, finely chopped
2 cups shelled fresh peas (about 1½
  pounds in pod), or 2 cups frozen
  from a poly bag

2 cans (13¾ ounces each) chicken
  broth, or 4 cups vegetable broth
  (see page 59)
1 tablespoon chopped fresh mint,
  or ½ teaspoon dried
1 teaspoon salt
¼ teaspoon freshly ground black
  pepper
1 cup heavy or light cream

1. In a heavy saucepan heat the butter and sauté the onion until tender but not browned. Add the celery, carrot, and garlic and cook 4 minutes, stirring often.
2. Add the peas, broth, mint, salt, and pepper. Bring to a boil, cover, and simmer 15 minutes, or until the vegetables are tender.
3. Purée in batches, if necessary, in an electric blender or a food processor and return to saucepan. Stir in the cream and reheat but do not boil.

SPLIT PEA SOUP
(Danish)

I enjoy this version which has no traditional ham flavor.
Makes 6 servings.

¼ cup (½ stick) butter or margarine
1 medium-size onion, finely chopped (½ cup)
1 carrot, finely diced
1 stalk celery with leaves, finely diced
1 small white turnip, finely diced
3 cans (13¾ ounces each) chicken broth, or 6 cups vegetable broth (see page 59), or water

1½ cups green or yellow split peas
1 bay leaf, crumbled
1 teaspoon salt
½ teaspoon freshly ground black pepper
½ teaspoon leaf thyme, crumbled
½ teaspoon leaf marjoram, crumbled

1. In a heavy kettle or Dutch oven heat the butter and sauté the onion, carrot, celery, and turnip until tender, about 10 minutes.
2. Add the broth, peas, and bay leaf. Bring to a boil, cover, and simmer 45 minutes. Add salt, pepper, thyme, and marjoram and cook, covered, 15 minutes, or until peas are tender.

PUMPKIN SOUP
(American)

For a dramatic effect serve in a hollowed-out pumpkin.
Makes 6 servings.

3 tablespoons butter or margarine
1 large onion, finely chopped
  (1 cup)
1 medium-size carrot, finely
  chopped
1 can (13¾ ounces) chicken broth,
  or 2 cups vegetable broth
  (see page 59)
1 cup water

1 can (1 pound) pumpkin
1 teaspoon salt
¼ teaspoon freshly ground black
  pepper
¼ teaspoon ground cinnamon
¼ teaspoon ground ginger
⅛ teaspoon ground nutmeg
1 cup light cream or half-and-half

1. Melt the butter in a heavy Dutch oven or casserole and sauté the
    onion and carrot until golden, about 8 minutes. Add the broth and
    water, bring to a boil, cover, and simmer 15 minutes.
2. Purée the vegetable broth mixture in an electric blender in batches
    and return to Dutch oven. Add pumpkin, salt, pepper, cinnamon,
    ginger, and nutmeg and heat while whisking until smooth. Simmer
    10 minutes.
3. Slowly stir in the cream and reheat but do not boil.

CREAM OF SPINACH SOUP
(French)

The pale green color, smooth texture, and delicate flavor will
make a soup lover out of anyone.
Makes 6 servings.

1½ pounds fresh spinach, or 3
  packages (10 ounces each) frozen
  chopped, thawed and squeezed
  dry
3 tablespoons butter or margarine
1 medium-size onion, finely
  chopped (½ cup)
3 tablespoons flour
1 can (13¾ ounces) chicken broth,
  or 2 cups vegetable broth
  (see page 59)

¼ teaspoon leaf savory, crumbled
¼ teaspoon leaf marjoram,
  crumbled
⅛ teaspoon ground nutmeg
1 teaspoon salt
¼ teaspoon freshly ground black
  pepper
2 cups heavy cream or half-and-half

1. Pick over, trim, and wash the fresh spinach and place in a kettle with just the water clinging to the leaves. Cook 5 minutes or until wilted. Purée in an electric blender or food processor.
2. Heat the butter in a large saucepan and sauté the onion until tender but not browned. Sprinkle with the flour and cook, stirring, 2 minutes. Gradually stir in the broth and bring to a boil, stirring.
3. Add the savory, marjoram, nutmeg, salt, pepper, and puréed or thawed frozen spinach. Simmer 5 minutes. Add cream and reheat but do not boil.

FRESH TOMATO SOUP
(French)

With this recipe on hand you'll never be at a loss to know what to do with extra fresh tomatoes.
Makes 8 servings.

¼ cup (½ stick) butter or margarine
2 tablespoons vegetable oil
1 large onion, finely chopped (1 cup)
½ teaspoon leaf thyme, crumbled
1 teaspoon leaf basil, crumbled or 1½ tablespoons chopped fresh
3 pounds ripe tomatoes (about 16 medium), peeled, seeded, and cut into eighths

4 tablespoons tomato paste
1 teaspoon salt
½ teaspoon freshly ground black pepper
¼ cup flour
1 quart vegetable broth (see page 59) or chicken broth
1 cup heavy or light cream

1. Heat the butter and oil in a heavy kettle or Dutch oven and sauté the onion until tender but not browned.
2. Add thyme, basil, tomatoes cut into eighths, tomato paste, salt, and pepper. Bring to a boil and simmer 20 minutes.
3. Mix the flour with a little of the broth until smooth and stir into kettle. Add remaining broth and bring to a boil, stirring. Simmer 30 minutes, stirring often.
4. Pass the mixture through a food processor or a fine sieve into a clean kettle. Reheat and stir in cream but do not boil.

MINESTRONE
(Italian)

Every major cuisine in the world has a vegetable soup, but this must be the best known and the most popular.
Makes 6 servings.

¼ cup olive or vegetable oil
1 large onion, finely chopped (1 cup)
1 clove garlic, finely chopped
1 stalk celery with leaves, finely chopped
1 large carrot, diced
1 large potato, diced
¼ pound green beans, cut in ½-inch lengths
1 medium-size zucchini, diced
1 can (2 pounds, 3 ounces) peeled Italian plum tomatoes
2 cups chicken or vegetable broth (see page 59), or water

½ cup dry red wine
1½ teaspoons salt
½ teaspoon freshly ground black pepper
1 teaspoon leaf oregano, crumbled
2 teaspoons leaf basil, crumbled
¼ cup orzo, broken spaghetti, or fine noodles
1 can (1 pound, 4 ounces) chick-peas, drained
2 tablespoons chopped fresh parsley
Freshly grated Parmesan

1. In a large heavy kettle or Dutch oven heat the oil and sauté the onion over low heat until tender, about 10 minutes.
2. Add the garlic, celery, carrot, and potato and cook, stirring, 5 minutes.
3. Add the green beans, zucchini, tomatoes, broth, wine, salt, pepper, oregano, and basil and bring to a boil. Cover and simmer 20 minutes.
4. Add the orzo and cook 10 minutes. Add the chick-peas and parsley and reheat. Serve with Parmesan and crusty Italian bread.

VEGETABLE BROTH
(American)

Collect parings from scrubbed carrots, potatoes, and turnips in a bag in the freezer between making batches of vegetable broth.

Makes about 3 quarts.

½ cup (1 stick) butter or margarine
6 carrots, scrubbed and sliced
4 leeks, cleaned and sliced
3 large onions, roughly chopped
6 stalks celery with leaves, sliced
2 large green peppers, seeded and diced
6 potatoes, scrubbed and diced
4 small turnips, scrubbed and diced
3 to 4 cups vegetable parings from potatoes, carrots, and turnips, optional

½ pound shredded spinach, escarole, chard, or kale, optional
Small bunch parsley sprigs
3 bay leaves, crumbled
1 tablespoon salt
8 peppercorns, bruised in mortar and pestle
1 tablespoon leaf thyme, crumbled
3 to 4 quarts water

1. Melt the butter in a large 6- to 8-quart heavy casserole or Dutch oven. Add the carrots, leeks, onion, celery, green pepper, potatoes, turnips, and parings and cook over medium-high heat about 20 minutes, stirring often.
2. Add remaining ingredients, including enough water to cover vegetables to a depth of an inch or two. Bring to a boil, cover, and simmer 2 to 3 hours. Strain and discard solids. Broth will keep in the refrigerator up to 3 days and in the freezer for 3 months. If it is to be served alone check the seasoning and concentrate by rapid boiling if needed.

VEGETABLE SOUP
(American)

Add a turnip or use winter squash instead of zucchini—the number of vegetable combinations is infinite and the choice should depend on what is on hand.
Makes 8 servings.

3 tablespoons butter or margarine
1 small onion, finely chopped (½ cup)
1 medium-size zucchini, diced
1 large carrot, diced
2 cans (13¾ ounces each) beef or chicken broth, or 4 cups vegetable broth (see page 59)
1 can (1 pound) plum tomatoes
1 package (10 ounces) frozen baby lima beans

½ cup orzo or small elbow macaroni
1 teaspoon salt
½ teaspoon freshly ground black pepper
¼ teaspoon leaf oregano, crumbled
¼ teaspoon leaf basil, crumbled
2 tablespoons freshly grated Parmesan
2 tablespoons chopped fresh parsley

1.   Heat the butter in a heavy Dutch oven or casserole. Sauté the onion, zucchini, and carrot until golden, about 8 minutes.
2.   Add broth, tomatoes, limas, orzo, salt, pepper, oregano, and basil. Bring to a boil, cover, and simmer 15 minutes, or until vegetables are tender. Stir in the cheese and parsley and serve immediately.

DILLED ZUCCHINI SOUP
(Italian)

Serve hot or cold with breadsticks.
Makes 4 servings.

¼ cup (½ stick) butter or margarine
1 large onion, finely chopped (1 cup)
1 clove garlic, finely chopped
4 medium-size zucchini, thinly sliced
2 cans (13¾ ounces each) chicken broth, or 4 cups vegetable broth (see page 59)

½ teaspoon salt
¼ teaspoon freshly ground black pepper
2 tablespoons snipped fresh dillweed
1 cup light cream, half-and-half, or plain yogurt

1. In a medium-size heavy saucepan heat the butter and sauté the onion until tender but not browned. Add the garlic and zucchini and cook, stirring, 3 minutes.
2. Add broth, salt, pepper, and dill. Bring to a boil, cover, and simmer 15 minutes. Purée in an electric blender or food processor in batches and return to clean saucepan. If serving hot add cream or yogurt and reheat but do not boil. If serving cold allow puréed mixture to cool and chill. Stir in the cream or yogurt.

YOGURT-BARLEY SOUP
(Armenian)

This soup has a strong mint flavor. Taste as you add the herb until it is to your liking.
Makes 4 servings.

½ cup pearl barley
Water
1 quart chicken broth or vegetable broth (see page 59)
¼ teaspoon freshly ground black pepper
3 tablespoons butter or margarine
1 medium-size onion, finely chopped (½ cup)

2 tablespoons chopped fresh parsley
2 tablespoons chopped fresh mint
2 containers (8 ounces each) plain yogurt
1 egg
Salt and freshly ground black pepper to taste

1. Rinse the barley and put in a medium-size bowl with cold water to cover. Let soak overnight.
2. Drain and place soaked barley in a kettle. Add the broth and pepper. Bring to a boil, cover, and simmer until barley is tender, about 45 minutes.
3. Meanwhile in a medium-size skillet heat the butter and sauté the onion until tender but not browned. Add the parsley and mint.
4. Add the onion mixture to the cooked barley. In a small bowl combine the yogurt with the egg. Add some of the hot soup to the yogurt mixture and beat well. Return to the kettle and heat, stirring, but do not boil. Taste and add salt and pepper to taste.

GAZPACHO
(Spanish Cold Salad Soup)

There are as many versions of this soup as there are minestrones but I promise you'll make this one again and again.
Makes 6 servings.

2 cloves garlic, crushed
2 pounds medium-size tomatoes (about 6), peeled and chopped
1 medium-size cucumber, peeled and cut into chunks
1 large green pepper, seeded and chopped
1 cup soft bread cubes, crusts removed
¼ cup red wine vinegar

2 cups tomato juice
1 cup water
¼ cup olive or vegetable oil
½ teaspoon salt
¼ teaspoon freshly ground black pepper
½ cup chopped green onions
½ cup garlic croutons
½ cup chopped green pepper

1. Put the garlic, tomatoes, cucumber, green pepper, bread, and vinegar in the container of an electric blender or food processor and whirl until smooth.
2. Pass the mixture through a fine sieve and discard the solids. To the liquid add the tomato juice, water, oil, salt, and pepper. Chill well.
3. Serve in chilled bowls and pass the garnishes of green onions, croutons, and green pepper.

FRUIT SOUP
(Swedish)

Good as a first course or dessert.
Makes 6 servings.

1 cup dried apricots, quartered
1 cup pitted dried prunes, quartered
½ cup raisins
6 cups water
½ lemon, cut into quarters
¾ cup sugar
3 tablespoons quick-cooking tapioca

1 orange, peeled, sliced, and slices halved
1 can (1 pound) pitted sour cherries with juice
¼ teaspoon salt
½ cup coarsely chopped walnuts
Heavy cream

1. In a heavy saucepan or kettle combine the apricots, prunes, raisins, water, lemon, sugar, and tapioca. Bring to a boil, stirring to dissolve the sugar. Cover and simmer 10 minutes, or until dried fruits are tender. Cool and chill.
2. Add the orange, cherries, and salt. Sprinkle with chopped walnuts and serve with a pitcher of heavy cream.

STRACCIATELLI
(Italian Egg Soup)

When I'm feeling under the weather or suffering from a head cold this is the medicine I take.
Makes 4 servings.

5 cups chicken broth or vegetable broth (see page 59)
3 eggs, lightly beaten
3 tablespoons cream of wheat
3 tablespoons freshly grated Parmesan

1 tablespoon chopped fresh parsley
Salt and freshly ground black pepper to taste

1. Reserve 1 cup of the broth and heat the remaining 4 cups to boiling in a heavy kettle or Dutch oven.
2. In a small bowl beat together the eggs, cream of wheat, cheese, and parsley. Gradually beat in the reserved cup of cold broth.
3. Slowly whisk the egg mixture into the boiling broth so that the egg forms ribbons. Simmer 4 to 5 minutes, stirring constantly. Add salt and pepper to taste and serve with more freshly grated Parmesan, if you wish.

EGG AND LEMON SOUP
(Greek)

Follow with a Greek vegetable main dish such as spinach pie or
stuffed eggplant, and fruit for dessert.
Makes 6 servings.

1 can (46 ounces) chicken broth, or   3 egg yolks, lightly beaten
  6 cups vegetable broth   ½ cup lemon juice
  (see page 59)   Salt
½ cup raw long-grain rice   1 tablespoon butter

1. In a heavy saucepan bring the broth to a boil. Stir in the rice, cover,
   and simmer 15 to 20 minutes, or until rice is tender.
2. Beat the egg yolks while adding the lemon juice slowly. Remove 2
   cups of the hot soup and add to the egg mixture, drop by drop, while
   beating vigorously.
3. Gradually beat the egg-broth mixture into the broth and rice in the
   saucepan. Reheat but do not boil. Taste and add salt if needed. Swirl
   in the butter.

NEW ENGLAND CLAM CHOWDER
(American)

Clam chowder and baked beans are two dishes in which I
always use salt pork, but I am suggesting a nontraditional
alternative. I cannot compromise with canned clams.
Makes 6 servings.

3 tablespoons butter, margarine, or   24 quahogs, opened, liquor strained
  ¼ cup diced salt pork   and reserved
1 large onion, finely chopped   1 quart milk or half-and-half
  (1 cup)   1 teaspoon salt
3 medium-size potatoes, peeled   ¼ teaspoon freshly ground black
  and diced (3 cups)   pepper

1. In a heavy saucepan heat the butter and sauté the onion until tender but not browned. Or render the fat from the salt pork, remove crisp pieces, and reserve. Sauté onion in fat as above.
2. Add potatoes and cook, stirring, 3 minutes. Measure the liquor from the clams and add water to make 2 cups. Add to potato mixture. Bring to a boil, cover, and simmer until potatoes are tender, about 20 minutes.
3. Grind or chop the quahogs and add with milk, salt, and pepper. Bring to a boil and simmer, but do not boil, 2 to 3 minutes, or until clams are tender. Return pork pieces.

MANHATTAN CLAM CHOWDER
(American)

Makes 6 servings.

24 quahogs, opened, strained, and liquor reserved
3 tablespoons butter or margarine, or ¼ cup diced salt pork
2 large onions, finely chopped (2 cups)
2 stalks celery, sliced
1 can (2 pounds, 3 ounces) Italian plum tomatoes
½ teaspoon leaf thyme, crumbled

1 bay leaf
3 medium-size potatoes, peeled and diced (3 cups)
½ teaspoon salt
¼ teaspoon freshly ground black pepper
Liquid red pepper seasoning
½ teaspoon Worcestershire sauce
2 tablespoons chopped fresh parsley

1. Grind or chop the quahogs and reserve. Measure the liquor and add water to make 3 cups. In a heavy saucepan heat the butter and sauté the onion until tender but not browned. Or render the fat from the salt pork, remove crisp pieces, and reserve. Sauté onion in pork fat. Add the celery and cook 1 minute.
2. Add the tomatoes, thyme, bay leaf, potatoes, salt, pepper, dash liquid red pepper seasoning, and Worcestershire. Bring to a boil, cover, and simmer 25 minutes, or until potatoes are tender.
3. Add clams and parsley and cook 5 minutes or until clams are tender. Return pork pieces.

FISH CHOWDER
(American)

Makes 6 servings.

¼ cup (½ stick) butter or margarine
1 small onion, finely chopped
  (¼ cup)
2 cups hot water
1 medium-size potato, peeled and
  diced (1 cup)
1 pound halibut, cod, or other firm
  white fish fillets, fresh or frozen,
  cut into bite-size pieces

2 cups light cream or half-and-half
¾ teaspoon salt
⅛ teaspoon freshly ground black
  pepper
2 tablespoons butter or margarine
2 tablespoons chopped fresh
  parsley

1. Heat the butter in a medium-size saucepan and sauté the onion until
   tender but not browned. Add the water and potatoes, cover, and cook
   until potatoes are barely tender, about 10 minutes.
2. Add the fish and simmer, covered, 5 minutes. Add the cream, salt,
   pepper, and butter and reheat but do not boil. Serve sprinkled with
   parsley.

TUNA CHOWDER
(American)

Hearty enough for a main course if you serve it with a chick-pea
salad and crusty bread.
Makes 6 servings.

3 tablespoons butter or margarine
1 medium-size onion, finely
  chopped (½ cup)
1 stalk celery, finely chopped with
  leaves
2 medium-size carrots, finely diced
  (1 cup)
4 medium-size potatoes, diced
  (4 cups)

2 teaspoons salt
¼ teaspoon freshly ground black
  pepper
2 cups water
1 can (6½ to 7 ounces) solid white
  tuna, drained and flaked
4 cups milk

1. Melt the butter in a heavy saucepan or Dutch oven. Add the onion, celery, and carrots and cook over low heat 10 minutes. Add the potatoes and cook 5 minutes.
2. Add the salt, pepper, and water. Bring to a boil, cover, and simmer 20 minutes or until potatoes are tender.
3. Add tuna and milk and reheat but do not boil. Serve sprinkled with chopped parsley, if you wish.

OYSTER BISQUE
(American)

I serve this as a first course at Thanksgiving and have no qualms about having an oyster dressing with the bird as an alternate to a sausage stuffing.
Makes 8 servings.

2 cans (8 ounces each) oysters or
1 quart freshly shucked
½ cup (1 stick) butter or margarine
1 tablespoon Worcestershire sauce
⅛ teaspoon celery salt
1 quart milk, scalded
3 cups light cream or half-and-half, scalded

1. Place the oysters and oyster liqueur in a medium-size saucepan with ¼ cup (½ stick) butter, Worcestershire, and celery salt. Heat over low heat until edges of oysters start to curl but do not boil.
2. Add the hot milk and cream and serve immediately dotted with remaining butter. Sprinkle with paprika, if you wish.

EGG DROP SOUP
(Chinese)

Homemade concentrated chicken broth is the best choice for this simple soup.
Makes 4 servings.

3 cups chicken broth or vegetable broth (see page 59)
2 teaspoons cornstarch
2 tablespoons water
2 green onions, chopped
1 egg, well beaten

1. Bring broth to a boil. Blend cornstarch with the water and whisk into broth slowly. When thickened add green onion.
2. While stirring the soup rapidly add the egg in a steady stream. Remove from heat and season with pepper, if you wish.

WONTON SOUP
(Chinese)

Delicate and delicious.
Makes 6 servings.

½ pound raw shelled and deveined
  shrimp, finely chopped
¼ cup finely chopped spinach
  leaves
1 tablespoon cornstarch
2 green onions, finely chopped
2 teaspoons soy sauce
¼ teaspoon salt
¼ cup finely chopped water
  chestnuts

1 small egg, lightly beaten
½ pound wonton skins (available in
  many supermarkets)
6 cups chicken broth or vegetable
  broth (see page 59)
½ teaspoon salt
1 tablespoon soy sauce
1 egg, lightly beaten
2 green onions, chopped

1. For the wonton filling combine the shrimp, spinach, cornstarch, green onions, soy sauce, salt, water chestnuts, and egg.
2. Place a teaspoonful of the shrimp mixture in center of each wonton skin. Fold in half to make a triangle and bring the opposite points together. Pinch and seal with water.
3. Heat 1 quart water to boiling. Add wonton and simmer, uncovered, 5 minutes or until they float. Drain and keep warm.
4. Heat broth, salt, and soy sauce to boiling. While stirring soup add the egg in a steady stream. Add wonton and sprinkle with green onion.

CELLOPHANE NOODLES
AND CHICKEN SOUP
(Japanese)

Even though I realize cellophane noodles are not on every supermarket shelf it is a favorite I could not resist including. Makes 4 servings.

1 ounce cellophane noodles
  (available in Oriental food stores)
  Warm water
2 cans (13¾ ounces each) chicken
  broth

½ whole chicken breast (about 6
  ounces)
1 tablespoon soy sauce
2 green onions, chopped, including
  green part

1. Soak the noodles in warm water to cover for 20 minutes. Drain and cut into 2-inch lengths.
2. In a medium-size saucepan heat the broth to boiling. Add the chicken breast, cover, and simmer 25 minutes, or until done. Remove breast, discard skin and bones, and dice finely.
3. Add noodles, chicken, soy sauce, and green onions to broth and reheat.

HOT-AND-SOUR SNOW PEA SOUP
(Chinese)

Have all the ingredients prepared ahead and the soup goes together in less than 10 minutes.
Makes 6 servings.

¼ cup vegetable oil
1 small green pepper, seeded and diced
¼ pound fresh snow or sugar snap peas (2 cups), or 1 package (7 ounces) frozen
¼ pound mushrooms, sliced (1 cup)
2 teaspoons finely chopped fresh ginger root, or ½ teaspoon ground
½ cup sliced water chestnuts

1 tablespoon soy sauce
2 cans (13¾ ounces each) chicken broth, or 4 cups vegetable broth (see page 59)
2 tablespoons white distilled vinegar
2 teaspoons honey
⅛ to ¼ teaspoon crushed hot red pepper flakes
¼ cup chopped green onion, green part only

1. Heat the oil in a large saucepan or Dutch oven and stir-fry the green pepper and snow peas until bright green, about 2 minutes.
2. Remove pepper and peas to warm paper-lined platter and keep warm. Add mushrooms, ginger, and water chestnuts to saucepan and cook, stirring, 2 minutes.
3. Add the soy sauce, broth, vinegar, honey, and red pepper flakes. Bring to a boil and simmer 2 minutes. Return the peas and peppers, reheat, and serve sprinkled with green onion.

BEAN CURD SOUP
(Chinese)

Makes 6 servings.

2 tablespoons vegetable oil
1 teaspoon finely chopped fresh
   ginger root, or ¼ teaspoon
   ground
2 cups shredded fresh spinach
½ teaspoon salt

½ cup (about one-eighth pound)
   thinly sliced fresh mushrooms
6 cups vegetable broth (see page
   59) or chicken broth
½ pound bean curd (tofu), diced

1. In a wok or heavy skillet heat the oil. Add the ginger, spinach, and
    salt and stir-fry until spinach is wilted. Add the mushrooms and
    stir-fry 2 minutes.
2. Add the broth, bring to a boil, and simmer 5 minutes. Add bean curd.

CHICKEN SOUP WITH NOODLES
(American)

Making a big kettle of soup or stew takes little extra effort and
gives extra servings for storing in the freezer. Do not add noodles and peas to chicken soup before freezing.
Makes 8 servings.

2 broiler-fryers (2½ to 3 pounds
   each), cut up
1 large onion, finely chopped
   (1 cup)
2 stalks celery, chopped
1 carrot, diced
1 tablespoon salt
1 teaspoon freshly ground black
   pepper
2 cans (13¾ ounces each) chicken
   broth

Water
1 bay leaf
1 teaspoon leaf thyme, crumbled
1 large potato, diced (about 2 cups)
2 cups fine noodles
1 cup peas, fresh or frozen
2 tablespoons chopped fresh
   parsley

1. Place the chicken pieces in a large heavy kettle or Dutch oven. Add the onion, celery, carrot, salt, pepper, broth, and enough water to cover chickens to a depth of 2 inches above.
2. Add bay leaf and thyme, bring to a boil, cover, and simmer 50 minutes or until chicken is done. When chicken is cool enough to handle remove and discard skin and bones and dice meat.
3. Add potatoes to broth and cook 10 minutes. Add noodles and peas and cook 8 minutes or until noodles are al dente. Return chicken meat to broth and sprinkle with parsley.

CREAM OF CHICKEN SOUP
(American)

I like to serve a cream soup with a main dish salad as a change of pace.
Makes 6 servings.

1 broiler-fryer (2½ pounds), cut up, or 2½ pounds chicken wings
2 stalks celery with leaves
1 small onion
1 bay leaf, crumbled
1 teaspoon salt
½ teaspoon freshly ground black pepper
½ teaspoon leaf thyme, crumbled
4 cups water
3 tablespoons butter or margarine
3 tablespoons flour
2 cups half-and-half
Salt and freshly ground black pepper to taste
1 egg yolk, lightly beaten

1. Place the chicken in a heavy kettle or Dutch oven. Add the celery, onion, bay leaf, salt, pepper, thyme, and water and bring to a boil.
2. Cover and simmer 1½ hours. Let cool until chicken can be handled. Remove skin and bones from chicken and discard. Shred meat.
3. Strain the broth. Taste and if it is weak in flavor add bouillon, or boil uncovered to concentrate. In a medium-size saucepan melt the butter and blend in the flour. Gradually stir in the half-and-half and bring to a boil, stirring until mixture is smooth, thick, and bubbly. Add salt and pepper to taste.
4. Pour ½ cup of the hot sauce into the egg yolk and mix well. Return to the body of the sauce. Add some of the strained broth to the white sauce, mix well, and return all to kettle of broth. Reheat but do not boil. Add chicken meat.

MULLIGATAWNY SOUP
(Indian)

This curried chicken soup has never been as well known here as it is in Europe.
Makes 6 servings.

1½ to 2 pounds chicken wings
1½ quarts water
1 large onion, chopped (1 cup)
1 carrot, diced
1 stalk celery, sliced
1 teaspoon salt
½ teaspoon freshly ground black pepper
3 tablespoons butter or margarine
1 medium-size onion, finely chopped (½ cup)

1½ tablespoons flour
½ teaspoon turmeric
½ teaspoon ground cumin
½ teaspoon ground coriander
½ teaspoon ground ginger
⅛ teaspoon crushed hot red pepper flakes
Salt to taste

1. Cut each wing into 3 joints and put into a heavy kettle or Dutch oven with water, onion, carrot, celery, salt, and pepper. Bring to a boil, cover, and simmer 1 hour. Let sit until cool enough to handle. Strain off the broth and reserve. Discard vegetables and wing tips.
2. Remove skin and bone from the other two wing joints and discard. Set chicken meat aside.
3. Heat the butter in a medium-size saucepan and sauté the onion until tender but not browned.
4. Sprinkle with flour, turmeric, cumin, coriander, ginger, and pepper flakes. Cook, stirring, 1 minute. Gradually stir in reserved broth, bring to a boil, and simmer until smooth and thick. Taste and add salt if needed. Return chicken meat and reheat.

Fish

BOUILLABAISE PROVENCAL
(French Fish Soup)

No fish soup made without the specialty fishes of the Marseilles region should be called bouillabaise but the fish soup below is a wonderful dish for entertaining. The more people, the greater variety of fish you can add. Also the soup base and rouille can be made ahead and the fish prepared for adding just before serving.
Makes 8 to 10 servings.

Soup Base

2 large onions, thinly sliced
  (2 cups)
1 medium-size leek, thinly sliced
  (1 cup)
2 stalks celery, finely chopped
¼ cup olive or vegetable oil
4 cloves garlic, finely chopped
1 can (2 pounds, 3 ounces) peeled
  plum tomatoes, coarsely chopped
3 quarts water
2 bay leaves, broken in half
½ teaspoon fennel seeds, crushed
1 teaspoon leaf basil, crumbled
¼ cup chopped fresh parsley,
  preferably flat Italian
½ teaspoon saffron threads
1 teaspoon freshly ground black
  pepper
  Fish heads and bones, if available

Fish

2½ pounds firm fish, fresh or frozen,
  such as cod, scrod, whiting,
  ocean perch, sole, haddock, bass,
  turbot, or blue fish, cut into
  2-inch chunks. If you buy from a
  fish store try to buy heads and
  bones to add to the soup base.
3 pounds shellfish, lobster tails,
  shrimp, crab (cut into bite-size
  pieces with shell left on for color),
  mussels, and clams

Rouille

This is a hot sauce with a
mayonnaise-like consistency.

3 tablespoons chopped drained
  roasted sweet red peppers sold in
  jars (pimiento can be substituted)
¼ to ½ teaspoon cayenne, or 1 small
  dried hot red pepper, soaked in
  warm water, drained, and
  chopped
1 teaspoon salt
  Pinch of ground cumin, optional
2 to 4 cloves garlic, finely chopped
1 small cooked potato or 1 slice
  (2 inches thick) French bread,
  soaked in a little of the soup base
  and drained
¼ cup olive or vegetable oil

Garnish

10 to 20 slices French bread
  sprinkled with Parmesan and
  toasted

1. To make the soup base sauté the onions, leek, and celery in the olive oil in a large stock pot or heavy Dutch oven until tender. Add garlic and toss.
2. Add tomatoes and cook 5 minutes. Add water and remaining ingredients, including fish heads and bones tied in muslin.
3. Bring to a boil and simmer, uncovered, over medium-high heat for about 30 minutes. If to be used immediately remove muslin bag but if base has been made ahead let muslin bag stay in soup, cool, and chill until ready to use.
4. To make rouille combine all the ingredients except the oil in an electric blender or a food processor. Blend or process until smooth and with the motor running add the oil drop by drop to get mayonnaise consistency. At the end oil can be added a bit more quickly. Taste sauce for seasonings. It should be hot and garlicky.
5. To finish soup heat the base to boiling and add the chunks of firm fish. Cook 2 minutes for fresh and 5 minutes for frozen or until fish flakes easily. Add shellfish and cook 2 minutes, or until pink and tender and mussels and clams open. DO NOT OVERCOOK.
6. To serve place a slice of French bread in each deep soup bowl and ladle fish and soup over. Serve rouille separately for stirring into the soup but warn guests that it is HOT. Sprinkle each bowl with more grated Parmesan, if you wish.

CIOPPINO
(American Fish Stew)

This is San Francisco's Fisherman's Wharf fish stew with a substitution suggestion for West Coast Dungeness crab so that everyone can enjoy.
Makes 6 servings.

½ cup olive or vegetable oil
2 large onions, finely chopped (2 cups)
2 large cloves garlic, finely chopped
1 can (2 pounds, 3 ounces) Italian plum tomatoes
1 can (6 ounces) tomato paste
1 cup dry red wine
2 teaspoons leaf basil, crumbled
1 teaspoon leaf oregano, crumbled
1 teaspoon salt
½ teaspoon freshly ground black pepper

1 pound striped bass, cod, halibut, haddock, or other firm white fish fillets, cut into 12 pieces
2 Dungeness crabs, cleaned and cracked, or 6 King crab claws, cracked
1 pound shrimp, shelled and deveined
18 littlenecks or cherrystone clams, well scrubbed
¼ cup chopped fresh parsley

1. Heat the oil in a large kettle or Dutch oven and sauté the onion until tender but not browned. Add the garlic and cook 2 minutes.
2. Add tomatoes, tomato paste, wine, basil, oregano, salt, and pepper. Bring to a boil and simmer 20 minutes.
3. Add the fish, crabs, shrimp, and clams. Cover and simmer 10 minutes, or until the fish flakes easily and clams have opened. Sprinkle with the parsley and serve with crusty garlic bread and red wine.

SPICY INDIAN FISH CURRY

Makes 4 servings.

½ cup vegetable oil
1 pound fresh or frozen firm white fish fillets, cut or sawed into bite-size pieces
1 large onion, finely chopped (1 cup)
1 clove garlic, finely chopped
¼ teaspoon turmeric

½ teaspoon ground ginger
½ teaspoon ground cumin
½ teaspoon chili powder
1 large tomato, peeled, seeded, and chopped
1 container (8 ounces) plain yogurt
½ teaspoon salt

1. Heat the oil in a large heavy skillet and fry the fish until browned and cooked, about 3 minutes on each side if fresh, longer if frozen. Remove fish to paper towels to drain.
2. Remove all but 2 tablespoons oil from skillet and sauté the onion until tender but not browned. Extra oil can be used again for frying fish. Add garlic, turmeric, ginger, cumin, and chili powder and cook, stirring, 2 minutes.
3. Add tomato and cook 1 minute. Stir in yogurt and salt. Reheat but do not boil. Return fish and reheat but do not boil. Serve sprinkled with chopped parsley (or fresh coriander) over hot cooked rice, if you wish.

BAKED FISH WITH COCONUT
(Indian)

An unusual presentation in foil packages.
Bake at 375° for 20 minutes.
Makes 4 servings.

⅓ cup vegetable oil
1 cup grated fresh coconut
1 large onion, finely chopped
 (1 cup)
2 cloves garlic, finely chopped
2 canned mild green chilies,
 chopped
½ teaspoon salt

1 teaspoon curry powder
2 tablespoons unsalted cashews or
 peanuts, chopped
1 pound frozen firm white fish
 fillets, thawed and finely
 chopped
1 tablespoon lemon juice
2 eggs, lightly beaten

1. In a small skillet heat 1 tablespoon of the oil and sauté the coconut until lightly browned.
2. In a large heavy skillet heat remaining oil and sauté the onion until tender but not browned. Add garlic, chilies, salt, and curry powder and cook, stirring, 2 minutes. Preheat oven to 375°.
3. Add coconut, nuts, and fish and cook 2 minutes. Cool slightly. Mix lemon juice with eggs and add to skillet. Divide the fish mixture among 6 oiled 7-inch squares of aluminum foil. Wrap tightly and place on a baking sheet.
4. Bake at 375° for 20 minutes or until set and fish is cooked. Serve with hot cooked rice, if you wish.

STEAMED BASS
(Chinese)

Steaming retains the delicate texture of the fish that is seasoned assertively with ginger and garlic.
Makes 4 servings.

1 whole (3 to 4 pounds) sea bass, striped bass, haddock, scrod, or other firm white fish, cleaned and dressed
1 tablespoon soy sauce
1 tablespoon dry sherry

3 teaspoons finely chopped fresh ginger root, or ½ teaspoon ground
3 cloves garlic, finely chopped
¼ cup vegetable oil
3 green onions, finely chopped

1. Place the fish on a rack in a deep roasting pan. Combine the soy sauce, sherry, ginger, and garlic and rub over fish and in cavity.
2. Pour boiling water under rack so that it does not touch fish. Return water to boil, cover tightly, and steam 25 minutes, or until fish flakes easily. Transfer to a serving platter.
3. Heat the oil in a saucepan and pour over fish. Scatter green onions over fish. Serve with fried rice, if you wish.

COLD POACHED BASS
(French)

This make-ahead buffet dish is not difficult to prepare. Finding the whole fish is usually the greatest challenge unless you live close to the New England coast as I do.
Makes 8 to 10 appetizer or 4 to 5 main dish servings.

1 4- to 5-pound striped bass, rock fish, salmon, or any fresh fish, cleaned, scaled, with or without head removed, and tail left on
2 onions, peeled and quartered
2 teaspoons salt
¼ teaspoon pepper

1 large bay leaf
¼ teaspoon leaf thyme, crumbled
5 sprigs parsley
2 cups dry white wine
2 cups water
1 tablespoon lemon juice
Watercress Sauce (see below)

1. Use a fish poacher or covered pan that will hold the whole fish and put the fish and 1 quart cold water into it. If the fish is not almost completely covered by water, double the stock recipe. Pour off the water and return the fish to the refrigerator while preparing stock.
2. In a large saucepan place onion, salt, pepper, bay leaf, thyme, parsley, wine, and water. Bring to a boil over high heat. Reduce heat to low and simmer 15 minutes.
3. Meanwhile sprinkle lemon juice inside fish. If you do not have a fish poacher with a rack it will be necessary to wrap fish in a double thickness of cheesecloth, tied at both ends, candy-wrapper style.
4. Strain stock into pan in which fish will be cooked. Bring to a boil, add fish, and simmer gently, allowing approximately 8 minutes per pound of fish.
5. Remove cooked fish to a large platter using 2 wide spatulas if there is no rack to facilitate lifting. Cover and chill several hours or overnight.
6. Remove cheesecloth, place fish on serving platter, and carefully lift away skin from top side of fish. To serve, scrape top layer of fish away from backbone and onto serving plates. Turn fish over and repeat with other side. Serve Watercress Sauce separately.

WATERCRESS SAUCE

Sauce can be prepared in a food processor in one batch or in an electric blender in two batches.
Makes 2 cups sauce.

1 bunch watercress, stems and leaves coarsely chopped
3 tablespoons snipped fresh dillweed
3 tablespoons sliced green onions
1 tablespoon lemon juice
1 cup mayonnaise
½ teaspoon salt
⅛ teaspoon freshly ground pepper

Place all ingredients in a food processor and process until sauce is smooth with tiny green flecks remaining. Cover and chill before serving.

WHITE CLAM SAUCE WITH SPAGHETTI
(Italian)

There are as many variations of this as there are Italian cooks but this is the way I like it.
Makes 4 servings.

2 to 2½ dozen littleneck or
  cherrystone clams, or 2 cans
  (7 ounces each) minced clams
⅓ cup olive or vegetable oil
1 small onion, finely chopped
  (¼ cup)
2 cloves garlic, finely chopped
¼ teaspoon salt

¼ teaspoon freshly ground black
  pepper
1 teaspoon leaf oregano, crumbled
1 pound thin spaghetti
2 tablespoons lemon juice
2 tablespoons chopped fresh
  parsley
Grated Parmesan

1. Scrub the clams well and place in a heavy saucepan or kettle with ¼ cup water. Cover and bring to a boil. Simmer until clams open, about 4 minutes.
2. Strain and reserve broth. Remove clam meat from shells and chop coarsely. If using canned clams, drain juice and reserve clams.
3. Meanwhile heat the oil in a medium-size heavy skillet and sauté the onion until tender but not browned. Add the garlic and cook 2 minutes.
4. Add salt, pepper, oregano, and reserved clam broth. Cook 5 minutes.
5. Cook the spaghetti according to package directions to al dente stage, drain, and set in deep platter.
6. Add lemon juice, parsley, and clams to sauce and reheat. Pour sauce over pasta and serve with grated Parmesan.

STUFFED CLAMS
(Portuguese)

Add 1 teaspoon crumbled oregano, and the dish is Italian.
Bake at 350° for 10 minutes.
Makes 6 servings.

36 littleneck or cherrystone clams,
  well scrubbed
¼ cup olive or vegetable oil
1 large onion, finely chopped
  (1 cup)
2 cloves garlic, finely chopped

½ cup seasoned stuffing mix
¼ cup chopped fresh parsley
  Salt and freshly ground black
  pepper to taste
⅓ cup freshly grated Parmesan

1. Place the clams in a kettle or Dutch oven with ¼ cup water. Cover and cook until clams open, about 10 minutes. Remove opened clams. Remove meat, reserving half the shells. Strain the clam broth and reserve.
2. In a heavy skillet heat the oil and sauté the onion until tender but not browned. Add the garlic and cook 2 minutes. Add 1 cup reserved clam broth. Heat to boiling and stir in the stuffing mix. Preheat oven to 350°.
3. Chop clams if large and add to skillet. Stir in the parsley and add salt and pepper to taste. Pile the mixture into the reserved shells and set on a baking sheet. Sprinkle with Parmesan and bake at 350° for 10 minutes or until very hot. Do not overcook or clams will be tough.

CLAM PIE
(American)

This is an old-fashioned New England recipe that deserves to have a revival.
Bake at 400° for 40 minutes.
Makes 6 servings.

Pastry for 9-inch double-crust pie
3 cups finely chopped or ground large clams (quahogs) with liquid, or 2 cans (7 ounces each) chopped clams
1 medium-size onion, finely chopped (½ cup)
¾ cup unsalted pilot cracker crumbs
2 tablespoons butter or margarine, melted
⅛ teaspoon freshly ground black pepper
Dash of liquid red pepper seasoning
¼ teaspoon leaf thyme, crumbled
1 egg, lightly beaten
½ cup light cream, half-and-half, or milk

1. Roll out half the pastry to a 12-inch round. Fit into a 9-inch pie plate.
2. Combine the clams and liquid, onion, crumbs, butter, pepper, red pepper, thyme, egg, and cream in a medium-size bowl. Pour into pie shell. Preheat oven to 400°.
3. Roll out remaining pastry to fit top of pie. Seal edges, fold lower pastry over top edge, and seal and flute. Make steam holes and bake at 400° for 40 minutes, or until pastry is golden. Let stand 10 minutes before cutting.

NORWEGIAN FISH PUDDING

This is one recipe where I would not recommend using frozen fish.
Makes 4 servings.

2 eggs
¼ cup milk
1 pound raw fresh cod, haddock, or ocean perch, cut into 1-inch pieces
1 teaspoon salt

¼ teaspoon freshly ground white pepper
⅛ teaspoon ground nutmeg
1 tablespoon snipped fresh dillweed
¾ cup heavy cream

1. Place the eggs and milk in the container of an electric blender or food processor. Start machine whirling and gradually add the pieces of fish to make a purée. Stop machine several times to scrape down the sides.
2. Scrape into a bowl and gradually beat in salt, pepper, nutmeg, dill, and the cream. Test 1 tablespoon of the mixture by dropping it into boiling salted water. It should hold its shape. If it is too soft add ¼ cup soft bread crumbs or if too stiff add more cream or milk.
3. Pour into a 1-quart mold which has been greased and sprinkled with bread crumbs. Cover mold with wax paper and set on a rack in a deep saucepan or in a steamer. Add boiling water to almost touch bottom of mold. Cover and simmer for 1 hour or until pudding is firm. Add more boiling water if necessary.

KEDGEREE
(British Rice and Fish)

Pallid versions of this dish have been standard British school lunch fare for decades but the results from this recipe prove it can be highly palatable.
Makes 4 servings.

¼ cup (½ stick) butter or margarine
1 medium-size onion, finely chopped (½ cup)
1 stalk celery, finely chopped
½ tart apple, peeled, cored, and finely chopped
2 tablespoons curry powder

1 cup raw long-grain rice
2¼ cups water
1 teaspoon salt
1 pound cod, haddock, or other firm white fish fillets, fresh or frozen
⅔ cup milk, approximately

1. In a medium-size skillet melt the butter and sauté the onion until tender but not browned. Add the celery and apple and cook 3 minutes.
2. Sprinkle with the curry powder and cook 1 minute. Add the rice, water, and salt. Bring to a boil, cover, and simmer until liquid has been absorbed, about 20 minutes.
3. Meanwhile place the fillets in a skillet and add ⅔ to ¾ cup milk to cover fish. Bring to a boil, cover, and simmer 10 minutes for fresh and 20 minutes for frozen, or until fish is done. Drain the fish, reserving the cooking liquid.
4. Flake the fish and add to cooked rice with enough reserved liquid to make it like a thick stew. Serve sprinkled with chopped parsley, if you wish.

POACHED COD WITH EGG SAUCE
(American)

A New England Fourth of July favorite served with new potatoes and fresh peas.
Makes 6 servings.

3 pounds cod, scrod, or haddock fillets
Boiling salted water
1 teaspoon leaf thyme, crumbled
1 onion, sliced
½ bay leaf
3 sprigs parsley

1 stalk celery, quartered
¼ cup (½ stick) butter or margarine
3 tablespoons all-purpose flour
¼ teaspoon salt
⅛ teaspoon freshly ground black pepper
2 hard-cooked eggs, chopped

1. Place the fish fillets in a large skillet. Add boiling salted water to cover, thyme, onion, bay leaf, parsley, and celery.
2. Bring to a boil, cover, and simmer 10 minutes. Turn off heat and let fish stand in water.
3. Meanwhile melt the butter and blend in the flour, salt, and pepper. Strain off 2 cups of the fish cooking water and, off the heat, gradually stir into the flour-butter mixture. Bring to a boil, stirring until thick and bubbly. Cook, stirring, 2 minutes. Add the chopped eggs. Drain the fish and place on a platter. Pour over the egg sauce and serve with parsleyed boiled potatoes and garden peas.

ESCABECHE
(Portuguese Pickled Fish)

The Portuguese are excellent fish cooks, and they make this
pickled fish using fresh sardines and conger eel.
Makes 8 servings.

2 pounds cod, scrod, haddock, or
  sole fillets
⅓ cup flour
1 teaspoon salt
½ teaspoon freshly ground black
  pepper
½ cup olive or vegetable oil

1 cup cider vinegar
1 bay leaf, crumbled
⅛ teaspoon saffron threads,
  crumbled
1 medium-size onion, finely
  chopped (½ cup)

1. Cut the fish into serving-size pieces and dredge in the flour mixed
   with the salt and pepper.
2. Heat the oil in a large heavy skillet and fry the fish, a few pieces at a
   time, until lightly browned on both sides and cooked through. Drain
   on paper towels. Place in a shallow serving dish and chill for 30
   minutes.
3. Combine the vinegar, bay leaf, saffron, and onion in a small bowl and
   pour over chilled fish. Chill 1 hour or longer before serving with
   boiled potatoes, if you wish.

CREAMED SALT COD
(French)

Even soaked salt cod needs a foil for its inherent saltiness.
More often than not this turns out to be potatoes, as in this
traditional recipe.
Makes 8 servings.

1 pound salt cod
2 medium-size hot baked potatoes
¾ cup heavy cream, scalded
1 cup olive or vegetable oil,
  warmed
2 cloves garlic, finely chopped

Freshly ground black pepper to
taste
Crustless bread triangles,
sautéed in butter or margarine
until golden

1. Cover the salt cod with water and soak 24 hours, changing the water several times.
2. Drain the cod and cut into four pieces. Place in a skillet with water to cover, bring to a boil, cover, and simmer 10 minutes, or until the fish flakes easily. Drain off water and flake fish into the bowl of an electric mixer.
3. Add the flesh of the baked potatoes to the cod in the mixing bowl. While beating vigorously gradually add the hot cream, warm oil, and garlic until mixture is smooth and thick. Season to taste with the pepper. Pile the cod mixture in the center of a platter, surround with the sautéed bread triangles, and serve lukewarm.

SALT COD WITH POTATOES
(Portuguese)

If you are entertaining culinarily adventurous guests for brunch this is an excellent choice. Serve with toast triangles.
Makes 6 servings.

1½ pounds dried salt cod
 1 large onion, finely chopped
   (1 cup)
 ½ cup olive or vegetable oil
 2 cloves garlic, finely chopped
 6 medium-size potatoes, cooked
   and diced
 3 tablespoons butter or margarine

 3 tablespoons flour
1½ cups half-and-half or milk
   Freshly ground white pepper to
   taste
 ⅛ teaspoon ground nutmeg
 ¼ cup chopped fresh parsley
 ¼ cup (1 ounce) shredded Swiss

1. Soak the cod in cold water to cover for 24 hours, changing the water several times.
2. In a heavy skillet sauté the onion in the oil over low heat until tender but not browned. Add the garlic and cook 2 minutes.
3. Remove onion with a slotted spoon to an ovenproof dish.
4. Flake cod and add to oil remaining in skillet. Add the potatoes and cook, stirring, 5 minutes.
5. Meanwhile melt the butter in a small saucepan, blend in the flour, and gradually stir in the half-and-half. Bring to a boil, stirring until bubbly and thick. Add pepper and nutmeg. Pour over cod and potatoes and cook gently, stirring, until cod is tender, about 5 minutes. Add parsley and pour over onions. Sprinkle with cheese and glaze under a preheated broiler.

MARINATED SEAFOOD WITH DILL
(Italian)

Delightful summer salad served on a bed of leaf lettuce and garnished with cherry tomatoes.
Makes 6 servings.

2 cups milk
1½ pounds cod, haddock, or other firm white fish fillets
12 large shrimp, peeled and deveined and split in half lengthwise
½ chopped green onion
⅓ cup chopped fresh parsley
3 tablespoons drained capers
3 tablespoons snipped fresh dillweed

½ teaspoon celery seeds, crushed
⅛ teaspoon liquid red pepper seasoning
½ cup olive or vegetable oil
½ cup white vinegar
1 teaspoon salt
½ teaspoon freshly ground black pepper

1. Pour the milk into a large heavy skillet and bring to a boil. Add the fish and shrimp, cover, and simmer gently 5 minutes, or until fish flakes easily and shrimp are pink.
2. Drain and arrange cod in a serving dish. Drain shrimp, cut into ½-inch pieces, and combine with the remaining ingredients. Spoon over cod and chill several hours.

CRABMEAT IMPERIAL
(American)

This recipe goes together fast and cooks in 15 minutes.
Bake at 350° for 15 minutes.
Makes 4 servings.

2 green onions, finely chopped
1 small green pepper, seeded and chopped
2 pimientos or roasted peppers, chopped
¼ teaspoon salt
⅛ teaspoon freshly ground white pepper
1½ teaspoons dry mustard
Mayonnaise

2 eggs, lightly beaten
¼ cup dry sherry
½ cup fresh soft bread crumbs (1 slice)
1 pound fresh lump crabmeat, or 2 cans (about 7 ounces each) crabmeat
2 tablespoons freshly grated Parmesan

1. In a medium-size bowl combine the green onions, green pepper, pimientos, salt, pepper, mustard, 2 tablespoons mayonnaise, eggs, sherry, and bread crumbs. Preheat oven to 350°.
2. Pick over the crabmeat for cartilage and gently fold into the bread crumb mixture. Spoon into individual buttered shells or ramekins.
3. Spread a thin layer of mayonnaise over each one, sprinkle with Parmesan, and bake at 350° for 15 minutes or until bubbly hot and lightly browned. Serve with lemon wedges, if you wish.

POACHED FINNAN HADDIE
(British)

It's well worth searching for the smoked fish to discover this simple but unusually good dish.
Makes 6 servings.

2 cups milk
2 bay leaves, broken in half
1 medium-size onion, finely chopped (½ cup)
⅛ teaspoon leaf thyme, crumbled
2½ pounds smoked haddock or finnan haddie, cut into 6 pieces (If very salty soak several hours in several changes of cold water.)

¼ cup (½ stick) butter or margarine
5 tablespoons all-purpose flour
½ cup heavy or whipping cream
⅛ teaspoon cayenne
Salt
2 hard-cooked eggs, sliced

1. In a large deep skillet combine the milk, bay leaves, onion, and thyme. Bring to a boil and add the smoked haddock in a single layer. Cover and simmer gently 10 minutes, or until the fish flakes easily. Time depends on how thick pieces are.
2. Drain fish, reserving liquid, and place in an au gratin or deep baking dish and keep warm. Remove and discard bay leaves from liquid.
3. Melt the butter in a medium-size saucepan and stir in the flour. Cook, stirring, 2 to 3 minutes. Gradually add the hot reserved liquid and onion to mixture. Stir in the cream and continue cooking and stirring until sauce is thick and smooth. Cook 2 minutes. Add cayenne and check seasonings. Add salt, if necessary. Pour over fish and garnish with egg slices.

BAKED FISH FILLETS
(American)

Here's proof that all fish needs is simple preparation and care to avoid overcooking.
Bake at 400° for 12 minutes for fresh, 24 minutes for frozen.
Makes 4 to 6 servings.

2 pounds fish fillets, fresh or frozen (flounder, sole, whiting, ocean perch, bass, cod, scrod)
⅓ cup chopped green onion
¼ pound mushrooms, sliced (1 cup)
1 teaspoon salt
¼ teaspoon freshly ground white pepper
1 teaspoon leaf marjoram, crumbled

2 tablespoons dry white wine
2 teaspoons lemon juice
¼ cup (1 ounce) shredded Monterey Jack or mild Cheddar
¼ cup fresh bread crumbs
½ cup (1 stick) butter or margarine, melted
2 tablespoons chopped fresh parsley

1. Butter a baking dish large enough to hold the fresh fish fillets in one slightly overlapping layer, or the frozen fish, cut into 6 pieces, in a single layer. Preheat oven to 400°.
2. Spread the green onions and mushrooms over the bottom of the dish and place fish on top, covering the thin part of 1 fresh fillet with the thick part of another to allow even cooking. Season with salt, pepper, and marjoram. Sprinkle with wine, lemon juice, cheese, and bread crumbs. Drizzle melted butter over crumbs.
3. Wet a piece of wax paper and wrinkle it to fit the top of the baking dish. Place directly on fish. Bake at 400° for 7 minutes, remove wax paper, and bake 5 minutes longer, or until fish is opaque at the thickest part and flakes easily for fresh fish. Increase cooking times to 14 minutes covered and 10 minutes uncovered for frozen fish, or until fish is opaque and flakes easily. Times depend on thickness of fillets in both cases. Sprinkle with parsley.

MUSSELS IN MUSTARD SAUCE
(French)

If you prefer, this recipe will serve 10 as an appetizer.
Makes 6 servings.

6 pounds mussels
¼ cup Dijon mustard
2 tablespoons red wine vinegar

3 tablespoons lemon juice
½ cup olive or vegetable oil
Freshly ground black pepper

1. Scrub the mussels very well and remove the beards. Discard any opened or damaged shells. Place cleaned mussels in a large kettle or Dutch oven. Add 1 cup water or enough to cover bottom of pan to a depth of ¼ inch.
2. Cover, bring to a boil, and simmer 5 minutes, or until mussels have opened. Remove from heat and set aside until cool enough to handle.
3. Meanwhile place the mustard in a small bowl. Whisk in the vinegar and lemon juice and then the oil. Add a few turns of the pepper mill.
4. When mussels are cool remove from shells and place in a medium-size bowl. Pour mustard dressing over, toss, cover, and chill several hours. Mussels can be served on lettuce leaves or in shell halves.

SPAGHETTI WITH MUSSELS
(Italian)

I prefer a red mussel sauce for pasta to a red clam sauce, perhaps because mussels are often more difficult to gather or purchase.
Makes 6 servings.

4 pounds mussels, well scrubbed and beards removed	6 plum tomatoes, peeled, seeded, and chopped, or 1 can (1 pound) Italian plum tomatoes, drained
½ cup olive or vegetable oil	3 tablespoons chopped fresh parsley, Italian flat variety if possible
2 cloves garlic, crushed	
¼ teaspoon crushed hot red pepper flakes, or to taste	1½ pounds thin spaghetti, cooked al dente and drained

1. Place the mussels in a large heavy kettle with ¼ cup water, cover, and cook over medium heat until mussels open, about 5 minutes. Cool until they can be handled.
2. Meanwhile heat the oil in a medium-size skillet and sauté the garlic until lightly browned. Remove and discard garlic.
3. Add pepper flakes, tomatoes, and about 1 cup of strained liquid from the mussels.
4. Bring to a boil and simmer, uncovered, 20 minutes. Remove mussels from the shells and add to skillet. Reheat, add parsley, and pour over spaghetti in a deep dish or bowl. Serve with Parmesan, if you wish.

ARROZ CON PESCADO
(Mexican Rice With Fish)

Everyone knows and likes Arroz Con Pollo (rice with chicken).
Here is a cousin that is equally delicious.
Makes 8 servings.

½ cup olive or vegetable oil
2 large onions, finely chopped
(2 cups)
2 cloves garlic, finely chopped
2 cups raw long-grain rice
1 can (1 pound, 12 ounces)
tomatoes
4 cups water
¼ cup chopped fresh cilantro
(Chinese parsley) or flat Italian
parsley

1½ teaspoons salt
½ teaspoon freshly ground black
pepper
2 pounds firm white fish fillets,
such as haddock, halibut, or cod,
cut into 2-inch chunks
½ pound shrimp, shelled and
deveined

1. In a large kettle or Dutch oven heat the oil and sauté the onion until
    tender but not browned. Add the garlic and cook 1 minute.
2. Add the rice and cook, stirring occasionally, until rice is lightly
    browned. Add tomatoes and water, bring to a boil, cover, and simmer
    20 minutes.
3. Add cilantro, salt, pepper, fish, and shrimp. Push fish down into rice
    mixture. Cover and simmer 10 minutes, or until fish flakes, shrimp
    are pink, and rice has absorbed the liquid.

SCALLOPED OYSTERS
(American)

Scalloped oysters often appear on Saturday night dinner tables
in New England along with the traditional ham and baked
beans.
Bake at 400° for 10 minutes.
Makes 4 servings.

½ cup (1 stick) butter or margarine
2 cups unsalted cracker crumbs
½ teaspoon salt
⅛ teaspoon freshly ground black
pepper
1 pint shucked oysters, drained
and liquid reserved

1 tablespoon lemon juice
2 tablespoons chopped fresh
parsley
¾ cup half-and-half or milk
Dash of liquid red pepper
seasoning

1. Melt the butter in a small skillet and add the crumbs, salt, and pepper. Spoon a third of the crumb mixture into a 7- × 9-inch shallow buttered baking dish. Cover with half the oysters. Sprinkle with half the lemon juice and parsley. Repeat the layers, ending with crumbs.
2. Preheat oven to 400°. Combine the reserved liquid with the half-and-half, add red pepper, and pour over oyster mixture.
3. Bake at 400° for 10 minutes, or until piping hot.

FRIED OYSTERS
(American)

Glorious food.
Makes 6 servings.

36 shucked fresh oysters with their juice, or 2 containers (12 ounces each) fresh oysters
1½ cups packaged bread crumbs
1½ cups flour
¼ cup milk

2 eggs, lightly beaten
1 teaspoon salt
⅛ teaspoon freshly ground black pepper
Oil for deep frying

1. Drain the oysters and use the liquor or juice in a fish soup or sauce for fish. On a piece of wax paper combine the crumbs and the flour.
2. In a shallow dish combine the milk, eggs, salt, and pepper. Roll oysters in crumb mixture, in egg mixture, and again in crumbs. Set aside for 15 minutes for coating to set.
3. In a deep heavy saucepan or a deep-fat fryer, add oil to a depth of 3 to 4 inches and heat it until it registers 350° on a deep-fat thermometer. Using a frying basket fry a few of the oysters at a time until they are golden, about 2 to 3 minutes. Drain on paper towels. Serve with lemon wedges or tartar sauce, if you wish.

RUSSIAN COULIBIAC
(Salmon and Rice in Puff Paste)

This recipe takes more effort than most in this book but my version is considerably simpler than the classical one calling for crêpes and real puff pastry or brioche dough.

Bake at 425° for 40 minutes.

Makes 6 servings.

1 recipe Quick Puff Pastry (see below) or 1 package frozen puff pastry, thawed
2 cups cooked rice (¾ cup raw)
1 recipe Mushroom Paste (see below)
1 pound poached boneless fresh salmon, flaked, or 1 can (1 pound) red salmon, drained, boned, skinned, and flaked

3 hard-cooked eggs, sliced
1 recipe thick Béchamel Sauce (see below)
1 egg mixed with 1 tablespoon cold water

1. Roll half the pastry dough into a rectangle 9 × 18 inches and place on an ungreased cookie sheet.

2. Spread half the rice to within ½ inch of the edges of the pastry. Mix Mushroom Paste and salmon and spread half over the rice. Top with egg slices and Béchamel Sauce. Repeat with remaining ingredients. Brush edges of pastry with water or lightly beaten egg white.

3. Roll out remaining pastry, retaining a small piece for decoration, into a slightly bigger rectangle and fit over the filling. Press edges together to seal. Cut 2 or 3 steam holes. Decorate with pastry leaves, if you wish. Brush all over with egg mixture. Chill at least 30 minutes. Preheat oven to 425°.

4. Bake at 425° for 40 minutes, or until the pastry is puffed and golden.

QUICK PUFF PASTRY

3 cups all-purpose flour
¾ cup (1½ sticks) cold butter or margarine, cut into small pieces

¾ cup ice water
¾ cup (1½ sticks) butter or margarine, thinly sliced

1. Place the flour in a medium-size bowl. With the fingertips or a pastry blender work the butter in until mixture resembles coarse meal. Stir in ice water to make a dough.

2. Roll out the dough on a lightly floured surface to an 11- × 24-inch rectangle. Place half of the butter slices over two-thirds of the rolled dough, leaving a margin near the edge. Fold unbuttered third of dough over to center and last buttered third over that. Press to seal edges. Give the dough a quarter turn to the right.

3. Roll out again into a rectangle and repeat the buttering and folding. Wrap in clear plastic wrap and chill 30 minutes. Roll dough and fold two more times. Chill 1 hour.

MUSHROOM PASTE

½ pound mushrooms, finely chopped (2 cups)
½ cup chopped shallots or green onions
2 tablespoons butter or margarine
¼ cup Madeira or sherry
Salt and freshly ground black pepper to taste
Pinch each of nutmeg, cinnamon, allspice, and cloves

In a medium-size skillet sauté the mushrooms and shallots in the butter until mushrooms give up their moisture and then long enough to evaporate that liquid. Add Madeira, salt, pepper, and spices and cook until almost dry.

BECHAMEL SAUCE

4 tablespoons (½ stick) butter or margarine
5 tablespoons all-purpose flour
1 cup milk
1 cup heavy cream or half-and-half
Pinch of nutmeg
Salt and freshly ground black pepper to taste

In a small saucepan melt the butter, stir in the flour, and cook 3 minutes. Remove from the heat and gradually blend in the milk and cream. Heat to boiling, stirring constantly, and cook until thickened, about 10 minutes. Season with nutmeg, salt, and pepper. Cool.

POACHED SALMON WITH SHRIMP
(American)

Makes 6 servings.

6 salmon steaks (about 8 ounces each), fresh or frozen
1 cup water
1 cup dry white wine
1 small stalk celery with leaves
2 sprigs parsley
½ bay leaf, crumbled
6 bruised black peppercorns
Pinch of salt

½ teaspoon leaf thyme, crumbled
½ pound shrimp, shelled and deveined
2 tablespoons butter
2 tablespoons flour
2 egg yolks, lightly beaten
1 tablespoon lemon juice
1 tablespoon chopped fresh parsley
Lemon slices

1. Place the steaks in a single layer in a large heavy skillet or sauté pan. Add water, wine, celery, parsley, bay leaf, peppercorns, salt, and thyme. Bring to a boil, cover, and simmer 8 minutes, or 12 minutes if fish is frozen.
2. Add the shrimp, cover, and simmer 3 minutes, or until shrimp is pink and salmon cooked. Arrange salmon and shrimp on a warm platter and keep them warm. Strain the cooking liquid and measure 2 cups.
3. Melt the butter in a small saucepan and blend in the flour. Gradually stir in the reserved cooking liquid. Bring to a boil, stirring. Cook 2 minutes.
4. Mix the egg yolks, lemon juice, and parsley together in a small bowl. Add a little of the hot sauce to the yolk mixture and mix well. Return to the bulk of the sauce and cook, stirring, until sauce thickens slightly but do not boil. Pour over fish and garnish with lemon slices.

SAUTEED SCALLOPS
(French)

Bay scallops have a delicate flavor that is brought out by very simple, quick cooking.
Makes 4 servings.

3 tablespoons butter or margarine
1 to 2 shallots or white part of green onion, finely chopped
1 pound scallops, fresh or frozen (if sea scallops, quarter)
¼ teaspoon salt

⅛ teaspoon freshly ground white pepper
2 tablespoons lemon juice or dry vermouth
2 tablespoons chopped fresh parsley

1. Heat the butter in a large heavy skillet and sauté the shallots until tender but not browned. Add the scallops and cook, stirring, 3 minutes, or until they turn opaque. Do not overcook.
2. Add the remaining ingredients and reheat. Serve immediately.

SEAFOOD QUICHE
(French)

With tossed salad and croissant, a delicious light main course, perfect for brunch.
Bake at 400° for 8 to 10 minutes and at 375° for 40 minutes.
Makes 8 appetizer servings or 4 main dish servings.

1 unbaked 9-inch pie shell
1 cup (4 ounces) shredded Swiss or Gruyère
2 tablespoons butter or margarine
2 shallots or white part of green onions, finely chopped
¼ cup dry white wine
½ pound fresh or frozen bay scallops or sea scallops, quartered

½ pound shelled deveined shrimp
2 tablespoons finely chopped fresh parsley
4 eggs, lightly beaten
1 cup heavy cream or half-and-half
2 tablespoons snipped fresh dillweed

1. Prick the bottom of the pie shell and bake at 400° for 8 to 10 minutes, or until set and lightly browned. Cool.
2. Sprinkle the bottom of the cooled pie shell with the cheese.
3. Melt the butter in a medium-size skillet and sauté the shallots until tender but not browned. Add the wine, scallops, and shrimp. Cover and simmer 3 minutes, or until scallops are opaque and shrimp are pink. Remove scallops and shrimp with slotted spoon and place over cheese in pastry shell. Sprinkle with parsley.
4. Strain and reserve ½ cup of the cooking liquid.
5. In a medium-size bowl combine the eggs, cream, dill, and reserved liquid. Pour over seafood and bake at 375° for 40 minutes or until quiche is set. Let cool 10 minutes before cutting.

COQUILLES ST. JACQUES
(French Scallops au Gratin)

There are some classic dishes that cannot be made without heavy cream sauces. If you are concerned about your intake of saturated fats forget this recipe and fix sautéed scallops using margarine on page 94.

Makes 12 appetizer servings or 6 main dish servings.

3 tablespoons butter or margarine
½ pound mushrooms, chopped
3 tablespoons chopped shallots or green onions
1 cup dry white wine
½ cup fish stock, bottled clam juice, or water
3 sprigs parsley
1 bay leaf
⅛ teaspoon leaf rosemary, crumbled
5 peppercorns, bruised

1 lemon slice
1 teaspoon salt
1½ pounds bay scallops, fresh or frozen
3 tablespoons butter or margarine
3 tablespoons flour
2 egg yolks
1 cup heavy cream or half-and-half
1 tablespoon butter or margarine, melted
¾ cup (3 ounces) freshly grated Parmesan

1. Melt the butter in a large heavy skillet and sauté the mushrooms and shallots until wilted, about 2 minutes. Add wine, stock, and parsley, bay leaf, rosemary, peppercorns, and lemon tied in a muslin bag. Add salt, bring to a boil, cover, and simmer 20 minutes.

2. Add scallops and simmer 2 minutes, or until opaque. Do not overcook.

3. Strain out scallops, place in a medium-size bowl, and keep them warm. Remove and discard the muslin bag from broth. Return broth to skillet and boil over high heat until liquid measures 1 cup.

4. Melt the 3 tablespoons of butter in a medium-size saucepan, blend in the flour, and cook 2 minutes, stirring. Remove from heat and gradually stir in the 1 cup reserved liquid. Cook, stirring, until thick and smooth. Cook 2 minutes.

5. Beat the egg yolks lightly in a small bowl and gradually beat in the cream. Stir 4 tablespoons hot thick sauce into yolk-cream mixture. Return all to the saucepan and cook until slightly thickened, but do not boil.

6. Add scallops to sauce and reheat. Spoon into 12 buttered coquille shells or 6 individual buttered au gratin dishes. Drizzle with butter and sprinkle with cheese. Place under a preheated broiler for 2 to 3 minutes, or until lightly glazed.

SCALLOPS AND ASPARAGUS
(Chinese)

Two delicate ingredients that are complemented and not over-
shadowed by Chinese vegetables.
Makes 6 servings.

2 tablespoons soy sauce
2 tablespoons dry sherry
4 green onions, finely chopped
1 tablespoon finely chopped fresh
  ginger root, or 1 teaspoon ground
1½ pounds sea scallops, cut in half
  crosswise
¼ cup vegetable oil
1½ pounds asparagus, trimmed and
  washed

¼ pound mushrooms, sliced (1 cup)
3 cups bean sprouts, fresh or
  canned, drained
1 teaspoon salt
1 can (6 ounces) water chestnuts,
  sliced
1 can (8 ounces) bamboo shoots
2 tablespoons cornstarch
2 tablespoons soy sauce
¾ cup water

1. In a large bowl mix together the soy sauce, sherry, green onion, and
    ginger. Add the scallops and toss to coat. Marinate 30 minutes.
2. Remove tips from asparagus and set aside. Cut stalks on bias into
    1-inch pieces, splitting lengthwise if they are fat. In a wok or skillet
    heat 2 tablespoons of the oil. Add asparagus stalks and stir-fry 2
    minutes. Add 2 tablespoons water, cover, and steam 3 minutes, or
    until stalks are crisp-tender. Add tips, cover, and cook 2 minutes.
3. With a slotted spoon remove asparagus to warm platter. Add mush-
    rooms to wok and stir-fry 3 minutes. Remove to platter.
4. Drain the scallops. Heat remaining oil in the wok and stir-fry the
    scallops until opaque, about 4 minutes. Add bean sprouts and stir-fry
    1 minute. Sprinkle with salt, add water chestnuts and bamboo shoots,
    and reheat while stirring.
5. In a small bowl mix the cornstarch with the soy sauce and water until
    smooth and stir into wok. Cook, stirring, until thickened. Stir in the
    asparagus and mushrooms. Serve over hot cooked rice, if you wish.

POLYNESIAN SHRIMP KEBABS

A low-fat barbecue idea.
Makes 6 servings.

2 tablespoons soy sauce
¼ cup dry sherry
1 teaspoon finely chopped fresh
  ginger root, or ¼ teaspoon
  ground
2 green onions, finely chopped
2 tablespoons vegetable oil

2 pounds large shrimp, shelled and
  deveined (about 30)
1 pineapple, peeled, halved,
  cored, and cut into chunks, or 1
  can (1 pound, 14 ounces) chunks
  in juice, drained

1. In a medium-size bowl combine the soy sauce, sherry, ginger, green onion, and oil. Add shrimp and toss to coat. Cover and chill 2 hours.
2. On 6 individual skewers alternate shrimp with pineapple chunks. Grill 5 to 6 inches from hot coals or oven broiler for about 6 minutes, brushing with remaining marinade several times. Serve over hot cooked rice.

SHRIMP WITH COCONUT
(Indian)

Spinach is the surprise ingredient in this coconut-flavored curry.
Makes 4 servings.

2 tablespoons flaked coconut
½ cup warm milk
3 tablespoons vegetable oil
1 large onion, finely chopped
  (1 cup)
2 cloves garlic, finely chopped
1 tablespoon curry powder (or to
  taste)
2 teaspoons chopped fresh ginger
  root, or ½ teaspoon ground

1 cup water
2 tablespoons tomato paste
1 pound shelled deveined shrimp
1 pound fresh spinach, or 1 bag
  (10 ounces), trimmed, washed,
  cooked, drained very well, and
  chopped

1. Soak the coconut in the milk for 10 minutes, strain, reserve liquid, and discard solids.
2. In a large heavy skillet heat the oil and sauté the onion until tender but not browned. Add the garlic, curry, and ginger and cook, stirring, 3 minutes.
3. Add the water and bring to a boil. Add reserved coconut milk to skillet.
4. Add the tomato paste and shrimp and cook, covered, until shrimp turn pink, about 3 to 5 minutes. Add spinach and reheat. Taste and add more salt if necessary. Serve over saffron rice (page 222), if you wish.

SHRIMP AND CABBAGE
(Chinese)

If you ever wondered what to do with that interesting-looking Chinese celery cabbage, this is a good place to begin.
Makes 4 servings.

4 tablespoons vegetable oil	1 green pepper, seeded and diced
1 small head of Chinese celery cabbage, cut into 1-inch squares	1 teaspoon sugar
	1 tablespoon dry sherry
3 green onions, chopped	1 tablespoon soy sauce
2 teaspoons finely chopped fresh ginger root, or ¼ teaspoon ground	½ teaspoon salt
	½ cup water
	1 pound raw, shelled and deveined shrimp
2 cloves garlic, finely chopped	1 tablespoon cornstarch
1 dried red chili pepper, finely chopped	¼ cup water

1. In a wok or skillet heat 2 tablespoons of the oil and stir-fry the cabbage 2 minutes. Add the green onions, ginger, garlic, chili pepper, green pepper, sugar, sherry, soy sauce, salt, and water and heat to boiling, stirring. Transfer to a warm deep platter and keep warm.
2. Clean the wok and add remaining 2 tablespoons oil. Stir-fry the shrimp until pink, about 2 minutes.
3. Mix the cornstarch with the water. Return the cabbage mixture to the wok. Stir in the cornstarch mixture and cook, stirring, until thickened. Serve at once over hot cooked rice, if you wish.

HOT-AND-SOUR SHRIMP
(Chinese)

Sweet-and-sour is probably one of the most popular Chinese flavor combinations, and in this recipe the element of heat is added through ginger and hot pepper.
Makes 4 servings.

1 pound medium-size shrimp, shelled and deveined, or ½ pound frozen shelled and deveined shrimp, thawed
1 teaspoon dry sherry
1 egg white
1 teaspoon cornstarch
2 cups peanut or vegetable oil
3 teaspoons finely chopped fresh ginger root, or ½ teaspoon ground
2 cloves garlic, finely chopped

1 dried hot red chili pepper, chopped
1 small green pepper, seeded and chopped
1 tablespoon sugar
1 tablespoon white vinegar
1 tablespoon catsup
1 tablespoon soy sauce
½ cup water
¼ teaspoon salt
2 teaspoons cornstarch
¼ cup water

1. In a medium-size bowl combine the shrimp, sherry, egg white, and cornstarch and let stand 30 minutes.
2. Heat the oil in a wok or deep heavy saucepan to 300° on a deep-fat thermometer. Fry the shrimp, a few at a time, until they turn pink, 30 to 45 seconds, drain, and keep warm.
3. Remove all but 2 tablespoons of the oil from the wok. Stir-fry the ginger, garlic, chili pepper, and green pepper briefly.
4. In a small bowl combine the sugar, white vinegar, catsup, soy sauce, water, and salt. Stir into the ginger mixture. Mix the cornstarch with the water and stir into the ginger mixture in the wok. Cook, stirring, until mixture thickens and clears. Return shrimp to wok and reheat. Serve with hot cooked rice, if you wish.

GREEK-STYLE SHRIMP WITH FETA

Make the tomato sauce ahead and then it only needs to be
reheated to cook the shrimp for 2 minutes. A foolproof recipe
for the inexperienced cook.
Makes 4 servings.

2 tablespoons olive or vegetable oil
1 large onion, sliced
2 cloves garlic, finely chopped
2 cups coarsely chopped, peeled, seeded, and drained fresh tomatoes, or 1 can (1 pound) tomatoes, drained and chopped
1 teaspoon leaf basil, crumbled
½ teaspoon fennel seeds, crushed
1 teaspoon salt
¼ teaspoon freshly ground black pepper
¼ cup chopped fresh parsley
1½ pounds large shrimp, shelled and deveined
1 cup (4 ounces) feta cheese, crumbled

1. Heat the oil in a medium-size skillet and sauté the onion and garlic until wilted but not browned, about 5 minutes. Add tomatoes and cook over high heat for 10 minutes, or until thickened.
2. Add basil, fennel, salt, and pepper and cook over medium-high heat 10 minutes.
3. Just before serving turn heat to medium-high. Add shrimp and cook 3 to 5 minutes, or until the shrimp turn pink. Add feta and turn off heat. Serve over hot cooked rice and garnish with lemon wedges, if you wish.

SHRIMP AND ARTICHOKES
(Italian)

Serve with rugola or spinach salad and rum cake for dessert.
Makes 4 servings.

3 tablespoons vegetable oil
1½ pounds large shrimp, shelled and
  deveined, with tails left on, if you
  wish
2 tablespoons chopped green onion
1 clove garlic, finely chopped
1 package (9 ounces) frozen
  artichoke hearts, cooked until
  thawed and drained, or 1 can
  (8 ounces) drained, cut in half

½ pound mushrooms, sliced
  (2 cups)
¼ teaspoon salt
¼ teaspoon freshly ground black
  pepper
½ teaspoon leaf thyme, crumbled
1 tablespoon chopped fresh parsley
2 tablespoons lemon juice

1. In a large heavy skillet heat the oil and cook the shrimp, stirring, until
    they turn pink, about 5 minutes.
2. Add the green onion and garlic and cook 1 minute. Add the artichoke
    hearts, mushrooms, salt, pepper, thyme, parsley, and lemon juice.
    Cook, stirring, 3 minutes. Serve over hot cooked fine noodles, if you
    wish.

SOLE DUGLERE
(French)

Dishes called Dugléré always have tomatoes among the ingre-
dients.
Bake at 350° for 12 minutes.
Makes 4 servings.

4 large sole, flounder, or fluke
  fillets (4 to 6 ounces each)
  Salt and freshly ground white
  pepper
3 large ripe tomatoes, peeled,
  seeded, and roughly chopped
¼ cup (½ stick) butter or margarine
2 shallots, finely chopped, or
  2 green onions, white part only
¼ pound mushrooms, sliced (1 cup)

2 teaspoons lemon juice
¾ cup dry white wine
2 tablespoons butter or margarine
3 tablespoons flour
1 cup half-and-half
¼ teaspoon freshly ground white
  pepper
¼ cup (1 ounce) freshly grated
  Parmesan

1. Season the fillets lightly with salt and pepper, fold in half lengthwise, and place in a single layer in a buttered shallow baking dish. Place tomatoes over fish. Preheat oven to 350°.
2. In a small skillet melt the butter and sauté the shallots until tender. Add the mushrooms and cook 3 minutes. Add lemon juice and wine. Bring skillet mixture to a boil and pour over fish. Top dish with crumpled damp wax paper and bake at 350° for 12 minutes, or until fish flakes easily. Pour off liquid but leave tomato and mushrooms with fish. Measure ½ cup.
3. In a small saucepan melt the butter and blend in the flour. Gradually stir in the half-and-half and white pepper. Stir in the reserved ½ cup cooking liquid. Bring to a boil, stirring, and cook 2 minutes.
4. Pour sauce over fish, sprinkle with cheese, and glaze under a pre-heated broiler, if you wish.

SQUID IN TOMATO SAUCE
(Italian)

Don't be put off by the appearance of the fresh squid. It is easy
to prepare for cooking following the directions below.
Makes 4 to 6 servings.

¼ cup olive or vegetable oil
1 large onion, thinly sliced (1 cup)
2 large cloves garlic, finely
  chopped
2 pounds squid, cleaned and cut
  into rings*
½ cup dry red wine
1 can (1 pound) peeled plum
  tomatoes, drained and coarsely
  chopped

2 to 4 tablespoons tomato paste
1 cup frozen peas
1 teaspoon salt
¼ teaspoon freshly ground black
  pepper
1½ teaspoons leaf oregano, crumbled
¼ cup chopped fresh parsley,
  preferably flat Italian

1. Heat the oil in a medium-size saucepan and sauté the onion and garlic
   until tender but not browned, about 5 minutes.
2. Add squid rings and tentacles and cook, stirring, 2 minutes. Add
   remaining ingredients except the parsley, bring to a boil, and cook
   uncovered 10 minutes. Test squid for tenderness. It may need up to 5
   minutes longer but do not cook past point of being tender or it will
   end up like rubber bands.
3. Sprinkle with parsley and serve over hot cooked rice or pasta in deep
   soup bowls.

*To clean squid: Pull the head from the body cavity just behind the eyes. Pull out
the quill-like backbone and innards and discard. Wash well inside and out. Peel
mottled skin from squid and cut into ½-inch slices or rings. Cut tentacles from
head, remove as much of mottled skin as possible, and cut into manageable-size
pieces.

SWORDFISH KEBABS
(Turkish)

Swordfish is one of the few fishes that is solid enough in texture
to stay on a skewer.
Makes 6 servings.

¼ cup olive or vegetable oil
¼ cup lemon juice
1 medium-size onion, finely
  chopped (½ cup)
2 bay leaves, crumbled
1½ teaspoons salt
½ teaspoon freshly ground black
  pepper

2 pounds swordfish, cut into
  1½-inch cubes
18 cherry tomatoes
1 large green pepper, seeded and
  cut into 1-inch pieces
¼ pound medium-size mushrooms

1. In a large bowl combine the oil, lemon juice, onion, bay leaves, salt,
   and pepper. Add the swordfish cubes. Toss to coat and let stand 30
   minutes at room temperature or up to 2 hours in the refrigerator.

2. On 6 individual skewers alternate the fish cubes with tomatoes, green
   pepper, and mushrooms. Brush vegetables with remaining marinade
   and grill 5 to 6 inches from hot coals or oven broiler for 8 to 10
   minutes, turning frequently, until fish is cooked through. Cut into 1
   cube to test. It should look opaque all the way through. Brush with
   the marinade throughout the cooking to prevent drying out. Serve
   over hot cooked rice, if you wish.

TROUT MEUNIERE
(French)

The most popular restaurant method of fixing trout.
Makes 4 servings.

2 cups milk
1 teaspoon salt
¼ teaspoon freshly ground black
pepper
4 trout (1 pound), fresh or
frozen and pan-dressed, with tails
and fins removed

⅓ cup flour
½ cup (1 stick) butter or margarine
½ pound mushrooms, sliced
(2 cups)
3 tablespoons lemon juice
3 tablespoons chopped fresh
parsley

1. In a shallow dish that can accommodate the fish in one layer combine the milk, salt, and pepper. Soak the trout in the milk mixture for 5 minutes, turning twice.
2. Drain the fish and dredge in the flour placed on wax paper.
3. Heat the butter in a large heavy skillet and brown the fish on both sides, two at a time if necessary, until fish flakes easily, about 8 minutes.
4. Place fish on a warm platter. Add mushrooms to skillet and sauté 3 minutes. Sprinkle with lemon juice. Spoon mushroom mixture over fish and sprinkle with parsley.

Chicken

BRUNSWICK STEW
(American)

Lima beans, potatoes, and corn are essential to this braised chicken dish. Add a few more vegetables and it stretches to serve unexpected guests.
Makes 8 to 10 servings.

1 roasting chicken (5 to 6 pounds), or 2 broiler-fryers (2½ to 3 pounds each), cut up
1 stalk celery
1 large onion, cut into eighths
1 carrot, quartered
6 bruised black peppercorns
2 teaspoons salt
3 sprigs parsley
1 teaspoon leaf thyme, crumbled
6 tablespoons butter or margarine
2 large onions, finely chopped (2 cups)

6 medium-size potatoes, cubed
6 tomatoes, peeled and chopped, or 1 can (1 pound, 12 ounces) tomatoes
2 packages (10 ounces each) frozen baby lima beans
3 cups corn kernels from the cob or canned drained
Salt and freshly ground black pepper to taste
¼ cup chopped fresh parsley

1. Place the chicken pieces in a large heavy kettle or Dutch oven. Add celery, onion, carrot, peppercorns, salt, parsley, and thyme and enough water to barely cover the chicken. Bring to a boil, cover, and simmer until chicken is tender, about 1½ hours for the roaster parts and 50 to 60 minutes for small chickens.
2. Set aside until cool enough to handle. Remove and discard bones and skin and leave chicken meat in serving size pieces. Strain the broth.
3. In a clean kettle or Dutch oven melt the butter and sauté the onions until tender but not browned. Add the potatoes and cook 5 minutes. Add tomatoes, bring to a boil, and cook 10 minutes.
4. Add limas and corn and enough strained broth to cover. Cover and simmer 3 minutes. Add the reserved chicken pieces and more broth to cover. Reheat, taste, and add salt and pepper, if needed. Serve in rimmed soup bowls and sprinkle with chopped parsley.

SANCOCHO
(Caribbean Chicken Stew)

Sweet potatoes and plantains or bananas make this chicken stew different and delicious.
Makes 8 servings.

2 broiler-fryers (2½ to 3 pounds each), cut up
2 tablespoons vegetable oil, approximately
2 large onions, sliced
1 clove garlic, finely chopped
1 can (13¾ ounces) chicken broth
1 can (1 pound, 12 ounces) tomatoes
½ cup dry red wine
1 green pepper, seeded and cut into strips

1½ teaspoons salt
½ teaspoon freshly ground black pepper
¼ teaspoon crushed hot red pepper flakes
½ teaspoon leaf thyme, crumbled
4 medium-size sweet potatoes, cut into ½-inch slices
2 plantains or bananas, peeled and cut into 1-inch slices

1. In a large heavy kettle or Dutch oven brown the chicken pieces, a few at a time, in the oil. Add the onion to the oil remaining in the kettle, adding more oil if necessary. Sauté onion until tender but not browned. Add garlic and cook 1 minute.

2. Return chicken to kettle and add broth, tomatoes, wine, green pepper, salt, pepper, red pepper flakes, and thyme. Bring to a boil, cover, and simmer 20 minutes. Add sweet potatoes and push down into liquid.

3. Cover and simmer 25 minutes longer, or until chicken is done. Add plantains and reheat. Serve over hot cooked rice, if you wish.

CHICKEN TAGINE
(Moroccan Chicken Stew)

Tagine indicates a stew, and this is an adaptation of one of the most popular.
Makes 6 servings.

2 broiler-fryers (2½ to 3 pounds each), cut up
¼ cup (½ stick) butter or margarine
1 large Bermuda or Spanish onion, cut into thin slices and separated into rings
3 cloves garlic, finely chopped
2 teaspoons salt

1 teaspoon ground ginger
½ teaspoon freshly ground black pepper
½ teaspoon turmeric
½ cinnamon stick
1 can (13¾ ounces) chicken broth
2 cans (20 ounces each) chick-peas, drained and rinsed
¼ cup chopped fresh parsley
Lemon wedges

1. Brown the chicken pieces in the butter, a few at a time, in a large kettle or Dutch oven. Keep them warm in a large bowl. Sauté the onion in the butter remaining in the kettle. Add the garlic and cook 1 minute.
2. Return chicken to kettle. Add salt, ginger, pepper, turmeric, cinnamon, and broth. Add water to barely cover chicken and bring to a boil. Cover and simmer 40 minutes, or until chicken is done.
3. Add chick-peas and reheat. Sprinkle with parsley, garnish with lemon wedges, and serve with rice or pita bread.

CHICKEN MARENGO
(French)

This dish is said to have been prepared for Napoleon after one of his victories over the Austrians in Italy.
Makes 8 servings.

2 broiler-fryers (2½ to 3 pounds each), cut up
½ cup all-purpose flour
2 teaspoons salt
½ teaspoon freshly ground black pepper
¼ cup vegetable oil
1 large onion, finely chopped (1 cup)

1 clove garlic, finely chopped
½ pound mushrooms, sliced (2 cups)
2 cans (1 pound each) tomatoes
1 teaspoon leaf thyme, crumbled
¼ teaspoon crushed hot red pepper flakes or to taste
¼ cup chopped fresh parsley

1. Coat the chicken pieces in the flour mixed with the salt and pepper and brown in the oil in a heavy skillet, a few pieces at a time. Keep chicken warm.
2. Add the onion to the oil remaining in the skillet and sauté until tender but not browned. Add the garlic and mushrooms and cook, stirring, 2 minutes. Add the tomatoes, thyme, and red pepper flakes. Bring to a boil. Return chicken to skillet, cover, and simmer 50 minutes on top of the stove or transfer to a casserole and bake at 350° for 1¼ hours.
3. If you prefer a thick sauce mix the remaining seasoned flour with water to make a smooth paste. Spoon some of the hot liquid in, return to skillet or casserole, and cook, stirring, until thickened. Sprinkle with parsley.

COQ AU VIN
(French Chicken in Red Wine)

A simplified version of the classic combination.
Makes 6 servings.

2 broiler-fryers (2½ to 3 pounds each), cut up	12 small white onions
3 tablespoons flour	½ pound mushrooms, sliced (2 cups)
1½ teaspoons salt	1 clove garlic, finely chopped
½ teaspoon freshly ground black pepper	1½ cups Burgundy or dry red wine
½ cup (1 stick) butter or margarine	½ cup chicken broth
¼ cup brandy	¼ cup chopped fresh parsley

1. In a brown paper or plastic bag dredge the pieces of chicken in the flour mixed with the salt and pepper. Reserve remaining flour mixture.
2. Heat the butter in a large heavy skillet and brown the chicken pieces on all sides. Heat the brandy, ignite, and pour over chicken.
3. When flame has subsided remove chicken. Add onions and mushrooms to skillet and sauté until lightly browned. Add garlic and cook 1 minute. Sprinkle with remaining flour mixture.
4. Add wine and broth and bring to a boil. Return chicken to skillet, cover, and simmer 30 minutes, or until chicken is tender. Sprinkle with parsley.

CHICKEN CACCIATORE
(Italian Chicken Hunter's-style)

This is a simplified version of an old favorite.
Makes 4 servings.

¼ cup flour
½ teaspoon salt
¼ teaspoon freshly ground black
   pepper
1 broiler-fryer (2½ to 3 pounds),
   cut into 8 pieces
2 tablespoons vegetable oil
2 tablespoons butter or margarine
1 medium-size onion, thinly sliced
1 medium-size green pepper,
   seeded and cut into thin strips
¼ pound mushrooms, thinly sliced
   (1 cup)

2 cloves garlic, finely chopped
½ cup dry white wine
1 can (2 pounds, 3 ounces) peeled
   plum tomatoes, drained and
   coarsely chopped
1 teaspoon leaf basil, crumbled
1½ teaspoons salt
½ teaspoon freshly ground black
   pepper
2 tablespoons chopped fresh
   parsley

1. Combine the flour, salt, and pepper in a paper or plastic bag. Drop the chicken, a couple of pieces at a time, into the flour mixture and shake to coat.
2. Heat the oil and butter in a heavy skillet and brown the chicken on all sides. Remove and drain on paper towels. In the fat remaining in the skillet sauté the onion, green pepper, mushrooms, and garlic until wilted, about 10 minutes. Add wine and tomatoes and cook over high heat 10 minutes to reduce liquid and thicken sauce.
3. Add basil, salt, and pepper and return the chicken to the pan. Cover and simmer gently 30 to 35 minutes, or until chicken is tender. Sprinkle with parsley.

Note: This dish can be fully prepared, simmered 15 minutes only, refrigerated, and reheated to finish cooking.

COUNTRY CAPTAIN
(*American*)

The Southern states lay claim to this tasty way to fix chicken.
An Indian curry it is not.
Makes 8 servings.

½ cup flour
1 teaspoon salt
½ teaspoon freshly ground black pepper
2 broiler-fryers (2½ to 3 pounds each), each cut into 8 pieces
¼ cup (½ stick) butter or margarine
¼ cup vegetable oil
1 large onion, chopped (1 cup)
2 medium-size green peppers, seeded and chopped
2 stalks celery, thinly sliced

3 to 4 teaspoons curry powder
1 can (2 pounds, 3 ounces) peeled plum tomatoes, undrained
1 teaspoon salt
¼ teaspoon freshly ground black pepper
1 teaspoon leaf thyme, crumbled
6 to 8 cups cooked rice (2 cups raw)
½ cup dried currants
½ cup sliced blanched almonds
½ cup chutney

1. Place flour, salt, and pepper in a paper or plastic bag. Drop the chicken pieces in two at a time and shake to coat with flour. Shake off excess. Repeat until all chicken is coated.
2. Divide the butter and oil between 2 large skillets and heat. Add chicken pieces in a single layer and brown on each side, about 5 minutes, in batches, if necessary. Remove chicken and place in a large casserole or Dutch oven with the dark meat on the bottom.
3. Add onion, green pepper, celery, and curry powder to one of the skillets and sauté until wilted, stirring occasionally. Coarsely chop the tomatoes and add to empty skillet. Heat and stir up all brown bits. Add to vegetables in second skillet.
4. Stir in salt, pepper, and thyme and pour sauce over chicken. Cover and simmer 30 to 40 minutes, or until chicken is tender. Serve with hot rice and side dishes of currants, almonds, and chutney.

Note: Chicken dish can be refrigerated after sauce is poured over. Then it will need cooking, covered, over low heat for 45 to 55 minutes or until chicken is tender.

CHICKEN PAPRIKASH
(Hungarian)

The calorie-conscious can substitute plain yogurt for the sour cream.
Makes 4 servings.

¼ cup (½ stick) butter or margarine
2 large onions, sliced and separated into rings
1 broiler-fryer (about 3 pounds), cut up
1 tablespoon flour
2 tablespoons sweet paprika
1 teaspoon salt

⅛ teaspoon freshly ground black pepper
1 can (1 pound) tomatoes
1 small green pepper, seeded and diced
1 container (8 ounces) sour cream, at room temperature
1 tablespoon chopped fresh parsley

1. Heat the butter in a large heavy skillet and sauté the onion until golden. Remove to a bowl with a slotted spoon. In the butter remaining in the skillet brown the chicken pieces on all sides.
2. Sprinkle with the flour and paprika. Return onions to skillet. Add the salt, pepper, tomatoes, and green pepper. Bring to a boil, cover, and simmer until chicken is tender, about 40 minutes. Arrange chicken in a serving dish.
3. Place sour cream in a bowl and gradually add liquid from skillet, stirring constantly. Pour over chicken. Sprinkle with parsley. Serve with noodles, nockerln, or tiny dumplings, if you wish.

CHICKEN NORMANDY
(French)

The designation Normande or Normandy usually means that apples in some form, here as Calvados or apple brandy, and cream are in the dish. Eliminating the cream and substituting all chicken broth requires that the pan liquid be thickened with 2 tablespoons flour mixed with 3 tablespoons water.
Makes 8 servings.

¼ cup olive or vegetable oil
¼ cup (½ stick) butter or margarine
2 broiler-fryers (2½ to 3 pounds each), each cut into 8 pieces
1 large and 1 medium-size onion, finely chopped (1½ cups)
½ cup Calvados or brandy, warmed
2 tart apples, cored and quartered

½ cup apple cider or juice
½ teaspoon leaf thyme, crumbled
¾ cup heavy or whipping cream
¾ cup chicken broth
1 teaspoon salt
¼ to ½ teaspoon freshly ground black pepper
¼ cup chopped fresh parsley

1. Divide the oil and butter between 2 large skillets and heat over medium heat. Add chicken in one layer and brown for about 5 minutes on each side. Add half the onions to each skillet and cook until wilted.
2. Pour ¼ cup Calvados into one skillet and ignite. Repeat with second skillet. Divide the remaining ingredients among the two skillets and bring to a boil. Cover, lower heat, and simmer 30 to 40 minutes, or until chicken is tender.

CHICKEN AND DUMPLINGS
(American)

Every grandmother and aunt has a different recipe for this old-fashioned favorite.
Makes 8 servings.

2 broiler-fryers (3 pounds each), cut up
1 large onion, quartered
1 stalk celery with leaves, quartered
2 carrots, quartered
6 bruised black peppercorns
2 teaspoons salt

1 chicken bouillon cube
1½ cups sifted all-purpose flour
½ teaspoon salt
1½ teaspoons baking powder
½ cup milk
2 tablespoons melted butter or margarine

1. Place the chicken in a heavy kettle or Dutch oven. Add the onion, celery, carrot, peppercorns, salt, and enough water to barely cover the chicken.
2. Bring to a boil, cover, and simmer 50 minutes, or until chicken is tender. Let chicken cool in broth. Chill. Remove chicken fat and reserve.
3. Remove chicken, discard skin and bones, and leave meat in as big pieces as possible. Set aside. Strain broth and boil rapidly until it measures about 4 cups. Add bouillon cube.
4. Melt 3 to 4 tablespoons of the reserved chicken fat in a clean kettle and blend in ¼ cup of the flour. Gradually stir in the reserved broth, bring to a boil, stirring, and cook until thickened and smooth. Check seasoning and add salt and pepper, if needed.
5. Meanwhile sift together the 1¼ cups remaining flour, ½ teaspoon salt, and the baking powder into a bowl. Stir in the milk and melted butter to make a soft dough. Put serving spoonfuls into the simmering chicken gravy. Cover tightly and cook without peeking for 15 minutes. Add chicken pieces and reheat.

WATERZOOI
(Belgian Chicken Stew)

A country-style stew enriched at the end with egg yolks and
perked up with lemon juice.
Makes 8 servings.

⅓ cup butter or margarine
1 large onion, finely chopped
  (1 cup)
3 medium-size leeks, cleaned and
  sliced
3 stalks celery with leaves, sliced
2 carrots, sliced
4 pounds drumsticks and thighs
3 cans (13¾ ounces each) chicken
  broth

1 bay leaf
½ teaspoon leaf thyme, crumbled
1 teaspoon salt
½ teaspoon freshly ground black
  pepper
3 tablespoons butter or margarine
¼ cup flour
2 egg yolks, lightly beaten
3 tablespoons lemon juice

1. In a large heavy kettle or Dutch oven heat ⅓ cup butter and sauté the
   onion and leeks until tender but not browned. Add celery and carrots
   and cook, stirring, 4 minutes. With a slotted spoon remove vegetables to a bowl.
2. In the butter remaining in the kettle brown the chicken pieces, a few
   at a time. Return vegetables and add broth, bay leaf, thyme, salt, and
   pepper. Bring to a boil. Return chicken pieces, cover, and simmer 30
   minutes, or until chicken is done.
3. With a slotted spoon remove chicken pieces to a deep serving dish.
   Strain broth and return to kettle.
4. In a medium-size saucepan melt the remaining butter and blend in
   the flour. Cook, stirring, 2 minutes. Gradually stir in 2 cups of the hot
   broth from the kettle. Bring to a boil, stirring.
5. Pour some of the hot sauce into the egg yolks and beat well. Return to
   rest of sauce in pan. Stir in another 2 cups of hot broth from the
   kettle. Return to the kettle. Add lemon juice. Reheat but do not boil.
6. Pour over chicken and sprinkle with chopped parsley, if you wish.

CHICKEN AND CORN CASSEROLE
(Chilean)

Cumin is a haunting spice and has a pleasant affinity for chicken
and corn. You will agree that this is a different way to fix the
popular broiler-fryer.
Bake at 350° for 35 minutes.
Makes 4 servings.

3 tablespoons vegetable oil
1 broiler-fryer (3 pounds), cut into 8 pieces
2 large onions, finely chopped (2 cups)
1 clove garlic, finely chopped
1 cup chicken broth
1 teaspoon salt
¼ teaspoon freshly ground black pepper
¼ cup raisins, soaked in ¼ cup water for 15 minutes and drained
1 teaspoon ground cumin
⅓ cup pitted black olives
2 cups fresh corn kernels, cut from the cob, or frozen, thawed, from a poly bag
2 tablespoons milk
1 tablespoon sugar

1. In a large heavy skillet heat the oil and brown the chicken pieces a
    few at a time. Transfer to a heavy casserole as they brown. Preheat
    oven to 350°.
2. In the oil remaining in the skillet sauté the onion until tender but not
    browned. Add the garlic and cook 1 minute. Add the broth, salt,
    pepper, raisins, cumin, and olives and cook, stirring up all browned-
    on bits. When boiling, pour over the chicken in the casserole. Cover
    tightly and bake at 350° for 15 minutes.
3. Meanwhile place the corn kernels and milk in the container of an
    electric blender. Whirl until puréed. Add more milk, if necessary.
4. Pour over the chicken in the casserole, sprinkle with the sugar, and
    bake, uncovered, at 350° for 20 minutes, or until chicken is cooked.
    Place under a preheated broiler for a minute or two if you prefer a
    browned surface.

ROAST CHICKEN WITH CORN BREAD STUFFING
(American)

Bake at 400° for about 1½ hours.
Makes 8 servings.

6 tablespoons (¾ stick) butter or margarine
¾ cup chopped celery
¾ cup finely chopped onion
¾ cup chopped green pepper
Corn bread (see below), crumbled, or 1 package corn bread mix, made according to package directions
½ cup packaged bread crumbs
½ cup chopped fresh parsley
1 teaspoon leaf thyme, crumbled
2 eggs, lightly beaten

3 cups chicken broth, approximately
2 hard-cooked eggs, chopped
½ teaspoon salt
¼ teaspoon freshly ground black pepper
1 roasting chicken (5 to 6 pounds), oven ready
5 tablespoons butter or margarine
3 tablespoons flour
Salt and pepper

1. Melt the 6 tablespoons butter in a skillet and sauté the celery, onion, and green pepper until tender but not browned. Place in a bowl with the crumbled corn bread, bread crumbs, parsley, thyme, eggs, and enough chicken broth just to moisten. Preheat oven to 400°.

2. Add the hard-cooked eggs, salt, and pepper, and mix well. Stuff the chicken cavity and under the neck flap. Melt 1 tablespoon of the butter in a roasting pan and turn the chicken in it to coat all surfaces. Set on one side.

3. Roast the chicken at 400° for 30 minutes, turn chicken to the other side, and roast 30 minutes. Baste several times. Turn chicken on its back and roast 30 minutes longer, or until juices run clear and thigh meat is tender.

4. Meanwhile place giblets, except liver, and remaining broth in a saucepan, bring to a boil, cover, and simmer 30 minutes. Add liver and cook 10 minutes. Strain and reserve broth. Chop liver, heart, and gizzard.

5. Melt the remaining 4 tablespoons butter. Blend in the flour and cook 1 minute. Gradually stir in the reserved broth. Bring to a boil, stirring until mixture thickens. Add chopped giblets. Season to taste with salt and pepper. Serve separately with roast chicken.

CORN BREAD

---

1 cup yellow cornmeal
1 cup flour
1 teaspoon sugar
½ teaspoon salt
4 teaspoons baking powder

1 egg, lightly beaten
1 cup milk
¼ cup (½ stick) butter or margarine, melted

1. Preheat oven to 425°. Sift cornmeal, flour, sugar, and salt into a bowl. Add egg, milk, and butter and mix until blended.
2. Pour mixture into a buttered 8- × 8- × 2-inch baking pan. Bake for 25 minutes, or until done.

BAKED CHICKEN
(*Swiss*)

Bake at 350° for 30 minutes.
Makes 6 servings.

⅓ cup flour
¾ teaspoon salt
¼ teaspoon freshly ground black pepper
1 tablespoon paprika
3 pounds chicken legs and thighs
3 tablespoons vegetable oil
1 large onion, finely chopped (1 cup)

1 clove garlic, finely chopped
1 large stalk celery, chopped
3 cups chicken broth
2 tablespoons Dijon mustard
1 cup (4 ounces) grated Swiss
2 tablespoons chopped fresh parsley

1. In a brown paper or plastic bag combine the flour, salt, pepper, and paprika. Dredge the chicken pieces, a few at a time, in the flour mixture. Reserve remaining flour mixture.
2. Heat the oil in a large heavy ovenproof skillet and brown the chicken on all sides. Remove and drain on paper towels.
3. To the oil remaining in the skillet add the onion and sauté until tender but not browned. Add the garlic and celery and cook 2 minutes. Preheat oven to 350°.
4. Stir in 2 cups of the broth and the mustard. Bring to a boil. Return chicken to the pan, cover, and bake at 350° for 30 minutes.
5. In a small bowl combine the reserved flour mixture and remaining broth. Stir into the chicken mixture and cook, stirring, over medium heat until mixture thickens.
6. Remove from heat and sprinkle with cheese. Place under a preheated broiler for 2 to 3 minutes, if you wish. Sprinkle with parsley.

CHICKEN COOKED IN A CLAY POT
(American)

Clay pots tend to be relegated to the top shelf in the cupboard but here's a good reason for getting them into action again. The flavor is outstanding.
Bake at 480° for 50 minutes.
Makes 4 servings.

¼ cup flour
2 teaspoons salt
½ teaspoon freshly ground black pepper
2 tablespoons butter or margarine
2 tablespoons vegetable oil
1 broiler-fryer (2½ to 3 pounds), cut into 8 pieces
1 clove garlic, finely chopped
½ cup dry white wine
½ cup chicken broth
½ teaspoon leaf savory, crumbled

½ teaspoon leaf thyme, crumbled
½ cup raw rice
2 small zucchini, thinly sliced
1 large onion, thinly sliced
½ pound mushrooms, sliced (2 cups)
2 carrots, thinly sliced
2 stalks celery, thinly sliced
1¼ teaspoons salt
½ teaspoon freshly ground black pepper

1. Soak the clay pot and cover according to manufacturer's instructions.
2. Mix the flour, salt, and pepper in a paper or plastic bag. Heat the butter and oil in a large heavy skillet. Drop the chicken pieces into the flour mixture and shake to coat. Fry a few at a time in the skillet. When golden transfer to the clay pot. Add garlic to skillet and cook 1 minute. Add to clay pot. Stir wine, broth, savory, thyme, and rice into skillet and cook, stirring to scrape up all the browned-on bits. Pour over chicken in clay pot.
3. Place zucchini, onion, mushrooms, carrots, and celery in a large bowl and toss with the salt and pepper. Spread over the chicken. Cover and place on bottom shelf in a cold oven. Turn heat to 480° and cook 50 minutes, or until chicken is done and rice has absorbed most of the liquid. Set on a wooden board or heavy cloth for 10 minutes before uncovering and serving.

CHICKEN PIE
(American)

This is one recipe where I do not think of cholesterol or calories because the sauce should be thick and rich under the crust.
Bake at 425° for 35 minutes.
Makes 6 servings.

2 broiler-fryers (2½ to 3 pounds each), cut up
1 medium-size onion, quartered
1 stalk celery with leaves, cut into quarters
1 carrot, quartered
2 cups chicken broth
1 teaspoon salt
½ teaspoon freshly ground black pepper

3 eggs, well beaten
2 cups heavy cream
1 small onion, finely chopped (¼ cup)
2 tablespoons chopped fresh parsley
1 teaspoon leaf thyme, crumbled
Salt and freshly ground black pepper to taste
Pastry for a one-crust 10-inch pie

1. Place the chicken pieces in a Dutch oven or deep casserole. Add onion, celery, carrot, chicken broth, salt, and pepper. Bring to a boil, cover, and simmer 50 minutes, or until chicken is tender.
2. Remove chicken pieces and when cool enough to handle remove meat from bones and discard skin and bones. Leave chicken in as big pieces as possible. Preheat oven to 425°.
3. Strain the broth and use in soup or stew. Combine the eggs and cream. Remove and reserve 1 tablespoon for pastry. Add onion, parsley, thyme, and chicken. Taste and add salt and pepper, if needed.
4. Turn chicken mixture into a deep 10-inch pie plate. Top with rolled-out pastry, flute edges, and make steam holes. Brush with reserved egg-cream mixture and bake at 425° for 35 minutes, or until pastry is golden.

CREAMED CHICKEN
(American)

This basic recipe can be served over rice, hot biscuits, noodles, or in patty shells.
Makes 6 servings.

2 broiler-fryers (2½ to 3 pounds each), cut up
1 carrot, sliced
2 stalks celery, sliced
2 sprigs parsley
1 medium-size onion, sliced
2 teaspoons salt
½ teaspoon freshly ground black pepper

½ cup (1 stick) butter or margarine
¼ cup flour
1 pound mushrooms, sliced (4 cups)
¼ cup heavy cream
2 tablespoons dry sherry, optional
2 tablespoons diced green pepper
2 tablespoons diced red pepper

1. Place the chicken pieces in a casserole or Dutch oven. Add the carrot, celery, parsley, onion, salt, pepper, and enough water to barely cover the chicken.
2. Bring to a boil, cover, and simmer for 50 minutes, or until chicken is tender. Remove chicken from broth and when cool enough to handle remove chicken from bones. Discard bones and skin.
3. Boil rapidly without a cover to reduce the broth by half. Strain and measure 2 cups.
4. Melt 4 tablespoons of the butter in a small saucepan. Blend in the flour and cook 4 minutes, stirring constantly. Remove from the heat and stir in the 2 cups of broth. Bring to a boil, stirring, and cook 3 minutes.
5. Meanwhile sauté the mushrooms in remaining butter in a skillet.
6. Add mushrooms, cream, sherry, green and red peppers, and chicken to sauce. Reheat and taste. Add salt and pepper, if needed.

BAKED BARBECUE-FLAVORED CHICKEN
(American)

The chicken can be barbecued over a charcoal fire and basted with the sauce during the last half of the cooking time, which will be reduced to about 1 hour, depending on the heat of the fire. Turn frequently.
Bake at 350° for 1½ hours.
Makes 8 servings.

4 medium-size onions, sliced
1½ cups catsup
1½ cups water
⅓ cup cider vinegar
3 tablespoons Worcestershire sauce
1 teaspoon paprika

1 tablespoon brown sugar
¼ teaspoon salt
⅛ teaspoon freshly ground black pepper
2 teaspoons chili powder or to taste
2 broiler-fryers (2½ to 3 pounds each), cut up

1. In a medium-size bowl combine the onions, catsup, water, vinegar, Worcestershire, paprika, brown sugar, salt, pepper, and chili powder. Preheat oven to 350°.
2. Place the chicken pieces in a shallow baking pan. Pour over the sauce and bake at 350° for 1½ hours, or until juices run clear and thickest part of the thigh is tender.

CHICKEN MOLE
(Mexican)

If you prefer, the whole cooked chicken pieces can be used in the finished dish and reheated in the mole sauce. The idea of chocolate in a savory sauce is hard to face the first time but once accepted it is addictive.
Makes 6 servings.

2 broiler-fryers (2½ to 3 pounds each), cut up
1 medium-size onion, quartered
1 stalk celery, quartered
2½ cups chicken broth (one 13¾-ounce can plus ½ cup water)
3 tablespoons lard or margarine
1 large onion, finely chopped (1 cup)
2 cloves garlic, finely chopped
2 to 3 tablespoons chili powder
½ teaspoon ground cinnamon
½ teaspoon ground cloves
½ teaspoon ground cumin

⅛ teaspoon cayenne
1 can (1 pound) tomatoes
2 six-inch stale tortillas, torn into pieces
3 tablespoons sesame seeds, toasted*
3 tablespoons raisins
1 ounce (1 square) unsweetened chocolate, grated
3 tablespoons chopped fresh cilantro (Chinese parsley) or Italian flat parsley
Salt to taste

1. Place the chicken pieces in a Dutch oven or deep casserole. Add the onion, celery, and chicken broth. Bring to a boil, cover, and simmer 50 minutes, or until chicken is tender.
2. Allow chicken to cool in the broth until it can be handled. Remove and discard skin and bones and leave chicken in as big pieces as possible. Strain broth and measure 2½ cups. Reserve.
3. Meanwhile heat the lard or margarine in a Dutch oven or heavy casserole and sauté the onion and garlic until tender but not browned. Stir in the chili, cinnamon, cloves, cumin, and cayenne. Cook 1 minute, stirring. Stir in the reserved broth.
4. Place tomatoes and juice, tortillas, sesame seeds, and raisins into the container of an electric blender. Blend until smooth. Add to Dutch oven.
5. Stir in the chocolate and simmer 5 minutes. Add chicken, cilantro, and salt to taste. Simmer 10 minutes to reheat chicken. Serve with warm tortillas, sour cream, and guacamole, if you wish.

*Place seeds in a small dry skillet and toast over low heat, shaking frequently until golden.

CHICKEN AND EGGPLANT
(Greek)

The hint of lemon and sweet spices is the secret of this chicken dish.
Makes 4 servings.

1 small eggplant (about ¾ pound)
Salt
1 broiler-fryer (3 pounds), cut up
3 tablespoons lemon juice
1 teaspoon salt
½ teaspoon freshly ground black pepper
3 tablespoons butter or margarine
3 tablespoons vegetable oil, approximately
1 large onion, finely chopped (1 cup)

3 large tomatoes, peeled, seeded, and chopped, or 1 can (1 pound) tomatoes
½ cup dry white wine
1 stick cinnamon, broken into 3 pieces
2 whole cloves
2 tablespoons chopped fresh parsley

1. Peel the eggplant, cut into ½-inch-thick slices, and sprinkle with salt. Set aside for 20 minutes. Rinse and pat dry on paper towels. Cut into 1½- × ½-inch pieces.
2. Rub the chicken with lemon juice and sprinkle with salt and pepper. In a large heavy kettle or Dutch oven heat the butter and oil and brown the chicken pieces on all sides. Remove to a large bowl and reserve.
3. Brown the eggplant on all sides. Add to chicken in bowl.
4. Sauté the onion in fat remaining in the kettle (add more oil if necessary) until tender but not brown.
5. Add tomatoes, wine, cinnamon, and cloves. Bring to a boil. Return chicken and eggplant to kettle. Cover and simmer 40 minutes, or until chicken is cooked. Sprinkle with parsley and season to taste with more salt and pepper, if needed. Serve with hot cooked rice, if you wish.

HAWAIIAN CHICKEN WITH PINEAPPLE

Makes 4 servings.

3 tablespoons flour
1 teaspoon salt
½ teaspoon freshly ground black pepper
¼ teaspoon ground ginger
1 broiler-fryer (2½ to 3 pounds), cut into 8 pieces
2 tablespoons butter or margarine
1 tablespoon vegetable oil
1 large onion, sliced

1 can (13¾ ounces) chicken broth
1 medium-size green pepper, seeded and diced
1 cup pineapple chunks, drained from juice pack, juice reserved and chunks halved
1 tablespoon soy sauce
3 tablespoons brown sugar
2½ tablespoons cornstarch

1. Combine the flour, salt, pepper, and ginger in a paper or plastic bag. Toss the chicken a piece at a time in the flour mixture to coat.
2. In a large heavy skillet heat the butter and oil and brown the chicken on all sides. With a slotted spoon remove chicken to a bowl. Add onion to skillet and cook until golden, about 5 minutes.
3. Stir in the broth and cook, stirring to scrape up all the browned-on bits. Return chicken to skillet, cover, and simmer gently 35 minutes, or until chicken is done. Remove chicken to bowl.
4. Add green pepper, pineapple chunks, soy sauce, and brown sugar to skillet. Mix the cornstarch with ¼ cup of the reserved pineapple juice and stir into the skillet. Bring to a boil and cook, stirring, until mixture thickens.
5. Return chicken to skillet and spoon sauce over. Reheat for 5 minutes.

CHICKEN SCARPARIELLO
(Italian Chicken Shoemaker-style)

This is considered a budget dish but the flavor makes everyone forget that aspect.
Makes 6 to 8 servings.

2 broiler-fryers (2½ to 3 pounds each), cut into 8 pieces, with backbone discarded
¼ cup olive or vegetable oil
2 cloves garlic, finely chopped
1½ teaspoons salt

½ teaspoon freshly ground black pepper
1½ teaspoons leaf rosemary, crumbled
1½ cups dry white wine
2 tablespoons chopped fresh parsley

1. Brown the chicken pieces, a few at a time, in the oil in a heavy skillet or Dutch oven. In the oil remaining in the skillet cook the garlic 1 minute.
2. Return chicken to skillet and add salt, pepper, rosemary, and wine. Bring to a boil, cover, and simmer 45 minutes, or until chicken is done.
3. Remove cover and boil rapidly for 2 to 3 minutes to reduce amount of liquid. Sprinkle with parsley and serve with hot cooked noodles, if you wish.

CHICKEN WITH EGGPLANT
(Italian)

Eggplant is a highly versatile vegetable and teams with chicken as easily as it does with other vegetables.
Bake at 350° for 50 minutes.
Makes 4 servings.

¼ cup olive or vegetable oil, approximately
1 broiler-fryer (2½ to 3 pounds), cut into 8 pieces, with backbone discarded
1 small eggplant (about ¾ pound)
Salt
1 can (1 pound) tomatoes

1 small onion, finely chopped (¼ cup)
1 green pepper, seeded and diced
1 clove garlic, finely chopped
1 teaspoon leaf basil, crumbled
1 teaspoon leaf oregano, crumbled
¼ teaspoon freshly ground black pepper
½ cup dry red wine

1. Heat the oil in a heavy casserole or Dutch oven and brown the chicken on all sides, a few pieces at a time.
2. Meanwhile peel and cut the eggplant into ½-inch slices. Sprinkle with salt and let stand 15 minutes. Rinse well, pat dry, and cut into 1-inch cubes. Preheat oven to 350°.
3. In the oil remaining in the casserole, adding more if necessary, brown the eggplant cubes on all sides. Add the tomatoes, onion, green pepper, garlic, basil, oregano, pepper, and wine. Bring to a boil. Return chicken to casserole. Cover tightly and bake at 350° for 50 minutes, or until chicken and eggplant are cooked. Taste for seasoning and add salt and pepper, if you wish. Serve over hot cooked rice or cooked orzo.

CHICKEN WITH ARTICHOKE HEARTS
(French)

Rich with cream and egg, this dish is outstanding for a special occasion. Double the wine, flour, and last quantity of butter and it is possible to eliminate the cream and egg, if you wish. Makes 4 servings.

1 broiler-fryer (2½ to 3 pounds), cut into 8 pieces
Salt and freshly ground black pepper
3 tablespoons butter or margarine
3 tablespoons vegetable oil
4 medium-size leeks, cleaned and thinly sliced
1 clove garlic, finely chopped
½ cup dry white wine
¼ teaspoon leaf thyme, crumbled
½ teaspoon leaf rosemary, crumbled
1 bay leaf
1 teaspoon salt

½ teaspoon freshly ground black pepper
1 package (9 ounces) frozen artichoke hearts, partially thawed, or 1 can (8½ ounces), drained
1 pound carrots, cut into 2-inch strips, ½ inch thick, cooked in a minimum of water and drained
½ teaspoon flour
½ teaspoon butter or margarine, softened
½ cup heavy cream or half-and-half
1 egg, lightly beaten

1. Rub the chicken pieces with salt and pepper. Heat the butter and oil in a heavy skillet and brown the chicken pieces on all sides.
2. Remove chicken pieces and keep them warm. Add leeks and garlic to skillet and cook until wilted and golden, about 8 minutes.
3. Add wine, thyme, rosemary, bay leaf, salt, and pepper and cook over high heat 1 minute. Return chicken to skillet, cover, and cook 25 minutes. Add artichoke hearts, cover, and cook 10 minutes.
4. Add carrots, cover, and cook 5 minutes, or until chicken is tender. Using a slotted spoon remove chicken and vegetables to a deep serving dish and keep them warm. Mix the flour and softened butter together and whisk into the skillet ¼ teaspoon at a time.
5. Combine the cream with the egg and slowly stir in 2 tablespoons of the hot sauce. Return to the skillet and heat slowly, stirring, until sauce thickens further but do not boil. Pour over the chicken and sprinkle with chopped parsley, if you wish.

CHICKEN WITH SEASONED RICE
(Indian)

Curry powder is bolstered with extra spices to give a more
authentic flavor to this chicken and rice dish.
Bake at 350° for 35 minutes.
Makes 6 servings.

1 container (8 ounces) plain yogurt
2 medium-size onions, finely
   chopped (1 cup)
2 cloves garlic, finely chopped
2 teaspoons curry powder
½ teaspoon cumin seeds
1 whole cardamom seed, crushed
1 two-inch piece stick cinnamon
½ teaspoon ground ginger
½ teaspoon salt
1 broiler-fryer (3 pounds), cut up
   into small pieces

¼ cup (½ stick) butter or margarine,
   approximately
2 large onions, finely chopped
   (2 cups)
2 cups raw long-grain rice
1½ teaspoons salt
3½ cups chicken broth or water
1 package (10 ounces) frozen peas
¼ cup unsalted cashews or
   blanched almonds, roughly
   chopped

1. In a large bowl combine the yogurt, onions, garlic, curry powder,
   cumin seeds, cardamom, cinnamon stick, ginger, and salt. Mix well.
2. Add the chicken pieces, turning to coat, and chill 4 to 6 hours.
3. In a large heavy saucepan or Dutch oven melt the butter and sauté
   the onion until tender but not browned, about 10 minutes.
4. Remove chicken from yogurt mixture and brown in the saucepan,
   adding more butter, if necessary. Add the rice and cook 5 minutes,
   stirring constantly. Preheat oven to 350°.
5. Stir in the yogurt spice mixture, salt, and broth. Bring to a boil,
   cover, and bake at 350° for 20 minutes. Add peas and bake 15 minutes, or until rice is tender and liquid has been absorbed.
6. Remove cinnamon stick, fluff up rice with fork, and serve sprinkled
   with the nuts.

ARROZ CON POLLO
(Spanish Chicken With Rice)

Makes 4 servings.

1 frying chicken (3 to 3½ pounds), cut up
¼ cup flour
1 teaspoon salt
½ teaspoon freshly ground black pepper
¼ cup vegetable oil
1 medium-size onion, finely chopped (½ cup)
1 can (13¾ ounces) chicken broth
1 cup water
1 cup raw rice

2 large tomatoes, peeled, seeded, and diced
½ bay leaf, crumbled
2 whole cloves
2 tablespoons chopped fresh parsley
⅛ teaspoon leaf saffron or ½ teaspoon turmeric
1 small green pepper, seeded and diced
1 small red pepper, seeded and diced

1. Dredge the chicken pieces in the flour mixed with the salt and pepper. Heat the oil in a heavy deep skillet and brown the chicken pieces on all sides. Drain on paper towels.
2. Add the onion to the oil left in the skillet and cook until limp. Add the broth, water, rice, tomatoes, bay leaf, cloves, parsley, and saffron. Bring to a boil.
3. Add the chicken pieces, cover, and cook 35 minutes, or until chicken is tender and liquid has been absorbed.
4. Stir in the green and red peppers just before serving.

BAKED MUSTARD CHICKEN BREASTS
(French)

The assertive mustard flavor is not for the faint-hearted.
Bake at 400° for 40 minutes.
Makes 6 servings.

3 whole chicken breasts, split
1 teaspoon salt
¼ teaspoon freshly ground black pepper
1 clove garlic, finely chopped
½ cup Dijon mustard
½ cup sour cream

1 cup packaged bread crumbs
½ teaspoon leaf oregano, crumbled
1 tablespoon finely chopped fresh parsley
3 tablespoons freshly grated Parmesan

1. Sprinkle the chicken with the salt and pepper. Combine the garlic, mustard, and sour cream in a small bowl. On a piece of wax paper combine the bread crumbs, oregano, parsley, and cheese. Preheat oven to 400°.
2. Spread mustard mixture over chicken pieces and roll in bread crumb mixture. Bake at 400° in a shallow baking pan for 40 minutes, or until golden and done.

BAKED CHICKEN KIEV
(Russian)

After baking, the butter in the middle of the chicken bundles will be hot and liquid and is likely to squirt out unless the chicken is cut with care.
Bake at 375° for 20 minutes.
Makes 4 servings.

⅓ cup butter or margarine
4 teaspoons chopped fresh chives, or 1 teaspoon freeze-dried
½ teaspoon leaf thyme, crumbled
⅛ teaspoon freshly ground black pepper
2 whole chicken breasts, boned, skinned, cut in half, and pounded between sheets of wax paper until as thin as veal scaloppini

Flour
1 egg, lightly beaten with 1 tablespoon water
1½ cups herbed stuffing mix, crushed in an electric blender
4 tablespoons (½ stick) butter or margarine, melted

1. Combine the butter, chives, thyme, and pepper. Form into 4 rectangles and freeze.
2. Place a frozen rectangle in the middle of each piece of chicken and fold up the chicken like a package so that butter is completely enveloped.
3. Dust with flour, dip in egg, and roll in seasoned crumbs. Pat well to make firm coating. Chill at least 1 hour or freeze if making ahead. Place on a jelly roll pan, drizzle butter over each, and bake at 375° for 20 minutes, or until chicken is done.

CHICKEN PARMIGIANA
(Italian)

Even though quality veal is very expensive and hard to get you
can enjoy the classic Parmigiana dish made with chicken.
Bake at 350° for 25 minutes.
Makes 6 servings.

3 tablespoons olive or vegetable oil
1 large onion, finely chopped
  (1 cup)
1 clove garlic, finely chopped
1 can (1 pound, 12 ounces)
  tomatoes
3 tablespoons tomato paste
¾ teaspoon salt
¼ teaspoon freshly ground black
  pepper
1 teaspoon leaf basil, crumbled
½ teaspoon leaf oregano, crumbled

3 whole chicken breasts, split,
  skinned, and boned
2 eggs, lightly beaten
2 tablespoons water
1 teaspoon salt
½ teaspoon freshly ground black
  pepper
¾ cup Italian seasoned bread
  crumbs
1 cup olive or vegetable oil
6 slices mozzarella from an 8-ounce
  package

1. Heat the oil in a medium-size saucepan and sauté the onion until
   tender but not browned. Add the garlic and cook 1 minute.
2. Add the tomatoes, tomato paste, salt, pepper, basil, and oregano.
   Bring to a boil and simmer, uncovered, 15 minutes.
3. Place the chicken pieces between sheets of wax paper and pound
   until as thin as veal scaloppini. Dip in the eggs mixed with the water,
   salt, and pepper, then in the bread crumbs. Pat crumbs and eliminate
   loose ones. Let sit 20 minutes or longer to set the coating. Heat the
   oil in a large heavy skillet and sauté the chicken pieces until golden
   on both sides. Preheat oven to 350°.
4. Pour half the tomato sauce in the bottom of a shallow baking dish.
   Top with slightly overlapping slices of the cooked chicken. Pour over
   remaining sauce and top with mozzarella. Bake at 350° for 25 minutes, or until cheese has melted and dish is bubbly-hot.

TARRAGON CHICKEN
(French)

Tarragon and chicken have an affinity which is hard to beat and easily seen in this presentation. This make-ahead version of the classic lets the busy cook serve a delicious dish without last-minute hassle.
Bake at 350° for 15 to 20 minutes.
Makes 6 servings.

½ cup flour
1 teaspoon salt
½ teaspoon freshly ground black pepper
½ teaspoon leaf tarragon, crumbled
4 large whole chicken breasts, boned and cut in half
¼ cup (½ stick) butter or margarine
1 small leek, thinly sliced (¾ cup)

⅓ cup dry white wine
Flour
¼ cup (½ stick) butter or margarine
1 cup chicken broth
1 cup light cream or milk
½ teaspoon Dijon mustard
½ cup lightly buttered bread crumbs

1. Combine the flour, salt, pepper, and tarragon on wax paper or in a paper bag. Coat the chicken pieces well with seasoned flour, reserving remaining flour mixture.
2. Heat the butter in a large heavy skillet and sauté the chicken pieces 2 minutes on each side. Drain on paper towels and arrange in a flat baking dish in single layer.
3. Add leek to butter remaining in skillet and cook until soft.
4. Stir in wine and scrape up all browned-on bits from bottom of pan. Cook, stirring, 3 to 4 minutes, or until the wine is reduced by half. Measure reserved flour mixture and add flour, if necessary, to make 5 tablespoons.
5. In a medium-size saucepan melt the ¼ cup butter, blend in the flour mixture, and cook 3 minutes, stirring constantly. Gradually stir in the broth and cream and whisk until smooth. Add mustard, bring to a boil, stirring, and cook 2 to 3 minutes, or until thickened. Taste and add more salt, pepper, and tarragon, if needed. Preheat oven to 350°.
6. Pour sauce over chicken, cover with aluminum foil, and bake at 350° for 15 to 20 minutes, or until chicken is tender. Sprinkle with crumbs and put under the broiler to brown lightly, if you wish.

Note: If this dish is made ahead of final cooking it should be stored in the refrigerator and brought back to room temperature before baking so that the chicken does not overcook.

CHICKEN FLORENTINE
(Italian)

This stretches a small quantity of chicken to serve four as a light main course.
Makes 4 servings.

1 whole chicken breast (about 14 ounces), cut in half
1 cup chicken broth
¼ teaspoon freshly ground black pepper
1 pound fresh spinach, trimmed and washed, or 1 bag (10 ounces), or 1 package (10 ounces) frozen chopped

⅛ teaspoon ground nutmeg
3 tablespoons butter or margarine
3 tablespoons all-purpose flour
Milk
½ teaspoon salt
Dash of cayenne
½ cup light cream, half-and-half, or milk
⅓ cup freshly grated Parmesan

1. Place the chicken breast in a small skillet or saucepan. Add broth and pepper. Bring to a boil, cover, and simmer 20 minutes, or until chicken is tender. Cool in broth until it can be handled.

2. Meanwhile cook the fresh spinach in the water clinging to the leaves until it is wilted. Drain very well and chop. Add nutmeg and place in the bottom of a buttered 6-cup shallow baking dish.

3. Remove meat from breasts and cut into thin slices. Place over spinach. Discard bones and skin and pour liquid into a 2-cup measure. In a small saucepan melt the butter, blend in the flour, and cook 1 minute. Add milk to the liquid in the cup to make 1½ cups and gradually stir it into the butter-flour mixture.

4. Bring to a boil, stirring, and simmer 3 minutes. Add the salt, pepper, and cream and return to boil. Add ¼ cup of the cheese and stir, off the heat, until cheese melts. Pour sauce over chicken and spinach. Sprinkle with remaining Parmesan and place under a preheated broiler until mixture bubbles and top is lightly browned.

CHICKEN PROVENCALE
(French)

Olive oil, garlic, thyme, and anchovies are among the flavors I associate with sun-drenched Provence, and they make this chicken dish special.
Makes 6 servings.

3 whole chicken breasts (about 12 ounces each), cut in half
1 teaspoon salt
½ teaspoon freshly ground black pepper
¼ cup lemon juice
2 tablespoons butter or margarine
2 tablespoons olive or vegetable oil
1 large onion, finely chopped (1 cup)
2 cloves garlic, finely chopped
½ cup dry white wine

2 large ripe tomatoes, peeled, seeded, and chopped, or 1 can (1 pound) tomatoes
2 tablespoons tomato paste
6 flat anchovy fillets, finely chopped
½ teaspoon leaf basil, crumbled
½ teaspoon leaf thyme, crumbled
12 pitted black olives
2 tablespoons chopped fresh parsley

1. Sprinkle the chicken breasts with the salt, pepper, and lemon juice. Heat the butter and oil in a heavy skillet and brown the chicken pieces on both sides.
2. Add the onion and cook until tender but not browned. Add the garlic and cook 1 minute.
3. Add the wine, tomatoes, tomato paste, anchovies, basil, thyme, and olives. Bring to a boil, cover, and simmer 20 minutes, or until chicken is done.
4. Transfer chicken pieces to a platter and keep warm. Boil the sauce rapidly until it is slightly thickened. Taste and season with salt and pepper, if you wish. Pour over chicken and sprinkle with parsley.

CHICKEN CHASSEUR
(French)

Quick-cooking dish for busy people.
Makes 6 servings.

3 whole chicken breasts, skinned,
   boned, and cut into 1-inch strips
⅓ cup flour
1½ teaspoons salt
½ teaspoon freshly ground black
   pepper
¼ cup vegetable oil
1 large onion, finely chopped
   (1 cup)

1 clove garlic, finely chopped
½ pound mushrooms, sliced
   (2 cups)
½ teaspoon leaf thyme, crumbled
½ teaspoon leaf tarragon, crumbled
1 can (13¾ ounces) chicken broth
3 large tomatoes, peeled, seeded,
   and chopped, or 1 can (1 pound)
   tomatoes

1.   In a paper or plastic bag dredge the chicken pieces in the flour mixed
     with the salt and pepper.
2.   Heat the oil in a large heavy skillet and brown the chicken pieces
     quickly. Remove with a slotted spoon and drain on paper towels.
3.   To the oil remaining in the skillet add the onion and sauté until
     tender but not browned. Add the garlic and mushrooms and cook 3
     minutes. Sprinkle with the thyme and tarragon. Add the broth and
     tomato and bring to a boil.
4.   Return chicken to pan and cook, covered, 10 minutes. Serve over rice
     or noodles.

CHICKEN VINDALOO
(Spicy Indian Chicken)

Adjust the amount of curry powder and chili peppers to suit
your tolerance and liking for fiery food.
Makes 4 servings.

¼ cup vegetable oil, butter, or
   margarine
2 large chicken breasts, split and
   skinned
2 large onions, finely chopped
   (about 2 cups)
2 cloves garlic, finely chopped
2 to 4 tablespoons curry powder

1 teaspoon salt
1 fresh hot green chili pepper,
   seeded and chopped, or 2 canned
   jalapeño peppers, seeded and
   chopped
½ teaspoon ground cumin, optional
2 tablespoons white vinegar
1 can (13¾ ounces) chicken broth

1. Heat the oil or butter in a large heavy skillet and sauté the chicken breast pieces until golden on both sides. Remove and keep warm.
2. Add onions and garlic to skillet and cook over low heat until tender, about 10 minutes. Sprinkle with the curry powder and salt and cook, stirring, 1 minute.
3. Add chili pepper, cumin, vinegar, and broth and bring to a boil. Return chicken to skillet, cover, and simmer 25 minutes, or until breasts are done. Serve over hot cooked rice with condiments such as currants, nuts, coconut, and chutney.

VELVET CHICKEN WITH SNOW PEAS
(Chinese)

The finished dish looks like snow dotted with snow peas and chopped green onion.
Makes 4 servings.

1 large whole chicken breast (about 14 ounces), skinned, boned, and finely chopped	3 tablespoons vegetable oil
2 teaspoons cornstarch	1 tablespoon cornstarch
½ teaspoon salt	¾ cup chicken broth
¼ cup water	1 tablespoon dry sherry
6 egg whites, beaten until fluffy*	¼ pound fresh snow peas or ½ package (10 ounces) frozen
	2 tablespoons chopped green onion

1. In a medium-size bowl combine the chicken, cornstarch, and salt. Gradually stir in the water. Fold in the egg whites.
2. Gently heat the oil in a wok or skillet. Stir-fry the chicken mixture over low to moderate heat, stirring constantly, until it turns opaque, 2 to 3 minutes. The chicken mixture should not brown. Remove chicken from wok to a warm platter.
3. In a small bowl combine the cornstarch with the broth slowly until smooth. Stir in the sherry. Pour into the wok and cook, stirring, until mixture thickens and clears. Add the snow peas and cook 1 minute. Pour over chicken, sprinkle with green onion, and serve with hot cooked rice, if you wish.

*Add ¼ cup water to yolks and use to make an omelet. Cut into strips and add to fried rice (see page 147).

FRUITED CHUTNEY CHICKEN CURRY
(Indian)

Simple curry that calls for relatively few ingredients.
Makes 4 servings.

2 tablespoons vegetable oil
1 medium-size onion, finely
  chopped (½ cup)
4 breast quarters from broiler-fryer
  chickens
2 cloves garlic, finely chopped
1 tablespoon curry powder or to
  taste

1 tablespoon flour
1 can (13¾ ounces) chicken broth
3 tablespoons mango chutney
1 can (8 ounces) pineapple chunks
  in juice, drained
1 banana, cut into thick slices

1. In a large heavy skillet heat the oil and sauté the onion until tender
    but not browned. Add chicken quarters and brown on all sides. Add
    garlic, curry powder, and flour, and cook, stirring, 2 minutes.
2. Pour in the broth, bring to a boil, and stir in the chutney and pine-
    apple. Cover and simmer 30 minutes, or until chicken is done.
3. Stir in the banana pieces and serve over hot coconut-flavored rice, if
    you wish.

CHICKEN AND CABBAGE
(Greek)

Cabbage is a neglected vegetable in most American kitchens
and usually reserved for coleslaw. The time has come to exper-
iment with new recipes, and here's a good place to start.
Makes 6 servings.

2 tablespoons flour
1½ teaspoons salt
½ teaspoon freshly ground black
  pepper
3 whole chicken breasts, halved,
  skinned, and boned
3 tablespoons vegetable oil
1 large onion, sliced
1 clove garlic, finely chopped
1 can (13¾ ounces) chicken broth

1 medium-size cabbage
  (2½ pounds), cut into 6 wedges
1 pound small red-skinned
  potatoes, scrubbed, with a 1-inch
  strip removed around the middle
¼ cup lemon juice
2 eggs, lightly beaten
2 tablespoons chopped fresh
  parsley

1. On a piece of wax paper combine the flour, salt, and pepper. Coat the chicken breast pieces on both sides with the flour mixture.
2. In a large deep skillet heat the oil and sauté the chicken breasts until lightly browned on both sides. Add the onion and garlic and cook, stirring, 3 minutes.
3. Sprinkle over any remaining seasoned flour mixture and gradually stir in the broth. Bring to a boil, cover, and simmer 20 minutes. Add the cabbage and potatoes and cook 20 minutes, or until potatoes are tender.
4. With a slotted spoon arrange the chicken, cabbage, and potatoes on a platter and keep them warm. Beat the lemon juice into the eggs. Gradually add the hot sauce from the skillet to the egg mixture. Return to the skillet and heat, stirring, until thick but do not boil. Pour over the chicken and vegetables and sprinkle with parsley.

SWEET-AND-SOUR CHICKEN
(Chinese)

Try this recipe with teenagers—I have found it to be a winner and it is not prohibitively expensive for family meals.
Makes 6 servings.

3 whole chicken breasts (about 12 ounces each)
3 tablespoons soy sauce
1 tablespoon dry sherry
½ teaspoon salt
4 teaspoons cornstarch
¼ cup vegetable oil
¼ cup chopped green onions
2 cloves garlic, crushed
1 large green pepper, seeded and cut into squares
1 can (8¼ ounces) pineapple chunks
2 tablespoons cider vinegar

1. Skin and bone the breasts and cut into 2- to 3-inch strips about ½ inch thick and place in a bowl with 1 tablespoon of the soy sauce, the sherry, salt, and 2 teaspoons of the cornstarch. Mix well and set aside.
2. In a wok or skillet heat the oil and stir-fry the green onions, garlic, and green pepper briefly. Remove and discard the garlic.
3. Add the chicken pieces to the wok and stir-fry until they turn opaque, about 3 minutes. Drain the pineapple and reserve the juice.
4. Mix remaining cornstarch with 1 tablespoon water, pineapple juice, remaining soy, and vinegar. Pour over chicken and cook quickly, stirring, until mixture thickens. Add pineapple and reheat. Serve with hot cooked rice, if you wish.

CHICKEN WITH PEPPERS
(Italian)

This dish goes together in less than 30 minutes.
Makes 4 servings.

¼ cup olive or vegetable oil
3 to 4 Italian-style long green peppers or bell green peppers, seeded and sliced lengthwise
1 large red pepper, seeded and sliced lengthwise
1 large onion, thinly sliced
2 cloves garlic, finely chopped
¾ teaspoon leaf oregano, crumbled
½ teaspoon leaf basil, crumbled
1 tablespoon red wine vinegar
½ teaspoon salt
⅛ teaspoon freshly ground black pepper
2 whole chicken breasts, boned, halved, and pounded between sheets of wax paper until the thickness of veal cutlets

¼ cup flour
¼ teaspoon salt
⅛ teaspoon freshly ground black pepper
1 egg, lightly beaten with 1 tablespoon water
⅓ cup packaged Italian bread crumbs
¼ cup (1 ounce) freshly grated Parmesan
3 tablespoons butter or margarine

1. In a large heavy skillet heat the oil and sauté the green and red peppers, onion, and garlic until wilted. Add oregano, basil, vinegar, salt, and pepper and cook over low heat, stirring occasionally, for 5 minutes.
2. Using a slotted spoon, remove vegetables to a medium-size bowl and keep them warm. Dip the chicken cutlets in the flour mixed with the salt and pepper, in egg and water, and then in bread crumbs mixed with Parmesan. Pat well to make a firm coating.
3. Add butter to the skillet and cook the chicken cutlets over high heat for about 2 minutes on each side, or until golden and cooked through.
4. Arrange chicken on a platter and spoon the vegetables over or around.

SUKIYAKI
(Japanese Chicken and Vegetables)

Prepare the chicken and vegetables ahead and cook the batches
while guests watch and enjoy.
Makes 4 servings.

2 whole chicken breasts, split,
boned, and skinned
1 package (4 ounces) bean thread
(cellophane) noodles, optional
1 cup boiling water
8 green onions, including green
part, cut into 1½-inch pieces
1 medium-size onion, sliced ½ inch
thick and separated into rings
6 mushrooms, sliced

1 can (8 ounces) bamboo shoots,
optional
2 cups shredded Chinese cabbage
or sliced celery
1 cake (12 to 16 ounces) bean curd
(tofu), cut into 1-inch cubes
2 tablespoons vegetable oil
½ cup soy sauce
3 tablespoons sugar
½ cup sake (rice wine) or dry sherry

1. Cut the chicken breast pieces into ⅛-inch-wide strips.
2. Add the noodles to the boiling water, return to the boil, drain, and
   cut them into thirds. Arrange the chicken, noodles, onion, mushrooms, bamboo shoots, Chinese cabbage, and bean curd attractively
   on a platter set near the cooking area.
3. Heat an electric skillet to 400° or heat a heavy skillet over a table
   heater. Rub skillet with some of the oil. Add a quarter of the chicken
   pieces, sprinkle with 2 tablespoons soy sauce and a quarter of the
   sugar. Cook, stirring, 1 minute and scrape to one side.
4. Add a quarter of the green onions, onion, mushrooms, bamboo
   shoots, cabbage, and bean curd. Sprinkle with 2 tablespoons of sake
   and cook, stirring, 3 to 4 minutes, or until vegetables are crisp-
   tender.
5. Divide the chicken and vegetable mixture among 4 warm plates and
   repeat the cooking with more oil and another one-quarter of the
   chicken and vegetables. The process is repeated three times in all.

CHICKEN SCALOPPINI
(Italian)

This recipe works well with turkey breast cutlets which are available in some markets.
Makes 6 servings.

3 whole chicken breasts
1 teaspoon salt
½ teaspoon freshly ground black pepper
¼ cup flour
2 eggs, lightly beaten
½ cup packaged bread crumbs

2 tablespoons freshly grated Parmesan
1 teaspoon leaf oregano, crumbled
2 tablespoons butter or margarine
2 tablespoons vegetable oil
¼ cup Marsala
Lemon slices

1. Split, bone, and skin the chicken breasts. Put each cutlet between sheets of wax paper and pound until as thin as veal cutlet.
2. Combine the salt, pepper, and flour on wax paper. Dip the chicken pieces in the seasoned flour, then in egg, and lastly in the bread crumbs mixed with the cheese and oregano. Pat well to remove loose crumbs. Let cutlets stand at room temperature 20 minutes or covered in the refrigerator longer to set the coating.
3. Heat the butter and oil in a large heavy skillet and sauté the chicken, so that the pieces do not touch, until brown. Turn and brown the other side. Remove to a warm platter and keep warm.
4. Add Marsala to skillet and cook, stirring. Strain over chicken and garnish with lemon slices.

CHICKEN WITH PEANUTS
(Chinese)

Like most stir-fried dishes this goes together in less than 10 minutes.
Makes 4 servings.

¼ cup soy sauce
2 tablespoons dry sherry
2 tablespoons cornstarch
2 whole chicken breasts, skinned, boned, and cut into thin strips
¼ cup vegetable oil
3 green onions, cut into ½-inch slices

1 teaspoon chopped fresh ginger root, or ¼ teaspoon ground
1 large green pepper, seeded and cut into strips
1 to 2 cups fresh bean sprouts
1 tablespoon Hoisin or A1 sauce
½ cup dry-roasted peanuts

1. In a medium-size bowl combine the soy sauce, sherry, and cornstarch and mix well. Add the chicken pieces. Toss to coat and allow to stand at room temperature 20 to 30 minutes. Remove with slotted spoon.
2. In a wok or skillet heat the oil. Stir-fry the chicken about 2 minutes, or until opaque. Remove and keep warm.
3. Add more oil if needed and stir-fry the green onions, ginger, and green pepper 1 to 2 minutes. Add bean sprouts and Hoisin sauce and reheat. Add chicken and any remaining marinade. Stir-fry until hot and glazed. Add nuts and serve.

CHICKEN TANDOORI
(Indian Grilled Chicken)

Cut-up broiler-fryers or other chicken parts can be substituted for the chicken breasts, and the cooking time would be increased to a total of about 40 minutes.
Makes 6 servings.

2 containers (8 ounces each) plain yogurt
¼ cup lime juice
2 cloves garlic, finely chopped
2 teaspoons salt
¼ teaspoon turmeric
½ teaspoon ground coriander
1 teaspoon ground cumin
1½ teaspoons ground ginger
⅛ teaspoon cayenne, optional
3 whole chicken breasts, split
1 large onion, finely chopped (1 cup)
1 large green pepper, seeded and chopped

1. In a large bowl combine the yogurt, lime juice, garlic, salt, turmeric, coriander, cumin, ginger, and cayenne. Stir to mix. Add chicken pieces and toss to coat. Sprinkle onion and green pepper over chicken, cover, and chill overnight.
2. Remove chicken from marinade and grill 5 inches from hot coals or preheated oven broiler for 10 minutes. Turn and cook 15 to 20 minutes longer, or until chicken is done. Baste with the marinade throughout the cooking. Serve with hot cooked rice, if you wish.

PEPPER CHICKEN
(Chinese)

Many dishes, especially stir-fried Chinese, that call for finely
cut pork or beef can be made successfully using chicken parts.
Makes 6 servings.

1½ teaspoons salt
 1 tablespoon dry sherry
 1 teaspoon finely chopped fresh
   ginger root, or ¼ teaspoon
   ground
 1 teaspoon sugar
 1 tablespoon soy sauce
 1 tablespoon cornstarch
   Pinch of freshly ground black
   pepper
 2 whole chicken breasts (about 12
   ounces each), skinned, boned,
   and cut into 2-inch pieces,
   ⅓ inch thick

 4 tablespoons vegetable oil
 1 bunch green onions, chopped
 3 large green peppers, seeded and
   sliced
 2 cloves garlic, finely chopped
 2 tablespoons cornstarch
 2 tablespoons soy sauce
 ½ teaspoon salt
 ⅛ teaspoon freshly ground black
   pepper
 1 cup water

1. In a medium-size bowl combine the salt, sherry, ginger, sugar, soy
   sauce, cornstarch, and pepper. Mix well. Add the chicken pieces and
   let stand 1 hour.
2. Heat 1 tablespoon of the oil in a wok or skillet and stir-fry the green
   onions and peppers 3 minutes. Add garlic and cook 1 minute.
3. Remove vegetables with a slotted spoon to a warm bowl.
4. Add remaining oil to wok and heat. Add chicken and marinade and
   stir-fry 5 minutes, or until lightly browned.
5. In a small bowl combine the cornstarch, soy sauce, salt, pepper, and
   water. Pour over chicken and cook, stirring, until mixture thickens.
6. Return the green onion mixture to wok and reheat, stirring. Serve
   with hot cooked rice.

CHICKEN SATAY
(Indonesian)

Those not familiar with Indonesian food will be surprised and, I guarantee, delighted with the peanuty flavor and colorful skewer presentation.
Makes 4 servings.

1 medium-size onion, finely chopped (½ cup)	⅛ teaspoon cayenne or to taste
1 clove garlic, crushed	2 whole chicken breasts, split, skinned, boned, and cut into
¼ cup soy sauce	1-inch cubes
¼ cup vegetable oil	8 cherry tomatoes
¼ cup chunk peanut butter	2 small green peppers, seeded and
1 tablespoon brown sugar	cubed
3 tablespoons lemon juice	1 small zucchini, cut into 8 chunks
1 teaspoon ground coriander	8 mushroom caps
¾ teaspoon salt	

1. Place the onion, garlic, soy sauce, oil, peanut butter, sugar, lemon juice, coriander, salt, and cayenne in the container of an electric blender and whirl until smooth.
2. Place chicken pieces in a shallow glass or ceramic dish and pour peanut mixture over. Stir to mix, cover, and marinate in the refrigerator 2 hours, turning a couple of times.
3. On 8 individual skewers alternate the chicken pieces with the tomatoes, green pepper, zucchini, and mushrooms.
4. Grill or broil skewers 6 inches from coals or heat for 10 to 12 minutes, turning and basting with remaining marinade several times. Serve over hot cooked rice.

TERIYAKI
(Japanese Broiled Chicken)

Great dish to prepare ahead that takes a short while to charcoal-broil.
Makes 4 servings.

2 whole chicken breasts
3 tablespoons lemon juice
3 tablespoons dry sherry
3 tablespoons soy sauce
2 teaspoons chopped fresh ginger
  root, or ½ teaspoon ground

1 clove garlic, crushed
1 teaspoon sugar
1 teaspoon cornstarch mixed with
  1 tablespoon water

1. Split and bone the chicken breasts but leave the skin on. In a small shallow glass or ceramic dish combine the lemon juice, sherry, soy sauce, ginger, and garlic. Add the chicken pieces in a single layer and turn several times to coat. Allow to marinate in the refrigerator 3 hours or overnight, turning several times.

2. Drain the chicken and broil, skin side down, over a charcoal fire or in oven broiler for 3 minutes. Brush with marinade and broil, skin side up, 3 minutes. Brush with marinade and broil, skin side down, for 3 more minutes, or until golden and done.

3. Remove garlic and place remaining marinade in a small saucepan. Add the sugar and cornstarch mixed with the water. Bring to a boil, stirring. Cook 1 minute. Pour over chicken and serve with hot cooked rice, parsley sprigs, and hot mustard powder mixed to a thick paste with water, if you wish.

CHICKEN AND CORNMEAL FRITTERS
(American)

Serve with cranberry sauce or applesauce for brunch or supper.
Makes 4 servings.

1 cup yellow cornmeal
½ cup sifted all-purpose flour
2 teaspoons baking powder
½ teaspoon salt
1½ cups diced raw chicken breasts
  (about 2 whole)
2 eggs, lightly beaten

¾ cup milk
1 small onion, finely chopped
  (¼ cup)
¼ cup finely chopped green pepper
¼ teaspoon freshly ground black
  pepper
Vegetable oil for deep frying

1. In a medium-size bowl combine the cornmeal, flour, baking powder, and salt. Add the chicken. Combine the eggs and milk and stir into cornmeal mixture. Stir in the onion, green pepper, and pepper.
2. Heat 2 inches of oil in a heavy straight-sided saucepan until it registers 375° on a deep-fat thermometer. Drop the chicken batter a tablespoon at a time, a few at a time, into the hot oil. Fry until golden, turning as needed, about 10 minutes. Drain on paper towels and keep fritters warm while cooking remainder.

FRIED RICE WITH CHICKEN
(Chinese)

Pork is usually the meat favored in this popular dish but you will find chicken works well.
Makes 6 servings.

2 tablespoons soy sauce	4 green onions, cut into ½-inch
2 tablespoons dry sherry	lengths
1 tablespoon cornstarch	2 small zucchini, cut into 2-inch
1 large whole chicken breast,	strips, ¼ inch thick
skinned, boned, and cut into	½ cup sliced bamboo shoots
2-inch strips, ¼ inch thick	1 cup bean sprouts
3 tablespoons vegetable oil	¼ pound mushrooms, sliced (1 cup)
3 eggs, lightly beaten	2 tablespoons vegetable oil
2 tablespoons water	3 cups cooked rice (1 cup raw)
¼ teaspoon salt	¼ teaspoon salt
3 tablespoons vegetable oil,	2 tablespoons soy sauce
approximately	

1. In a medium-size bowl combine the soy sauce, sherry, cornstarch, and chicken pieces. Toss to coat. Marinate 20 to 30 minutes. Heat the oil in a wok or skillet.
2. Mix the eggs with the water and salt and pour into the wok. Stir gently until mixture begins to set and make an omelet. When set turn out onto a board and cut into strips.
3. Heat the oil in the wok and stir-fry the green onions and zucchini for 2 minutes. Add the bamboo shoots, bean sprouts, and mushrooms and stir-fry 2 minutes. Remove with slotted spoon and keep warm.
4. Add 2 more tablespoons oil and heat. Add chicken and marinade and stir-fry 3 to 4 minutes, or until chicken is opaque. Add rice, salt, and soy sauce and reheat. Add vegetables and egg pieces. Reheat and serve immediately.

RISOTTO WITH CHICKEN
(Italian)

In Italy this would be served as a separate course before a fish
and vegetable main course.
Makes 4 servings.

1 whole chicken breast (about 14 ounces)
2 cups chicken broth or water
1 small onion, halved
½ bay leaf, crumbled
1 stalk celery, sliced
¼ cup (½ stick) butter or margarine
1 medium-size onion, finely chopped (½ cup)

1 cup raw long-grain rice
1 clove garlic, finely chopped
¼ pound mushrooms, sliced (1 cup)
¾ teaspoon salt
¼ teaspoon freshly ground black pepper
½ teaspoon Italian seasoning
¼ cup (1 ounce) freshly grated Parmesan

1. Place the chicken breast in a large heavy skillet with the broth, onion,
    bay leaf, and celery. Bring to a boil, cover, and simmer 25 minutes or
    until chicken is done. Let cool until chicken can be handled.
2. Meanwhile, in a heavy saucepan or Dutch oven heat the butter and
    sauté the onion until soft. Add the rice and garlic and cook, stirring,
    until rice is lightly golden. Add the mushrooms and cook 2 minutes
    longer.
3. Strain the broth off the chicken and measure 2 cups. Add to rice
    mixture with salt, pepper, and Italian seasoning. Bring to a boil,
    cover, and simmer until rice is tender and liquid has been absorbed.
    Bone and skin the breast and dice the meat.
4. Stir the chicken and cheese into the hot rice. Serve immediately.

POULTRY-STUFFED CABBAGE
(Hungarian)

Raw ground turkey, available in many meat cases, can be used.
The cooking time in step 3 will be increased to 8 minutes while
stirring until all pinkness has disappeared.
Bake at 350° for 50 minutes.
Makes 8 servings.

1 head of cabbage (3 to 3½ pounds)
6 tablespoons (¾ stick) butter or
 margarine
1 large onion, finely chopped
 (1 cup)
3 cups ground cooked chicken or
 turkey
2 teaspoons paprika
3 cans (13¾ ounces each) chicken
 broth

2 cups seasoned packaged bread
 crumbs
1 teaspoon salt
½ teaspoon freshly ground black
 pepper
1 teaspoon leaf sage, crumbled
2 eggs, lightly beaten
¼ cup chopped fresh parsley
 Tomato Sauce (see page 188)

1. Remove tough outer leaves from cabbage and cut away the tough part
 of the core. Set in a big saucepan and cover with boiling salted water.
 Cook, covered, about 5 minutes, or until the leaves can be separated
 easily.
2. Remove the leaves and drain on paper towels.
3. Heat the butter in a large skillet and sauté the onion until tender but
 not browned. Stir in the chicken and paprika and cook 2 minutes.
4. Heat the chicken broth and pour 1 cup of the hot broth over the
 bread crumbs. Stir to moisten and add to chicken mixture.
5. Add the salt, pepper, sage, eggs, and parsley and mix. Mixture
 should be moist and stick together when pressed. Add more broth, if
 needed.
6. Place 2 tablespoons on each cabbage leaf, using 2 if small or torn. Roll
 up, tucking in the sides. Place in a double layer of cheesecloth and
 squeeze the ends to shape the roll. Remove from cloth and place in a
 heavy casserole, seam side down. Continue filling and shaping until
 all filling is used.
7. Pour remaining hot chicken broth over the cabbage rolls. It should
 almost cover them. Cover the casserole and simmer 30 minutes or
 bake at 350° for 50 minutes.
8. Serve the broth as soup and the rolls with hot tomato sauce.

CHICKEN LIVER-STUFFED POTATOES
(American)

Bake at 400° for 50 minutes.
Makes 4 servings.

4 medium-size baking potatoes,
well scrubbed
3 tablespoons flour
1 teaspoon salt
¼ teaspoon freshly ground black
pepper

1 pound chicken livers, trimmed
and quartered
3 tablespoons butter or margarine
1 medium-size onion, finely
chopped (½ cup)
¼ teaspoon leaf thyme, crumbled
½ cup chicken broth or water

1. Bake the potatoes at 400° for 50 minutes or until tender. Cut a small
    slice from the top and scoop out a one-inch-deep hole in each potato.
    Dice the potato removed. Keep potatoes warm.
2. Place the flour, salt, and pepper on wax paper and coat the chicken
    livers with the mixture. Heat the butter in a medium-size skillet.
    Sauté the onion until tender but not browned. Add the chicken livers
    and cook, stirring, about 3 minutes until done but still pink in the
    middle.
3. Add the thyme and broth and cook, stirring, until sauce thickens and
    bubbles. Add the diced potato. Spoon mixture into the potatoes.
    Some will spill over the sides, but as the skin should be eaten too this
    is an advantage and is more attractive-looking to serve.

CHICKEN POJARSKI
(Russian Chicken Patties)

Makes 6 servings.

½ cup (1 stick) butter or margarine
1 medium-size onion, finely
chopped (½ cup)
3 whole raw chicken breasts,
skinned, boned, and finely
ground
1½ cups fresh soft white bread
crumbs (3 slices)
¾ cup milk
½ cup heavy cream or skim
evaporated milk

1 teaspoon salt
½ teaspoon freshly ground black
pepper
¼ teaspoon ground nutmeg
Flour
¼ cup (½ stick) butter or margarine
¼ pound mushrooms, sliced (1 cup)
2 tablespoons drained capers
½ cup chicken broth
½ cup heavy cream or skim
evaporated milk

1. Heat the butter in a small skillet and sauté the onion until tender but not browned. Turn off the heat, add the chicken, and stir to mix. Soak the bread crumbs in the milk, squeeze, and add to chicken.
2. Add the cream, salt, pepper, and nutmeg and mix well. Form into 6 oval patties or traditional chop shape. Coat with flour and chill several hours.
3. Heat the butter in a large heavy skillet and sauté the ovals until well browned on both sides and chicken is cooked, about 15 minutes.
4. Remove patties with a spatula and drain on paper towels. Keep them warm. Add mushrooms to skillet and cook 5 minutes. Add capers, broth, and cream and cook, stirring, until mixture is thick. Pour over patties.

CHINESE CHICKEN SALAD

A change from standard chicken, celery, and mayonnaise salad.
Makes 4 servings.

1 whole chicken breast, split, or 1½ cups chopped cooked chicken
¼ pound fresh snow peas, or 1 package frozen (10 ounces), defrosted and dried on paper towel
¼ cup vegetable oil
2 tablespoons cider vinegar
1 tablespoon soy sauce
2 teaspoons finely chopped fresh ginger root, or ½ teaspoon ground

Pinch of sugar
¼ teaspoon salt
2 green onions, sliced
1 cup bean sprouts
1 medium-size head Chinese cabbage, shredded (about 4 cups)
1 tablespoon sesame seeds, toasted lightly in a dry skillet
½ cup coarsely chopped walnuts

1. Place the chicken in a saucepan, cover with salted water, and bring to a boil. Cover and simmer 15 minutes, or until cooked. Cool slightly, skin, bone, and chop chicken.
2. Trim snow peas and add to chicken. In a screw-cap jar combine the oil, vinegar, soy sauce, ginger, sugar, and salt. Shake to mix.
3. Add green onion and sprouts to chicken. Pour over dressing and toss. Arrange cabbage in a bowl and top with chicken mixture. Sprinkle with sesame seeds and walnuts.

HOT CHICKEN SALAD
(American)

A tried and true favorite that goes together fast. Make it with diced cooked turkey, if you wish.
Bake at 450° for 15 minutes.
Makes 6 servings.

3 cups diced cooked chicken
½ teaspoon salt
¼ teaspoon freshly ground black pepper
1½ tablespoons grated onion
3 cups diced celery

1½ cups mayonnaise
3 tablespoons lemon juice
¼ cup slivered almonds
¾ cup (3 ounces) grated sharp Cheddar
¾ cup buttered croutons

1. Combine all the ingredients except the cheese and croutons and turn into a greased baking dish or casserole.
2. Combine cheese and croutons and sprinkle over top. Bake at 450° for 15 minutes or until bubbly-hot.

Main and Side
Vegetable Dishes

EGGS AND ASPARAGUS
(American)

I like to think that spring and mimosa blossoms inspired this
tasty dish. Super for a vegetarian main dish.
Bake at 350° for 20 minutes.
Makes 6 servings.

2½ pounds asparagus, or 2 packages
(10 ounces each) frozen asparagus
spears
6 hard-cooked eggs, sliced
2 tablespoons butter or margarine
2 tablespoons flour
1½ cups half-and-half or milk
½ teaspoon salt

¼ teaspoon freshly ground black
pepper
Pinch of cayenne
½ cup (2 ounces) grated sharp
Cheddar
½ cup buttered fresh bread crumbs
2 tablespoons freshly grated
Parmesan

1. Break the asparagus stalks where the white part meets the green and
   wash well. Drain. Heat 2 to 3 inches salted water in the bottom of a
   double boiler. Set the stalks into the boiling water, tips up, and cover
   with the double boiler insert, or cook in a skillet. Boil until crisp-
   tender, about 5 minutes. Drain and rinse under cold water. Cook
   frozen asparagus according to package directions until crisp-tender.
2. Place spears in a greased shallow baking dish. Arrange egg slices on
   top. In a small saucepan melt the butter and blend in the flour. Cook
   2 minutes. Preheat oven to 350°.
3. Gradually stir in the half-and-half and bring to a boil, stirring. Add
   salt, pepper, cayenne, and cheese. Stir until cheese melts. Pour over
   eggs and asparagus and sprinkle with the crumbs and Parmesan. Bake
   at 350° for 20 minutes. Glaze under broiler, if needed.

CHOWAN MUSHI
(Japanese Steamed Egg Custard)

Excellent served with stir-fried vegetables to follow sushi,
sashimi, or soup.
Makes 4 servings.

8 eggs, lightly beaten
1 teaspoon salt
2 tablespoons dry sherry

½ cup cooked fresh peas or thawed
frozen
¼ pound shelled deveined shrimp,
finely chopped

154

1. While continuing to beat the eggs add the salt, sherry, peas, and shrimp. Divide among 4 greased custard cups.
2. Set the custard cups on a rack in a deep sauté pan or Dutch oven. Cover with a piece of wax paper. Pour boiling water down the sides of the pan to come one quarter of the way up the cups.
3. Cover the pan and simmer so that the custard steams for about 20 minutes, or just until set. Do not boil.

CURRIED EGGS
(Indian)

The larger amount of curry powder is for the dedicated lover of curries.
Makes 4 servings.

¼ cup vegetable oil, butter, or margarine
2 large onions, finely chopped (2 cups)
2 cloves garlic, finely chopped
2 to 4 teaspoons curry powder
½ teaspoon ground cumin
½ teaspoon turmeric
½ teaspoon ground ginger

2 large potatoes, cubed
2 cups coconut milk*
2 cups frozen or fresh peas
1 tablespoon lemon juice
8 hard-cooked eggs, shelled and halved
¼ cup chopped fresh parsley, preferably the Italian flat variety or cilantro (Chinese parsley)

1. Heat the oil in a skillet and sauté the onion and garlic over low heat until tender but not browned, about 10 minutes.
2. Sprinkle over the curry powder, cumin, turmeric, and ginger and cook 2 minutes. Add potatoes and cook 2 minutes, stirring often.
3. Add the coconut milk and cook, covered, 10 minutes, or until potatoes are almost tender. Add peas and cook 5 minutes for frozen, 10 to 15 minutes for fresh.
4. Stir in the lemon juice. Add the hard-cooked eggs and reheat. Sprinkle with parsley and serve over hot cooked rice with chutney.

To make coconut milk: Place 1 cup shredded fresh coconut or unsweetened shredded coconut in a blender with 2 cups warm water. Blend on high speed for 1 minute. Strain through double muslin into a 2-cup measure. Discard pulp.

EGGS FLORENTINE
(Italian)

Can be prepared ahead up to the final baking, which makes it
great for brunch or lunch.
Bake at 350° for 10 minutes.
Makes 4 servings.

2 pounds fresh spinach, or 2
  packages (10 ounces each) frozen
  chopped
1 clove garlic, finely chopped
¼ teaspoon ground nutmeg
2 tablespoons butter or margarine
2 tablespoons flour

1 cup half-and-half or milk
½ teaspoon salt
¼ teaspoon freshly ground black
  pepper
8 eggs
½ cup (2 ounces) freshly grated
  Parmesan

1. Trim, wash, and drain the fresh spinach and place in a large saucepan
   with the garlic and just the water clinging to the leaves. Cook, covered, until wilted. Drain, squeeze dry, and chop. Place in a bowl.
   Add nutmeg.
2. In a small saucepan melt the butter, sprinkle with the flour, and cook,
   stirring, 1 minute. Gradually stir in the half-and-half and bring to a
   boil, stirring. Cook 1 minute, or until thick. Add the salt and pepper.
   Stir half the sauce into the spinach. Preheat oven to 350°.
3. Spread the spinach mixture in a shallow baking dish. Make 8 depressions in the spinach mixture and break 1 egg into each hole.
   Spoon a tablespoon of the remaining sauce over each egg, sprinkle
   with the cheese, and bake at 350° for 10 minutes, or until the eggs are
   set.

EGG FOO YONG
(Chinese)

This classic dish can make an important contribution to a
Chinese vegetarian meal.
Makes 4 servings.

6 eggs
4 green onions, chopped
6 mushrooms, sliced
1½ cups bean sprouts

1 tablespoon soy sauce
½ teaspoon salt
1 stalk celery, finely chopped
  Vegetable oil

1. In a large bowl beat the eggs until frothy. Stir in the green onions, mushrooms, sprouts, soy sauce, salt, and celery.
2. Heat a small 6-inch skillet or a large griddle. Oil well.
3. If using the skillet, pour in one-quarter of the egg mixture and cook until set and lightly browned. Turn and brown the other side. Keep warm while repeating with remaining three-quarters of the mixture. If using a griddle ladle onto griddle in serving-spoon amounts and cook as above.
4. Serve with hot cooked rice and extra soy sauce, if you wish.

PIPERADE
(French Scrambled Eggs With Onions and Peppers)

Good cold, too, if there are any leftovers.
Makes 6 servings.

¼ cup olive or vegetable oil
1 large onion, thinly sliced and separated into rings
1 clove garlic, finely chopped
1 medium-size green pepper, seeded and cut into strips
1 medium-size sweet red pepper, seeded and cut into strips

3 tomatoes, peeled, seeded, and chopped
1 teaspoon salt
¼ teaspoon freshly ground black pepper
8 eggs, lightly beaten

1. In a large heavy skillet heat the oil and sauté the onion until tender but not browned. Add the garlic and green and red pepper and cook 3 minutes.
2. Add the tomato, salt, and pepper and bring to the simmer point. Simmer, uncovered, until most of the tomato liquid has evaporated and the mixture is thick.
3. Stir in the eggs and cook, stirring gently, until they are just set. Spoon to serve, or cook longer until solid and lightly browned on the bottom, and serve in wedges.

HUEVOS RANCHEROS
(Mexican)

This is a great dish for breakfast, brunch, or a late snack.
Makes 4 servings.

2 tablespoons peanut oil
1 large onion, finely chopped
  (1 cup)
2 cloves garlic, finely chopped
1½ cups canned tomatoes, drained
  and chopped
2 canned serrano chili peppers,
  seeded and chopped
1 teaspoon salt
¼ teaspoon freshly ground black
  pepper
2 teaspoons dried coriander or
  dried parsley

2 tablespoons peanut oil
8 corn tortillas, canned, thawed
  frozen, or refrigerated
8 eggs
¼ cup (½ stick) butter or margarine
  Salt and freshly ground black
  pepper to taste
  Shredded Monterey Jack,
  optional
  Sour cream
  Avocado slices

1. Heat the oil in a medium-size skillet. Add the onion and garlic and
    cook until soft. Add the tomatoes, chilies, salt, pepper, and coriander
    and cook, uncovered, until sauce is thick, about 20 minutes or so.
2. In another skillet heat the remaining 2 tablespoons oil and fry the
    tortillas, one at a time, until they are soft but not crisp. Drain on
    paper towels and keep warm.
3. In the same skillet fry the eggs in the butter and season with salt and
    pepper. To serve place 1 or 2 tortillas on each plate, top with eggs,
    and surround with sauce. Sprinkle with shredded Monterey Jack
    cheese, if you wish, and pass the sour cream and avocado slices
    separately.

Variation: After the sauce has cooked down place in a shallow baking dish or au
gratin dish. Make 8 depressions in the sauce and drop an egg into each one.
Season with salt and pepper and bake at 350° for about 25 minutes, or until eggs
are set. Serve each egg on a tortilla surrounded by sauce.

EGGS WITH POTATO SAUCE
(Peruvian)

Makes 4 servings.

4 medium-size boiling potatoes
1 medium-size onion, finely chopped (½ cup)
3 tablespoons vegetable oil
½ cup cottage cheese
½ cup (2 ounces) shredded Muenster
2 jalapeño peppers, seeded and chopped
1 teaspoon salt
¼ cup warm heavy cream, approximately
4 hard-cooked eggs, shelled and cut in half lengthwise

1. Cook the potatoes in boiling salted water until tender, about 30 minutes. Meanwhile sauté the onion in the oil until tender. Peel potatoes and mash in a bowl.
2. Add the cottage cheese, Muenster, and jalapeño peppers. Beat well. Stir in the onion mixture, salt, and enough of the cream, which has been heated, to make a smooth thick sauce. Spoon over the eggs.

EGGS IN TOMATO SAUCE
(Italian)

Makes 6 servings.

3 tablespoons olive or vegetable oil
1 large Spanish or Bermuda onion, thinly sliced
1 clove garlic, finely chopped
6 ripe tomatoes, peeled and chopped, or 2 cans (1 pound each) tomatoes
1 teaspoon salt
½ teaspoon freshly ground black pepper
1 teaspoon leaf oregano, crumbled
6 eggs
Hot cooked rice

1. In a medium-size heavy skillet heat the oil and sauté the onion until tender but not browned. Add the garlic and cook 1 minute.
2. Add the tomato, salt, pepper, and oregano and cook, uncovered, until slightly thickened.
3. The eggs can be dropped into the tomato sauce to poach for 4 minutes. Lift out with a slotted spoon, set on rice, and spoon sauce over. Or lightly beat the eggs and pour into the tomato sauce. Stir briefly. Let cook over medium heat until mixture starts to set and stir gently to scramble. Serve over rice.

EGGS WITH RICOTTA
(Italian)

I think there are more exciting and different ways to cook and present eggs in Italian cooking than in any other cuisine.
Bake at 325° for 35 minutes.
Makes 6 servings.

¼ cup (½ stick) butter or margarine
2 tablespoons olive oil
2 medium-size green peppers, finely chopped
1 medium-size onion, finely chopped (½ cup)
2 fresh hot chili peppers, seeded and chopped, or 2 canned jalapeño peppers, seeded and chopped
2 tomatoes, peeled, seeded, and chopped

2 tablespoons chopped fresh parsley
1 cup ricotta
8 eggs, lightly beaten
1 teaspoon salt
¼ teaspoon freshly ground black pepper
1 can (14 ounces) artichoke hearts, drained and halved, optional
2 tablespoons freshly grated Parmesan

1. In a large heavy skillet heat the butter and oil and sauté the pepper and onion until tender but not browned.
2. Add the hot pepper and tomato and cook 1 minute. Add parsley. Preheat oven to 325°.
3. In a bowl combine the ricotta, eggs, salt, pepper, and artichoke hearts, if you wish. Add the tomato mixture. Mix, turn into a greased shallow baking dish, and sprinkle with Parmesan. Bake at 325° for 35 minutes, or until the mixture is set.

EGGS A LA TRIPE
(French)

Don't be put off—there is no tripe or meat product of any kind in this classic recipe that is perfect for brunch.
Makes 8 servings.

3 large onions, thinly sliced and separated into rings
¼ cup (½ stick) butter or margarine
3 tablespoons all-purpose flour
1 cup half-and-half
1 cup milk

1 cup (4 ounces) shredded Gruyère or Swiss
1 teaspoon salt
8 hard-cooked eggs, sliced
1 tablespoon soft butter or margarine

1. In a large heavy saucepan cook the onions with the butter until golden and wilted but not brown. Sprinkle with the flour and cook, stirring, 2 minutes.
2. Off the heat gradually stir in the half-and-half and the milk. Bring to a boil, stirring constantly until thickened and bubbly. Cook, stirring, 3 minutes. Stir in the cheese until melted. Stir in the salt.
3. Spread a layer of the onion mixture in the bottom of a greased shallow baking dish. Top with the egg slices and cover with remaining onion mixture. Dot with butter and place under a preheated broiler until bubbly and lightly browned.

ARTICHOKE FRITTATA
(Italian Artichoke Omelet)

Frittata, that combination of eggs and vegetables subtly seasoned, is one of the many joys of Italian cooking.
Makes 4 servings.

2 tablespoons olive or vegetable oil
1 clove garlic, finely chopped
1 medium-size onion, thinly sliced
2 flat anchovy fillets, chopped
1½ cups cooked artichoke hearts (2 ten-ounce packages frozen)
¼ teaspoon leaf thyme, crumbled
1 teaspoon leaf oregano, crumbled

6 eggs, lightly beaten
½ teaspoon salt
¼ teaspoon freshly ground black pepper
½ cup packaged coarse bread crumbs
¼ cup (1 ounce) freshly grated Parmesan

1. In a medium-size heavy skillet heat the oil and sauté the garlic, onion, and anchovies over low heat until wilted, about 10 minutes.
2. Add artichokes, thyme, and oregano. Cook 4 minutes over medium heat. Turn heat to medium-high and pour in eggs mixed with salt and pepper. Cook 1 minute. Reduce heat to medium, sprinkle bread crumbs and Parmesan over surface, and cook until bottom is set but top still shimmers.
3. Place 4 to 6 inches from preheated broiler and cook until top is set and lightly browned.

CHILI-CHEESE OMELET
(Mexican)

I prefer to make individual omelets to order rather than divide
a larger one.
Makes 1 serving.

1½ teaspoons butter or margarine
2 eggs, beaten
¼ teaspoon salt
Freshly ground black pepper to
taste

¼ cup (1 ounce) shredded
Monterey Jack or mild Cheddar
1 to 2 mild green chilies, seeded
and chopped

1. Heat the butter in an omelet pan or small skillet until it starts to foam.
   Beat the eggs with the salt and pepper.
2. Pour the eggs into the pan and cook until the bottom starts to set
   (almost immediately). Sprinkle with the cheese and chilies and cook,
   picking up the edges to allow liquid to drain under set portion. When
   set but soft fold over onto a warm plate and serve immediately.

MUSHROOM OMELET
(French)

For a light breakfast for two, halve the recipe and use a 7- or
8-inch omelet pan.
Makes 3 servings.

3 tablespoons butter or margarine
½ pound mushrooms, sliced
(2 cups)
2 shallots or 4 green onions, finely
chopped
1 tablespoon snipped fresh
dillweed, or ½ teaspoon dried
¾ teaspoon salt
⅛ teaspoon freshly ground black
pepper

2 tablespoons chopped fresh
parsley
¼ cup sour cream
6 large eggs, lightly beaten
⅛ teaspoon liquid red pepper
seasoning
3 tablespoons water
2 tablespoons butter or margarine

1. Melt the butter in a medium-size skillet and sauté the mushrooms
   and shallots until wilted. Stir in the dill, ¼ teaspoon of the salt,
   pepper, parsley, and half the sour cream. Keep warm.
2. In a medium-size bowl combine the eggs, remaining salt, red pepper
   seasoning, and water. Heat a 9- or 10-inch omelet pan or heavy skillet
   until a drop of water skitters over the surface and disappears. Add the
   butter and swirl to coat pan surface.

3. Pour in the egg mixture and stir quickly with a fork until mixture starts to set on the bottom. As omelet continues to cook lift up sides to let uncooked mixture flow under, or scratch a hole to let it flow through.
4. When omelet is set but still soft and barely browned on the underside spoon half the mushroom mixture in a strip across the middle. Holding the pan with the left hand under the handle, fold omelet in three and tip onto a warm platter over the edge of the pan.
5. Spoon remaining mushroom mixture over middle of omelet, top with remaining sour cream, and serve to 2 or 3 immediately.

TORTILLA
(Spanish Potato Omelet)

A tortilla in Spain is an omelet and in Mexico, a flat thin cake of corn or wheat.
Makes 4 servings.

¼ cup olive or vegetable oil, approximately	1 teaspoon salt
1 large onion, finely chopped (1 cup)	¼ teaspoon freshly ground black pepper
2 cups diced cooked potato	6 eggs, lightly beaten
	2 tablespoons water

1. In a large heavy skillet or an omelet pan heat the oil and sauté the onion over low heat until golden and tender but not browned. Add the potato, salt, and pepper and cook, stirring, until potato is hot.
2. In a medium-size bowl beat the eggs with the water. With a slotted spoon remove onion and potato from skillet and add to egg mixture. Reheat skillet, adding more oil if necessary.
3. Pour in the egg-potato mixture and cook until lightly browned on the bottom. Loosen around the edges, place a plate over skillet, and invert. Remove any bits left in the skillet. Reheat skillet, adding more oil if necessary and slide omelet back, uncooked side down.
4. Cook until underside gets a brown crust. Serve immediately, or cool and serve at room temperature.

BAKED LEEK OMELET
(French)

Leeks are one of my favorite vegetables and they will be yours too when you discover this baked omelet recipe.
Bake at 325° for 30 minutes.
Makes 4 servings.

8 medium-size leeks, well washed and sliced
6 eggs, lightly beaten
1 teaspoon salt
¼ teaspoon freshly ground black pepper

1 cup (4 ounces) grated Swiss or Gruyère
½ cup fresh soft bread crumbs

1. Steam the leeks over boiling water until tender, about 10 minutes. Drain well and place in a greased shallow baking dish.
2. Combine the eggs, salt, pepper, cheese, and crumbs. Pour over leeks and bake at 325° for 30 minutes, or until set.

ZUCCHINI FRITTATA
(Italian Zucchini Omelet)

Think of frittatas as quiches without the crust, although undoubtedly the Italian version came first.
Makes 4 servings.

1 medium-size zucchini, shredded (2 cups)
Salt
¼ cup olive or vegetable oil
1 medium-size onion, sliced
2 cloves garlic, finely chopped
8 eggs

½ teaspoon salt
½ teaspoon freshly ground black pepper
¼ teaspoon leaf basil, crumbled
2 tablespoons freshly grated Parmesan

1. Place the zucchini in a colander or strainer and sprinkle lightly with salt. Let stand 30 minutes, rinse briefly, and dry thoroughly on paper towels and squeeze dry in the corner of a clean dish towel.
2. Heat the oil in a medium-size skillet with an ovenproof handle and sauté the onion until soft. Add the garlic and cook 1 minute. Add zucchini, toss to mix, and cook 1 to 2 minutes.

3. Beat the eggs, salt, pepper, and basil in a small bowl until frothy. Pour over zucchini in skillet and cook over medium-high heat until bottom and sides are set but top is still soft. Sprinkle with cheese and put under preheated broiler until top is set and lightly browned. Cut into wedges and serve with tomato sauce, if you wish.

CHEESE SOUFFLE
(French)

A classic that is spectacular enough to make often. Vary the flavor by adding ½ cup ground cooked chicken or turkey to the sauce with the cheese.
Bake at 375° for 40 to 45 minutes.
Makes 6 servings.

¼ cup (½ stick) butter or margarine
¼ cup all-purpose flour
1½ cups hot milk
1 teaspoon salt
Freshly ground black pepper to taste
Pinch of cayenne

1 teaspoon Dijon mustard
1½ cups (6 ounces) shredded Swiss, Gruyère, or mild Cheddar
6 eggs, separated and at room temperature
⅛ teaspoon cream of tartar

1. Preheat oven to 400°. Grease a 2-quart soufflé dish.
2. Melt the butter in a medium-size saucepan and stir in the flour. Cook, stirring, 2 minutes over low heat. Remove from heat and gradually stir in the milk until smooth. Bring to a boil, stirring, and cook 3 to 4 minutes. Remove from heat.
3. Add salt, pepper to taste, cayenne, mustard, and cheese. Stir until cheese melts.
4. Beat the egg whites and cream of tartar until stiff but not dry. Beat the yolks, one at a time, into the slightly cooled sauce. Stir in ½ cup of the egg whites. Gently fold in the remaining egg whites until no streaks of white remain. Carefully spoon mixture into prepared soufflé dish.
5. Place in the middle of the oven and immediately reduce the oven temperature to 375°. Bake 40 to 45 minutes, or until well puffed and brown on top and still slightly soft in the middle for the French version, or until firm in the center, if you prefer.

EGGPLANT SOUFFLE
(French)

A one-dish meal, if you add crusty bread and a tossed green salad.
Bake at 400° for 30 minutes, then at 375° for 30 minutes.
Makes 6 servings.

2 medium-size eggplants (about 1 to 1½ pounds each)
Vegetable oil
Salt and freshly ground black pepper
1 medium-size onion, finely chopped (½ cup)
1 clove garlic, finely chopped
4 tablespoons (½ stick) butter or margarine

5 tablespoons all-purpose flour
1½ cups milk
2 cups (8 ounces) grated Swiss
6 eggs, separated
1 teaspoon leaf rosemary, crumbled
Salt and pepper to taste
¼ cup (1 ounce) freshly grated Parmesan

1. Preheat oven to 400°. Cut the eggplants in half lengthwise and place, cut side up, in a baking dish. Brush liberally with oil and sprinkle lightly with salt and pepper. Bake at 400° for 30 minutes or until tender.
2. Reduce oven to 375°. When eggplant is cool enough to handle scoop out the flesh and chop.
3. Meanwhile, heat 2 tablespoons oil in a heavy skillet and sauté the onion until tender but not browned. Add the garlic and chopped eggplant and cook, stirring, 2 to 3 minutes.
4. Melt the butter in a medium-size saucepan and blend in the flour. Gradually stir in the milk. Bring to a boil, stirring until mixture bubbles and thickens. Cook 2 minutes. Stir in the cheese off the heat until it melts.
5. Lightly beat the egg yolks. Add a cup of the hot sauce to the yolks and mix well. Return to bulk of sauce, reheat, but do not boil.
6. Stir in the rosemary, eggplant mixture, salt, and pepper. Beat the egg whites until stiff but not dry and fold into the eggplant mixture. Turn into a greased 2-quart soufflé dish, sprinkle with Parmesan, and bake at 375° for 30 minutes or until puffed, golden, and set around the edges but still soft in the middle. Serve immediately.

VEGETABLE SOUFFLE
(French)

Once you've mastered beating egg whites until they are stiff but not dry and have enough confidence to make family and guests eat when the dish is ready, you are ready to try many more variations.
Bake at 350° for 1 hour.
Makes 6 servings.

6 tablespoons (¾ stick) butter or margarine
⅓ cup all-purpose flour
1¼ teaspoons salt
¼ teaspoon freshly ground black pepper
1¼ cups milk

¼ cup chopped green onion
1½ cups chopped broccoli
1 cup frozen peas
6 eggs, separated
¾ cup (3 ounces) shredded sharp Cheddar

1. Melt 5 tablespoons of the butter in a saucepan, blend in the flour, and cook, stirring, 3 minutes. Remove from heat and add salt and pepper. Gradually stir in the milk. Return to heat and bring to a boil, stirring until thickened and smooth. Cook 2 minutes, stirring.
2. Melt remaining tablespoon of butter and sauté green onion and broccoli 5 minutes. Stir in peas.
3. Beat egg yolks with whisk and gradually beat in hot sauce. Stir in the vegetable mixture and cheese. Preheat oven to 350°. Beat the egg whites until they form soft peaks and are stiff but not dry. Stir half the whites into vegetable mixture. Fold in remaining whites and pour into a buttered 8-cup soufflé dish. Bake at 350° for 1 hour.

RATATOUILLE QUICHE
(French Vegetable Stew Quiche)

Great way to use up leftover ratatouille.
Bake at 375° for 40 minutes.
Makes 6 servings.

2 cups ratatouille (see page 229)
½ cup (2 ounces) shredded Gruyère
3 eggs, lightly beaten

1 cup milk or half-and-half
1 baked 9-inch pie shell, cooled
   slightly

Combine the ratatouille, cheese, eggs, and milk and pour into the pie shell. Bake at 375° for 40 minutes, or until set.

TOMATO QUICHE
(French)

Save this recipe for local tomato harvest time.
Bake at 450° for 12 minutes, then at 375° for 40 minutes.
Makes 6 servings.

1 unbaked 9-inch pie shell
1 cup (4 ounces) shredded Swiss or
   Gruyère
8 large ripe tomatoes, peeled,
   seeded, and chopped
1 small onion, finely chopped
   (¼ cup)
¼ teaspoon leaf thyme, crumbled

1 teaspoon leaf basil, crumbled
1 teaspoon salt
¼ teaspoon freshly ground black
   pepper
4 eggs
1 cup light cream or half-and-half
1 teaspoon sugar

1. Prick the shell with a fork and bake in a preheated 450° oven for 12 minutes or until golden. Cool slightly and sprinkle with cheese.
2. Place the tomatoes in a large heavy skillet. Add onion, thyme, basil, salt, and pepper and cook, stirring occasionally, until a very thick purée, about 30 minutes. Lower oven to 375°.
3. Beat the eggs and gradually add the cream. Add sugar and tomato mixture. Pour into the baked pie shell and bake at 375° until set, about 40 minutes. Let cool 10 minutes before cutting. Garnish with sautéed tomato slices, if you wish.

VEGETABLE QUICHE
(French)

Other vegetables cooked to the crisp-tender stage may be substituted. This is great for using up leftovers.
Bake pastry shell at 425° for 15 minutes.
Bake quiche at 450° for 15 minutes, then at 350° for 15 minutes.
Makes 4 main dish servings or 8 appetizer servings.

1 baked 10-inch pie shell
(see page 170)
2 tablespoons butter or margarine
1 large shallot or 2 green onions,
finely chopped
1 cup thinly sliced zucchini
(1 small)
¼ pound mushrooms, sliced
(about 1 cup)
1 cup peeled, diced eggplant
(½ small)

1 cup (4 ounces) shredded
Monterey Jack, mild Cheddar, or
Muenster
¾ cup milk*
¾ cup heavy or whipping cream*
4 eggs, lightly beaten
2 teaspoons salt
¼ teaspoon freshly ground black
pepper
¼ teaspoon summer savory or leaf
marjoram, crumbled

1. Prepare the pastry shell.
2. Heat the butter in a large skillet and sauté the shallot, zucchini, mushrooms, and eggplant until limp, about 5 to 10 minutes.
3. Spoon evenly over the bottom of the cooled pastry shell. Sprinkle cheese over vegetables. Preheat oven to 450°.
4. Combine the milk, cream, eggs, salt, pepper, and savory in a bowl. Place the quiche pan on the oven shelf and pour in the egg mixture. Bake at 450° for 15 minutes, reduce oven heat to 350°, and bake 15 minutes longer, or until almost set in the middle. Let stand 5 to 10 minutes before cutting.

*1½ cups of milk can be substituted for the milk and cream, if you wish.

BAKED PIE SHELL

Bake at 425° for 15 minutes.
Makes one 10-inch quiche shell.

1 cup all-purpose flour
½ teaspoon salt
⅛ teaspoon summer savory,
optional

⅓ cup (⅔ stick) butter or margarine
3 tablespoons cold water

1. Combine the flour, salt, and savory in a medium-size bowl. With the fingertips or a pastry blender work in the butter until the mixture resembles coarse meal. With a fork stir in enough water to make a dough. Gather dough into a ball, wrap in wax paper, and chill 30 minutes or until manageable. Preheat oven to 425°.
2. Roll out the dough into a 12- or 13-inch circle and fit into a 10-inch quiche pan or pie plate. Prick the bottom and sides with a fork. Line with aluminum foil, fill with dried beans or raw rice, and bake at 425° for 12 minutes or until set. Remove foil, beans or rice, and bake 3 to 4 minutes longer, or until lightly browned. Cool slightly before filling.

ZUCCHINI AND BROCCOLI QUICHE
(French)

Bake at 450° for 8 to 10 minutes, then at 350° for 40 minutes.
Makes 6 servings.

Pastry

1¼ cups sifted all-purpose flour
⅛ teaspoon salt
⅓ cup butter or margarine
2 to 3 tablespoons ice water

Filling

3 tablespoons butter or margarine
1 medium-size onion, thinly sliced
1 green pepper, seeded and diced
1 medium-size zucchini, thinly sliced
1 medium-size carrot, diced
2 cups broccoli flowerets
5 eggs, lightly beaten
2 cups (8 ounces) shredded Swiss or Gruyère
1 teaspoon salt
½ teaspoon freshly ground black pepper
½ teaspoon summer savory, crumbled

1. To make the pastry shell place the flour and salt in a medium-size bowl. With the fingertips or a pastry blender work in the butter until mixture resembles coarse oatmeal. With a fork stir in enough of the ice water to make a dough. Preheat oven to 450°.
2. On a lightly floured board roll out the dough to a 12-inch round and fit it into a 9-inch pie plate. Make a fluted, stand-up edge and prick shell all over with a fork.
3. Bake at 450° for 8 minutes or until set and lightly browned. Cool on a wire rack. Lower oven to 350°.
4. For the filling melt the butter in a large skillet and sauté the onion until golden, about 5 minutes. Add the pepper, zucchini, and carrot and cook over low heat, stirring occasionally, until vegetables are crisp-tender, about 10 minutes. Do not brown. Meanwhile steam the broccoli flowerets 5 minutes, or until crisp-tender. Allow vegetables to cool slightly.
5. Combine the eggs, cooled vegetables, cheese, salt, pepper, and savory and pour into a cooled crust. Bake at 350° for 40 minutes or until set. Let stand 10 minutes before serving.

PAN BAGNA
(French Fancy Sandwich)

Because the sandwich improves if kept cold for an hour or two, it is ideal to take on a picnic in an insulated container.
Makes 4 servings.

1 loaf French bread, cut into 4 pieces, or 4 crusty "hero" rolls
½ cup olive or vegetable oil
1 tablespoon red wine vinegar
2 cloves garlic, finely chopped
Lettuce leaves
2 tomatoes, halved and thinly sliced

1 medium-size red onion, sliced
1 green pepper, seeded and cut into strips
1 can (2 ounces) anchovy fillets
8 pitted black olives, halved
2 tablespoons lemon juice

1. Split the bread or rolls horizontally and pull out some of the crumbs. Combine the oil, vinegar, and garlic and drizzle a tablespoon or two over the inside of the rolls.
2. Fill rolls with layers of lettuce, tomato slices, onion slices, and green pepper strips. Arrange anchovies and olives over and drizzle with remaining oil mixture and the lemon juice.
3. Wrap the rolls loosely and store in the refrigerator for 1 hour or longer.

PIZZA RUSTICA
(Italian)

Simple to put together using frozen bread dough.
Bake at 450° for 15 minutes.
Makes 4 to 6 servings.

1 pound frozen plain bread dough, thawed overnight in the refrigerator
1 can (2 pounds, 3 ounces) Italian plum tomatoes, drained
½ teaspoon salt
¼ teaspoon freshly ground black pepper
½ cup (2 ounces) freshly grated Parmesan

1 container (15 ounces) ricotta
2 cups (8 ounces) shredded mozzarella
1 teaspoon leaf oregano, crumbled
¼ cup chopped fresh parsley
1 small onion, finely chopped (¼ cup)
6 to 8 flat anchovy fillets, chopped
2 tablespoons olive or vegetable oil

1. Roll and stretch the dough over an oiled 14- or 15-inch pizza pan. Cover with a damp cloth and let rise 20 minutes.
2. Combine the tomatoes, salt, and pepper in a skillet and cook, uncovered, until thick, about 20 minutes. Sprinkle dough with the Parmesan.
3. In a medium-size bowl combine the ricotta, mozzarella, oregano, parsley, onion, and anchovies. Preheat oven to 450°.
4. Spread the tomato mixture over the cheese, top with the ricotta mixture, and drizzle the oil over. Bake at 450° for 15 minutes, or until the dough is cooked.

PISSALADIERE
(French Pizza)

Frozen bread dough eliminates a lot of work when making this
French variation of a pizza.
Bake at 450° for 15 minutes.
Makes 4 servings.

2 very large Spanish or sweet
onions, cut into thin slices and
separated into rings
2 cloves garlic, finely chopped
2 tablespoons olive or vegetable oil
1 can (2 pounds, 3 ounces) Italian
plum tomatoes, drained
½ teaspoon salt
¼ teaspoon freshly ground black
pepper

1 teaspoon leaf thyme, crumbled
1 pound frozen plain bread dough,
thawed overnight in the
refrigerator
½ cup (2 ounces) freshly grated
Parmesan
2 cans (3½ ounces each) flat
anchovy fillets
12 to 16 pitted black olives

1. Place the onion, garlic, and olive oil in a heavy saucepan. Cover and
   cook over low heat until onions are golden and tender, about 30
   minutes. Stir occasionally to prevent sticking or browning.
2. Place tomatoes in a skillet and cook, uncovered, until thick, about 20
   minutes. Season with the salt, pepper, and thyme.
3. Roll and stretch the dough on a lightly oiled 14-inch pizza pan. Cover
   with a damp cloth and let rise 20 minutes. Preheat oven to 450°.
4. Spread the risen dough with the Parmesan. Spread the onion mixture
   over the cheese and top with the tomatoes. Arrange the anchovies
   crisscross in a lattice pattern over the tomatoes and put an olive in
   each space. Bake at 450° for 15 minutes, or until crust is done and top
   is bubbly.

CHEESE-FILLED CALZONE
(Italian)

Fun to take on a picnic. If there's a barbecue fire going, wrap
the calzone in foil and warm them around the edges of the grill.
Bake at 400° for 18 minutes.
Makes 4 servings.

1 envelope active dry yeast
1 cup very warm water
2 tablespoons sugar
1 teaspoon salt
½ cup (1 stick) butter or margarine, softened
3½ cups unsifted, unbleached, all-purpose flour, approximately
1 egg, lightly beaten
2 tablespoons vegetable oil
1 large onion, finely chopped (1 cup)
1 clove garlic, finely chopped
½ pound mushrooms, sliced (2 cups)

1 large green pepper, seeded and cut into strips
3 large tomatoes, peeled, seeded, and chopped
3 tablespoons tomato paste
½ teaspoon leaf oregano, crumbled
1 teaspoon leaf basil, crumbled
¼ teaspoon freshly ground black pepper
2 cups (8 ounces) shredded Monterey Jack or mild Cheddar
⅓ cup freshly grated Parmesan

1. Sprinkle yeast over very warm water, stir in sugar, and let stand 5
    minutes in a warm place. Add salt and butter and stir until butter
    melts.
2. Add 2½ cups of the flour and beat at medium speed with an electric
    mixer 5 minutes. Beat in the egg and beat until mixture is smooth and
    elastic. Beat in enough of the remaining flour to make a soft dough.
3. Place dough in a clean buttered bowl, turn dough in bowl, cover, and
    let rise in a warm place until doubled in bulk, about 1 hour.
4. Meanwhile heat the oil in a skillet and sauté the onion until tender
    but not browned. Add the garlic, mushrooms, and pepper and cook 3
    minutes. Add tomatoes, tomato paste, oregano, basil, and pepper.
    Simmer, uncovered, 25 minutes. Cool.
5. Punch dough down, divide into 4 pieces, and roll each piece out to an
    8-inch circle. Divide onion mixture among the 4 circles, spreading it
    to within ½ inch of edges. Sprinkle with the cheeses.
6. Moisten edges of dough. Fold over and pinch to seal. Place on a large
    greased cookie sheet at least 2 inches apart. Cover and let rise in a
    warm place about 20 minutes. Bake at 400° for 18 minutes, or until
    golden and the dough is cooked. Brush with melted butter, if you
    wish.

BEAN AND CHILI ENCHILADAS
(Mexican)

This is an excellent addition to a combination platter along with
chili-and-cheese-stuffed peppers, omelets, and salsa.
Bake at 350° for 15 minutes.
Makes 4 servings.

3 tablespoons peanut oil
1 teaspoon ground cumin
1 tablespoon grated onion
3 tablespoons flour
¾ cup chicken broth or vegetable broth (see page 59)
½ cup (2 ounces) shredded Monterey Jack or mild Cheddar
2 cups cooked black, pink, or pinto beans, mashed
3 to 4 serrano chili peppers, seeded and finely chopped
½ teaspoon salt
1 cup cooked rice (⅓ cup uncooked)

2 tablespoons peanut oil
1 small onion, finely chopped (¼ cup)
2 cloves garlic, finely chopped
1 can (2 pounds, 3 ounces) peeled plum tomatoes, drained
2 cans (4 ounces each) mild green chilies, seeded and chopped
1 teaspoon salt
2 tablespoons peanut oil
8 to 10 corn tortillas, canned, thawed frozen, or refrigerated
¼ cup (1 ounce) shredded Monterey Jack or mild Cheddar

1. Heat 3 tablespoons oil in a medium-size saucepan. Add cumin and onion and sauté 3 to 4 minutes. Stir in the flour and cook, stirring, 2 to 3 minutes. Slowly stir in the broth and bring to a boil, stirring until mixture is thick. Remove from heat. Stir in the ½ cup cheese and set aside to cool.
2. Combine the cooled sauce, beans, chili peppers, salt, and rice.
3. Heat 2 tablespoons oil in a medium-size skillet, add onion and garlic, and sauté until soft. Add tomatoes, chilies, and salt and cook over medium-high heat until thickened.
4. Heat remaining 2 tablespoons oil in a small skillet and sauté tortillas briefly on both sides to soften but not to brown or crisp. Preheat oven to 350°.
5. Fill each tortilla with 1½ to 2 tablespoons of the bean mixture. Roll up and place, seam side down, in a baking dish big enough to hold them in a single layer. Spread the tomato sauce down the center of the enchiladas. Sprinkle with the cheese, cover with foil, and bake at 350° for 10 minutes. Remove foil and bake another 5 minutes to melt cheese.

SWISS-STYLE ENCHILADAS
(Mexican)

Although this sounds like a recent innovation it is a classical
Mexican dish.
Bake at 350° for 25 minutes.
Makes 4 servings.

3 tablespoons vegetable oil
1 medium-size onion, finely
  chopped (½ cup)
1 clove garlic, finely chopped
2 packages (10 ounces each) frozen
  chopped spinach, thawed and
  squeezed dry
½ teaspoon salt
2 cups (8 ounces) shredded Swiss

8 thawed frozen, homemade,
  canned, or refrigerated tortillas
1½ tablespoons butter or margarine
1½ tablespoons flour
1½ cups milk
½ cup sour cream
⅓ cup diced mild green chilies
¼ teaspoon salt

1. In a medium-size heavy skillet heat the oil and sauté the onion until
   tender but not browned. Add the garlic and cook 1 minute. Add the
   spinach and toss with onion. Stir in the salt.
2. Wrap the tortillas in aluminum foil and heat in a toaster oven or oven
   set at 250° for 6 to 10 minutes, or until soft and pliable.
3. Spread a heaped tablespoon cheese down middle of each tortilla and
   top with 2 tablespoons of spinach mixture. Roll up enchilada and
   place, seam side down, in a greased shallow baking dish in a single
   layer. Preheat oven to 350°.
4. Melt the butter, blend in the flour, and cook, stirring, 2 minutes.
5. Gradually stir in the milk and bring to a boil, stirring. Cook until
   thick and smooth. Add a little hot sauce to the sour cream and return
   all to saucepan. Stir in chilies, salt, and remaining cheese.
6. Pour sauce over enchiladas and bake at 350° for 25 minutes, or until
   bubbly and lightly browned. Serve with extra sour cream, if you
   wish.

VEGETABLE ENCHILADAS
(Mexican)

You won't miss the chicken or beef in the filling.
Bake at 400° for 10 minutes.
Makes 4 servings.

¼ cup vegetable oil
2 large onions, finely chopped
(2 cups)
3 cloves garlic, finely chopped
½ pound mushrooms, sliced
(2 cups)
1 large green pepper, seeded and
chopped
3 tomatoes, peeled and coarsely
chopped (1½ cups)
2 canned green chili peppers,
seeded and chopped

2 teaspoons leaf basil, crumbled
1 teaspoon leaf thyme, crumbled
1 teaspoon salt
¼ teaspoon freshly ground black
pepper
2 containers (8 ounces each) sour
cream
8 canned, frozen, or refrigerated
tortillas
Vegetable oil
1 cup (4 ounces) shredded
Monterey Jack or mild Cheddar

1. In a large skillet heat the oil and sauté 1½ cups of the onion until tender but not browned. Add the garlic and cook 2 minutes.
2. Add the mushrooms and green pepper and cook, stirring, 3 minutes. Stir in 1 cup of tomatoes, the chili peppers, basil, thyme, salt, and pepper. Bring to a boil and simmer 3 minutes.
3. Stir in the sour cream and remove from the heat.
4. Combine remaining onion and tomato for a filling.
5. Soften the tortillas either by dipping in hot oil for 5 seconds and draining or by wrapping in plastic wrap and cooking 20 to 30 seconds on high power in a microwave oven.
6. Preheat oven to 400°. Oil a shallow baking dish big enough to hold 8 rolled tortillas in a single layer. Divide the onion-tomato mixture among the tortillas, top with some sauce, and roll. Place seam side down. Pour over remaining sauce and sprinkle with cheese. Bake at 400° for 10 minutes, or until bubbly and cheese has melted.

VEGETABLE-FILLED PANCAKES
(Chinese)

Unlike egg rolls these heavenly packages do not have to be
deep-fried.
Bake at 350° for 15 minutes.
Makes 6 servings (3 pancakes each).

2 eggs, lightly beaten
1½ cups milk, approximately
1½ cups sifted all-purpose flour
¼ cup vegetable oil
⅛ teaspoon salt
4 green onions, finely chopped
2 tablespoons vegetable oil
2 cans (16 ounces each) Chinese
   mixed vegetables, drained
1 cup chopped celery

4 green onions, sliced
1 clove garlic, finely chopped
1 can (8 ounces) water chestnuts,
   drained and sliced
3 tablespoons cornstarch
⅓ cup soy sauce
⅓ cup dry sherry
1 cup water
1 teaspoon salt

1. Place the eggs in a 2-cup measure and add milk to make 2 cups. In a
    medium-size bowl combine the flour, oil, salt, green onions, and
    egg-milk mixture. Beat until smooth. Set aside for 20 minutes.
2. Lightly oil a 5- or 6-inch skillet or crêpe pan. Heat and add about 2
    tablespoons of the batter. Tip to spread all over pan and cook until
    golden. Turn and cook second side. If batter is too thick to spread add
    more milk. Keep pancakes warm while using remainder of batter.
3. Heat the oil in a large skillet or wok. Add the mixed vegetables and
    stir-fry 1 minute. Add the celery, green onions, garlic, and water
    chestnuts and stir-fry 4 minutes.
4. Mix the cornstarch with the soy sauce, sherry, and water until
    smooth. Stir into skillet. Add salt and cook, stirring, until mixture
    thickens. Preheat oven to 350°.
5. Fill each pancake with about ¼ cup vegetable mixture. Roll up and
    place, seam-side down, in a shallow baking dish. Bake at 350° for 15
    minutes, or until piping hot.

CHEESE AND CHILI TACOS
(Mexican)

Tacos are fun for people who like to get involved in putting food together.
Makes 4 servings.

Peanut oil or lard
8 corn tortillas, canned, frozen, homemade, or refrigerated
3 cups (12 ounces) shredded Monterey Jack or mild Cheddar
1 can mild green chilies, seeded and chopped
1½ cups shredded iceberg lettuce
1½ cups Chili Tomato Sauce (see recipe below)
1 avocado, peeled, pitted, sliced, and dipped in lemon juice
1 container (8 ounces) sour cream

1. In a medium-size heavy skillet heat enough oil or lard to make a ¼-inch layer. Drop the tortillas in, one at a time, and cook quickly on both sides. Fold in half and return to the oil to crisp.*
2. Drain on paper towels and keep warm in a slow oven while cooking rest of tortillas.
3. Assemble tortillas and fill with cheese, chilies, lettuce, sauce, avocado, and sour cream, in that order.

*Preformed taco shells can be used, if you wish, but they will not have the same fresh flavor.

CHILI TOMATO SAUCE

Combine 1 small onion, finely chopped, 1½ cups fresh or canned tomatoes, peeled, seeded, and drained, 1 jalapeño pepper, seeded and finely chopped, and 1 teaspoon salt. Chill at least 1 hour before using.

TORTILLA CASSEROLE
(Mexican)

This casserole is a way of using up leftovers. The proportions
and ingredients may be changed to suit your needs and the
leftovers on hand.
Bake at 350° for 20 minutes.
Makes 4 servings.

2 tablespoons peanut oil
1 small onion, finely chopped
  (¼ cup)
2 cloves garlic, finely chopped
1 can (2 pounds, 3 ounces) peeled
  plum tomatoes, drained and
  chopped (1½ to 2 cups)
2 cans (4 ounces each) mild green
  chilies, drained, seeded, and
  chopped

1 teaspoon salt
¼ cup peanut oil
8 stale tortillas
1½ cups refried beans (see page 238)
1 cup (4 ounces) shredded
  Monterey Jack or mild Cheddar
  Sour cream

1. Heat 2 tablespoons oil in a medium-size skillet and sauté the onion
    and garlic until soft. Add the tomatoes and cook over medium-high
    heat until thickened, about 15 minutes. Add chilies and salt.
2. In a second smaller skillet heat the ¼ cup peanut oil and fry the
    tortillas, one at a time, until just slightly crisp but not brown, about 1
    minute on each side. Drain on paper towels and break into thin strips
    no more than 1 inch wide. Preheat oven to 350°.
3. In a deep 2-quart baking dish arrange the ingredients in the following
    order: one-third of the tortilla strips, half the tomato sauce, half the
    beans, one-third of the cheese. Repeat layers, finishing with tortillas
    and cheese. Cover with foil and bake at 350° for 20 minutes. Serve
    topped with sour cream and pass more at the table.

TOSTADAS
(Mexican)

A filling snack or luncheon dish that's easy on the budget.
Makes 4 servings.

6 to 8 tablespoons peanut oil
8 corn tortillas, thawed frozen, canned, or refrigerated
1½ to 2 cups refried beans (see page 238)
2 cups shredded iceberg lettuce
1 large onion, finely chopped (1 cup)

Fresh Tomato and Chili Sauce (see recipe below)
1 cup (4 ounces) shredded Monterey Jack or mild Cheddar
Hot Avocado Sauce (see recipe below)

1. Heat oil in a small deep skillet or saucepan and fry tortillas, one at a time, until crisp and lightly browned. Add more oil as needed. Drain tortillas on paper towels and keep warm until all are done.
2. Let everyone fix his or her own and pile on what pleases. Traditionally the order is tortilla, beans, lettuce, onion, tomato sauce, cheese, and avocado sauce. Tostadas are picked up with the fingers and eaten out of hand.

FRESH TOMATO AND CHILI SAUCE

Combine 1 cup peeled, seeded and chopped fresh tomatoes with 2 cans (4 ounces each) drained and seeded mild green chilies, ⅓ cup chopped onion, 1½ teaspoons salt, and 1 or 2 seeded and finely chopped canned jalapeño chilies or to taste.

HOT AVOCADO SAUCE

Mash 2 ripe avocados and combine with one 8-ounce package of softened cream cheese, 2 to 3 cloves garlic, finely chopped, ½ jalapeño chili pepper, seeded and chopped, and salt to taste. If made ahead, cover the surface of the sauce with plastic wrap, cover container, and chill.

CHILAQUILES
(Mexican)

Here is more proof that stale tortillas have an important role to
play in casserole dishes.
Bake at 375° for 20 minutes.
Makes 6 servings.

Vegetable oil
8 stale corn tortillas, cut into
  1-inch-wide strips
2 tablespoons lard or margarine
1 large onion, finely chopped
  (1 cup)
1 can (4 ounces) mild, diced green
  chilies
1 clove garlic, finely chopped
1 can (1 pound) tomatoes, drained
  and chopped

½ teaspoon salt
½ cup light cream or half-and-half
2 tablespoons chopped fresh
  cilantro (Chinese parsley) or
  parsley
2 cups (8 ounces) shredded
  Monterey Jack or mild Cheddar
1 avocado, peeled, pitted, and
  sliced
½ cup pitted black olives, sliced
  Parsley sprigs

1. In a deep heavy saucepan pour oil to a depth of 2 inches. Heat to 360°
    on a deep-fat thermometer. Fry the tortilla strips, a few at a time, in
    the hot oil until crisp. Drain on paper towels.
2. Heat the lard or margarine in a medium saucepan and sauté the onion
    until tender but not browned. Add the chilies, garlic, and tomatoes.
    Bring to a boil and simmer 15 minutes until of sauce consistency. Add
    some of drained tomato liquid, if necessary. Preheat oven to 375°.
3. Stir in salt, cream, and parsley. Pour ½ cup sauce into a 2-quart
    casserole. Top with tortillas, remaining sauce, and cheese.
4. Bake at 375° for 20 minutes, or until top is lightly browned. Serve
    garnished with avocado, olives, and parsley.

FONDUE
(Swiss)

Makes 6 servings.

1 pound (4 cups) shredded natural Swiss, Gruyère, or Emmenthal cheese or a combination of two or three (Do not use processed cheese.)
1 tablespoon flour
1½ cups dry white wine

2 tablespoons kirsch
1 tablespoon cornstarch
⅛ teaspoon ground nutmeg
1 clove garlic, bruised
1 loaf French bread, cut into cubes, or cubes of green pepper, pieces of celery, cauliflowerets, and broccoli flowerets

1. Toss the cheese with the flour. In a heavy saucepan heat the wine slowly but do not boil. When bubbles start showing add the cheese gradually, stirring with a wooden spoon. Let the first batch of cheese melt before adding the second.
2. Mix the kirsch and cornstarch and stir into melted cheese mixture. Stir in the nutmeg.
3. Rub a heatproof ceramic or metal chafing dish with the garlic and discard. Pour in the cheese mixture and keep warm but do not boil. If mixture becomes too thick add more wine. Test consistency by spearing a cube of bread or raw vegetable on a long-handled fork and dipping in the cheese mixture. It should coat the bread.

WELSH RAREBIT
(British)

The British version of fondue can be served with raw vegetable dippers if you choose.
Makes 6 servings.

1 tablespoon Worcestershire sauce
½ teaspoon dry mustard
Pinch of cayenne
½ cup beer

4 cups (16 ounces) grated sharp Cheddar
2 tablespoons flour

1. In a medium-size heavy saucepan heat the Worcestershire, mustard, cayenne, and beer. Toss the cheese with the flour and add to saucepan. Heat, stirring, over low heat until cheese melts.
2. Serve over toast or English muffins, if you wish.

VEGETABLE-FILLED CHEESE PUFF
(French)

The French call the puff part of this recipe a gougère.
Bake at 400° for 40 minutes.
Makes 6 servings.

1 cup water
½ cup (1 stick) butter or margarine
1 cup sifted all-purpose flour
Pinch of salt
4 eggs
½ cup (2 ounces) shredded sharp Cheddar
¼ cup (½ stick) butter or margarine
1 large onion, finely chopped (1 cup)
1 clove garlic, finely chopped
1 medium-size green pepper, seeded and cut into strips
1 medium-size sweet red pepper, seeded and cut into strips

½ pound mushrooms, sliced (2 cups)
2 tablespoons flour
1¼ cups chicken or vegetable broth (see page 59)
1 teaspoon salt
¼ teaspoon freshly ground black pepper
1 can (1 pound) tomatoes, drained and chopped
2 tablespoons chopped fresh parsley

1. Place the water and butter in a small saucepan and heat gently until butter melts. Bring to a boil and quickly stir in the flour all at once. Add salt and continue stirring over low heat until mixture leaves the sides of the pan clean. Cool slightly. Preheat oven to 400°.
2. With a wooden spoon beat in the eggs one at a time, making sure the mixture stays smooth and silky-looking. Add the cheese.
3. Spoon the dough around the outside edge of a buttered 10-inch ovenproof skillet or shallow baking dish, leaving the center empty. Bake at 400° for 30 minutes.
4. Meanwhile in a medium-size skillet melt the butter and sauté the onion until tender but not browned. Add the garlic, green and red peppers, and mushrooms and cook, stirring, 3 minutes.
5. Sprinkle the flour over vegetables and cook, stirring, 1 minute. Stir in the broth gradually. Add salt, pepper, and tomatoes and cook, uncovered, until mixture is thick.
6. Spoon vegetable mixture into center of cheese puff and bake 10 minutes, or until golden brown. Sprinkle with parsley.

CHEESE-FILLED MANICOTTI
(Italian)

For family or friends this will always be a winner.
Bake at 350° for 40 minutes.
Makes 8 servings.

3 tablespoons olive or vegetable oil
1 large onion, finely chopped
 (1 cup)
2 cloves garlic, finely chopped
1 can (2 pounds, 3 ounces) peeled
 Italian plum tomatoes
1 can (6 ounces) tomato paste
1 teaspoon leaf basil, crumbled
½ teaspoon leaf oregano, crumbled
1 teaspoon salt
½ teaspoon freshly ground black
 pepper

16 manicotti shells
 2 packages (10 ounces each) frozen
 chopped spinach, thawed
 1 container (15 ounces) ricotta
½ cup (2 ounces) freshly grated
 Parmesan
¼ teaspoon nutmeg
¼ teaspoon freshly ground black
 pepper
 1 tablespoon chopped fresh parsley

1. In a heavy kettle or Dutch oven heat the oil and sauté the onion until soft but not browned. Add the garlic and cook 1 minute. Add tomatoes, tomato paste, basil, oregano, salt, and pepper. Cover and simmer 30 minutes.
2. Cook the manicotti according to package directions, drain, and rinse with cold water.
3. Squeeze the water out of the spinach and place in a medium-size bowl. Add the ricotta, Parmesan, nutmeg, pepper, and parsley. Mix well.
4. Stuff the manicotti with the cheese-spinach mixture. Preheat oven to 350°.
5. In a shallow baking dish pour in a thin layer of tomato sauce and arrange the filled manicotti in a single layer (use 2 dishes if necessary). Top with remaining sauce and bake at 350° for 40 minutes, or until bubbly hot.

CHEESE-FILLED CANNELLONI
(Italian)

You won't miss the meat in this tasty cheese filling.
Bake at 350° for 15 minutes.
Makes 6 servings.

2 packages (10 ounces each) frozen chopped spinach, thawed and squeezed dry
1 cup whole milk ricotta
½ cup (2 ounces) shredded mozzarella
½ cup (2 ounces) freshly grated Parmesan
2 cloves garlic, finely chopped
2 teaspoons salt
¼ teaspoon crushed hot red pepper flakes
2 eggs, lightly beaten
1 package (12) manicotti tubes or homemade pasta squares

1 tablespoon olive or vegetable oil
¼ cup (½ stick) butter or margarine
1 clove garlic, finely chopped
5 tablespoons flour
2 cups hot milk
⅛ teaspoon ground nutmeg
¼ cup chopped fresh parsley, preferably flat Italian
Salt and freshly ground black pepper to taste
2 tablespoons freshly grated Parmesan

1. In a medium-size bowl combine the spinach, ricotta, mozzarella, Parmesan, garlic, salt, red pepper flakes, and eggs.
2. Cook the pasta tubes according to package directions until al dente and the pasta squares according to recipe. Drain and toss with 1 tablespoon of oil. When cool enough to handle stuff the tubes with the ricotta mixture or roll in squares of dough.
3. Place in a single layer in one large or two small greased baking dishes. Keep them warm. Meanwhile melt butter in a medium-size saucepan and sauté the garlic for 1 minute. Do not brown. Stir in flour and cook 2 minutes. Preheat oven to 350°.
4. Remove from the heat and gradually stir in the milk until smooth. Bring to a boil, stirring, and cook 2 to 3 minutes. Stir in nutmeg, parsley, salt, and pepper. Pour sauce over pasta to completely cover. Sprinkle with Parmesan and bake at 350° for 15 minutes, or until bubbly and lightly browned.

Note: If prepared ahead, cover and refrigerate. Cover with foil and bake 30 minutes. Remove foil and cook 10 minutes longer, or until brown and bubbly.

RICOTTA-STUFFED SHELLS
(Italian)

The stuffing is piquant with anchovies, capers, and pesto.
Bake at 350° for 15 minutes.
Makes 6 servings.

1 tablespoon vegetable oil
1 medium-size onion, chopped
(½ cup)
4 flat anchovies, finely chopped
2 cans (2 pounds, 3 ounces each)
peeled plum tomatoes, drained
and coarsely chopped
2 teaspoons capers, drained
3 tablespoons chopped fresh
parsley, preferably flat Italian
5 tablespoons pesto sauce
(see page 190)
Salt and pepper to taste

2 pounds whole milk ricotta
2 eggs, lightly beaten
¼ cup chopped fresh parsley,
preferably flat Italian
Pinch of freshly grated nutmeg
2 teaspoons salt
½ teaspoon freshly ground black
pepper
¼ cup (1 ounce) freshly grated
Parmesan
1 package (12 ounces) large
macaroni shells

1. Heat the oil in a medium-size saucepan and sauté the onion and anchovies until onions are wilted, about 5 minutes. Add tomatoes and cook over high heat until thickened slightly, about 15 minutes.
2. Stir in the capers, parsley, and pesto sauce and cook 5 minutes. Season with salt and pepper to taste.
3. Combine the ricotta, eggs, parsley, nutmeg, salt, pepper, and half the Parmesan.
4. Cook the shells according to package directions until al dente and drain. Rinse with cold water and drain well. Stuff the shells with the cheese mixture. Preheat oven to 350°.
5. Spread half the tomato sauce over the bottom of a 13- × 9- × 2-inch baking dish. Arrange the shells over the sauce and pour remaining sauce over. Sprinkle with remaining Parmesan and bake at 350° for 15 minutes, or until heated through.

CHEESE LASAGNA
(Italian)

This recipe can easily be doubled for a larger group or for an extra casserole to freeze.
Bake at 350° for 30 minutes.
Makes 4 servings.

Tomato Sauce

- 3 tablespoons olive oil
- 1 large clove garlic, finely chopped
- 1 small carrot, shredded
- 1 stalk celery, chopped
- ½ green pepper, seeded and chopped
- 1 large onion, finely chopped (1 cup)
- ½ cup dry red wine
- ¼ cup chopped fresh parsley, preferably flat Italian
- 1 teaspoon leaf basil, crumbled
- 1 can (2 pounds, 3 ounces) plus 1 can (1 pound) peeled plum tomatoes, drained and coarsely chopped
- 1 can (6 ounces) tomato paste
- 2 teaspoons salt
- ¾ teaspoon freshly ground black pepper

Cheese Filling

- 2 cups whole milk ricotta
- ¼ cup chopped fresh parsley, preferably flat Italian
- 1 egg, lightly beaten
- 1 cup (4 ounces) shredded mozzarella
- 2 tablespoons freshly grated Parmesan or Romano
- 1 teaspoon salt
- ¼ teaspoon freshly ground black pepper
- 2 large cloves garlic, finely chopped

- ½ pound lasagna noodles
- 1 tablespoon olive oil
  Freshly grated Parmesan

1. To make the tomato sauce heat the oil in a heavy casserole or Dutch oven and sauté the garlic, carrot, celery, green pepper, and onion until wilted. Add wine and cook over high heat 3 minutes.
2. Add remaining tomato sauce ingredients, bring to a boil, and cook, uncovered, until thickened, about 20 minutes.
3. Combine all the ingredients for the cheese filling (except the lasagna noodles and oil) in a medium-size bowl and beat until smooth.
4. Cook the noodles until barely tender, drain, and rinse generously with cold water. Drain and toss with 1 tablespoon olive oil. Preheat oven to 350°.
5. In a 7- × 12-inch shallow casserole spread a layer of tomato sauce, layer of noodles, more sauce, cheese mixture, noodles, and so on until all are used, ending with tomato sauce.

6. Sprinkle with more grated Parmesan, if you wish, and bake at 350° for 30 minutes, or until hot and bubbly. Brown under broiler if necessary. Dish may be prepared to the end of step 5 a day before, or several hours ahead. Cover and chill. Allow to return to room temperature and bake 30 to 40 minutes, or until hot and bubbly.

NOODLES WITH ZUCCHINI AND NUTS
(Italian)

Zucchini and walnuts have an affinity for each other whether you are making a simple vegetable combination, zucchini bread, or this quick pasta dish.
Makes 4 servings.

1 clove garlic, finely chopped
2 tablespoons chopped fresh parsley
½ teaspoon leaf oregano, crumbled
1 tablespoon pine nuts (pignoli), chopped
1⅓ cups walnuts, finely chopped
1 teaspoon salt
½ teaspoon freshly ground black pepper

1 cup heavy cream
1 cup ricotta
2 pounds zucchini, cut in half lengthwise and into ½-inch pieces
½ cup (1 stick) butter or margarine
1 pound macaroni or ziti
½ cup coarsely chopped walnuts, lightly toasted in a skillet

1. Place the garlic, parsley, oregano, pine nuts, walnuts, salt, pepper, cream, and cheese in a blender or food processor. Blend or process until smooth.
2. Blanch the zucchini in boiling water for 3 minutes and drain. Sauté in the butter until lightly browned, add sauce, and reheat. Cook macaroni or ziti according to package directions. Drain.
3. Toss pasta with sauce and top with toasted walnuts. Serve immediately.

PASTA WITH TOMATO SAUCE
(Italian)

Simple and superb!
Makes 4 servings.

¼ cup olive or vegetable oil,
approximately
1 large eggplant, peeled and cubed
(3 to 4 cups)
1 medium-size onion, thinly sliced
1 green pepper, seeded and sliced
lengthwise
3 cloves garlic, finely chopped
2 cans (2 pounds, 3 ounces each)
Italian plum tomatoes
1 teaspoon leaf basil, crumbled

1 teaspoon leaf oregano, crumbled
1½ teaspoons salt
½ teaspoon freshly ground black
pepper
1 tablespoon drained capers,
optional
¼ cup sliced pitted black olives,
optional
1 pound linguine
1 cup (4 ounces) shredded
mozzarella

1. Heat 2 tablespoons of the oil in a large heavy skillet. Add the eggplant
    and cook, stirring, until lightly browned. Remove to a bowl. Add
    more oil if needed.
2. Add remaining 2 tablespoons oil and sauté onion, green pepper, and
    garlic until wilted. Add tomatoes and cook over high heat until mix-
    ture thickens, about 10 minutes.
3. Add eggplant, basil, oregano, salt, and pepper and cook briefly until
    eggplant is tender. Just before serving add the capers and olives, if
    you wish. Cook pasta al dente according to package directions.
4. Toss pasta with sauce and cheese.

PASTA WITH PESTO I
(Italian)

This sauce is also delicious stirred into minestrone, drizzled on
tomato slices, or added to homemade tomato sauce.
Makes 6 servings.

¼ cup (1 ounce) freshly grated
Parmesan
3 cloves garlic, finely chopped
¼ cup pine nuts (pignoli) or walnuts
2 cups fresh basil*
1 to 1½ teaspoons salt

½ teaspoon freshly ground black
pepper
1 cup olive oil
1½ pounds linguine or other pasta
cooked al dente and drained

1. Combine all the ingredients except the pasta in an electric blender or a food processor and blend or process until smooth. It can be done in 2 or 3 batches in the blender.
2. Toss sauce with drained pasta and serve at once with more freshly grated Parmesan, if you wish.

*The pesto can be made with ½ cup olive oil, if you wish, and if fresh basil is not available an acceptable sauce can be made by substituting flat parsley for the basil and adding 2 teaspoons dried basil. This is an excellent way to preserve fresh basil. Float extra oil over the surface of the sauce, cover, and store in the refrigerator for 10 to 14 days or in the freezer for 3 months.

PASTA WITH PESTO II
(Italian)

Heavenly flavor of fresh basil.
Makes 4 servings.

1½ cups fresh basil leaves
⅓ cup fresh flat Italian parsley leaves
3 cloves garlic
⅓ cup pine nuts or walnuts
½ teaspoon salt
⅛ teaspoon nutmeg
¾ cup (3 ounces) freshly grated Parmesan
¾ cup olive or vegetable oil
1 pound tagliarini, trenette, or narrow noodles

1. Place the basil, parsley, garlic, nuts, salt, and nutmeg in the container of an electric blender or in a food processor. Whirl to blend. Add the cheese and blend again.
2. While the machine is running gradually add the oil until you have a thick smooth mixture.
3. Cook the noodles al dente according to package directions. Drain. Pour the pesto into a large bowl. Top with hot pasta and toss to mix. Serve immediately with more freshly grated Parmesan cheese, if you wish.

PASTA PRIMAVERA
(Italian Pasta With Vegetable Sauce)

This is an excellent dish to use up leftover vegetables provided they were not overcooked in the first coming.
Makes 4 servings.

½ pound mushrooms, sliced (2 cups)

2 large cloves garlic, finely chopped

1 small onion, sliced (⅓ cup)

½ cup vegetable oil

4 ounces cream cheese, at room temperature

1¼ cups light cream

½ teaspoon leaf basil, crumbled

2 tablespoons chopped fresh parsley

1 teaspoon salt

½ teaspoon freshly ground black pepper

½ teaspoon crushed hot red pepper flakes, optional

2 cups green beans, cut into ½-inch lengths and cooked until crisp-tender

2 cups cauliflower or broccoli pieces, cooked until crisp-tender

1 pound spaghetti or thin noodles cooked al dente, drained, and tossed with 1 tablespoon oil

1. In a large heavy skillet sauté the mushrooms, garlic, and onion in the oil slowly for 7 to 10 minutes. Add cream cheese, cream, basil, parsley, salt, pepper, and red pepper flakes. Heat and stir well until smooth. Add vegetables.
2. Heat the mixture through and serve immediately over hot pasta.

MACARONI AND CHEESE PIE
(Greek)

A take-off on pastitsio, the macaroni and ground lamb dish.
Bake at 350° for 25 minutes.
Makes 4 to 6 servings.

½ pound small elbow macaroni

6 tablespoons unsalted butter or margarine, melted

2 eggs, lightly beaten

¼ cup (1 ounce) freshly grated Parmesan

1 cup (about 4 ounces) small cubes feta cheese

1 package (10 ounces) frozen chopped spinach, thawed and squeezed dry

½ teaspoon salt

¼ teaspoon freshly ground black pepper

¼ teaspoon ground nutmeg

8 sheets phyllo or strudel dough

1. Cook the macaroni according to package directions until al dente. Drain, rinse with cold water, drain well, and place in a large mixing bowl.
2. Add 2 tablespoons of the butter, eggs, Parmesan, feta, spinach, salt, pepper, and nutmeg to macaroni. Mix well.
3. Butter a 9- × 9- × 2-inch baking dish. Halve the sheets of phyllo and cut to fit the dish. Place 1 piece of phyllo in the bottom and brush with remaining butter. Continue layering 7 more pieces of phyllo and butter each piece. Preheat oven to 350°.
4. Spoon in the macaroni mixture and layer the remaining pieces of phyllo, brushing each with butter. Score the top layers into squares with the point of a sharp knife. Bake at 350° for 25 minutes or until pastry is crisp and done. Cut into squares to serve.

FETTUCINE WITH SPINACH
(Italian)

Pasta, especially noodles, has infinite possibilities for being combined with vegetables, sauces, and cheeses. This is one of my favorites.
Makes 4 servings.

¼ cup olive or vegetable oil
1 large onion, finely chopped (1 cup)
2 cloves garlic, finely chopped
1 pound or 1 bag (10 ounces) fresh spinach, washed, trimmed, and shredded, or 1 package (10 ounces) frozen chopped spinach, partially thawed

1 cup ricotta
¼ cup (1 ounce) freshly grated Parmesan
Heavy cream
1 pound fettucine or other thin noodles cooked al dente and drained

1. In a large heavy skillet heat the oil and sauté the onion until tender but not browned. Add the garlic and spinach, cover, and cook 5 minutes or until spinach has wilted.
2. Remove pan from the heat and stir in the ricotta, Parmesan, and enough cream to make a creamy sauce consistency. Place noodles in a deep serving platter and top with sauce. Toss and serve with extra Parmesan cheese, if you wish.

MACARONI, VEGETABLES, AND CHEESE
(American)

Use a variety of leftover vegetables such as corn, lima beans, cauliflower, or peas, if you wish.
Bake at 375° for 25 minutes.
Makes 4 servings.

3 tablespoons butter or margarine
3 tablespoons flour
1½ cups half-and-half or milk
1 teaspoon salt
1 teaspoon dry mustard
¼ teaspoon freshly ground black pepper
1½ cups (6 ounces) shredded sharp Cheddar

2 cups diced cooked carrot or green beans
1 package (10 ounces) frozen chopped broccoli, cooked and well drained
1 package (8 ounces) elbow macaroni, cooked according to package directions and drained
Freshly grated Parmesan

1. Melt the butter in a small saucepan and blend in the flour. Gradually stir in the half-and-half and bring to a boil, stirring until smooth and thick. Cook 3 minutes.
2. Stir in the salt, mustard, pepper, and cheese. Stir until cheese melts. Place the carrots, broccoli, and macaroni in a greased 1-quart casserole. Preheat oven to 375°.
3. Pour the sauce over the vegetables. Toss gently to mix, sprinkle with grated Parmesan, and bake at 375° for 25 minutes, or until bubbly hot and lightly browned.

NOODLE AND GREEN PEPPER CASSEROLE
(Hungarian)

Bake at 375° for 30 minutes.
Makes 6 servings.

¼ cup vegetable oil
2 large onions, thinly sliced and separated into rings
1 clove garlic, finely chopped
3 large green peppers, seeded and cut into strips
2 teaspoons sweet paprika
1 teaspoon caraway seeds

½ teaspoon salt
1 container (8 ounces) sour cream
1 container (8 ounces) cottage cheese
3 cups narrow egg noodles, cooked al dente and drained
1 cup fresh soft bread crumbs
2 tablespoons melted butter

1. In a large heavy skillet heat the oil and sauté the onions until tender but not browned. Add the garlic and cook 1 minute.
2. Add the green pepper strips and cook, stirring, 3 minutes. Sprinkle with the paprika, caraway seeds, and salt. Remove from heat and stir in the sour cream and cottage cheese. Preheat oven to 375°.
3. Fold in the noodles and turn into a buttered 2-quart casserole. Toss bread crumbs with melted butter and sprinkle over casserole. Bake at 375° for 30 minutes, or until thoroughly hot.

POLENTA
(Italian)

An old favorite that often gets overlooked.
Bake at 350° for 15 minutes.
Makes 4 servings.

1 quart water	1 can (1 pound) tomatoes, drained
1 cup yellow cornmeal	2 tablespoons chopped fresh
1½ teaspoons salt	parsley
¼ cup (½ stick) butter or margarine	1 teaspoon leaf basil, crumbled
1 medium-size onion, finely	½ teaspoon salt
chopped (½ cup)	¼ teaspoon freshly ground black
1 clove garlic, finely chopped	pepper
½ pound mushrooms, sliced	1 cup (4 ounces) freshly grated
(2 cups)	Parmesan

1. Mix 1½ cups of the water with the cornmeal and salt. In a heavy saucepan heat remaining water to boiling and gradually stir in the cornmeal mixture. Bring to a boil, stirring constantly. Lower heat and cook, stirring, about 20 minutes. Pour into an oiled 8- × 8- × 2-inch pan. Cool.
2. In a large skillet heat the butter and sauté the onion until tender but not browned. Add the garlic and mushrooms and cook, stirring, 3 minutes.
3. Add the tomatoes, parsley, basil, salt, and pepper. Bring to a boil and simmer 10 minutes. Preheat oven to 350°.
4. Cut the cooled polenta into eight pieces and arrange overlapping in four individual au gratin dishes or in one shallow casserole. Spoon the sauce over, sprinkle with the Parmesan, and bake at 350° for 15 minutes, or until hot and cheese has melted.

Note: Polenta can be served hot with melted butter and freshly grated Parmesan or shredded mozzarella.

STIR-FRIED BEAN CURD
WITH VEGETABLES
(Chinese)

Bean curd is a bland, white spongy product that takes on the flavors of other ingredients, especially seasonings.
Makes 6 servings.

2 to 4 tablespoons vegetable oil
1 pound bean curd (tofu), cut into 1-inch cubes
¼ pound snow peas
½ pound mushrooms, sliced if large

2 cups bean sprouts
1 teaspoon salt
1 tablespoon cornstarch
1 tablespoon soy sauce
½ cup water

1. In a wok or heavy skillet heat the oil and stir-fry the bean curd pieces until lightly browned. Remove with slotted spoon and keep them warm.
2. Add the snow peas to wok and stir-fry 2 minutes. Add to bean curd. Stir-fry the mushrooms 2 minutes. Add the bean sprouts and stir-fry 1 minute. Sprinkle with the salt.
3. In a small bowl mix the cornstarch with the soy sauce and the water very well. Stir into bean sprout mixture and cook until thickened, 30 seconds.
4. Return the bean curd and snow peas to wok and reheat. Sprinkle with toasted sesame seeds, if you wish.

Note: Sesame seeds can be toasted in a small skillet over medium heat while shaking frequently to prevent burning.

BEAN-TAMALE PIE
(Mexican)

This dish is good, if not better, when reheated the following day.
Bake at 350° for 50 minutes.
Makes 6 to 8 servings.

3 tablespoons peanut oil
1 large onion, finely chopped (1 cup)
2 cloves garlic, finely chopped
2 to 3 tablespoons chili powder
1 teaspoon ground cumin
1 small green pepper, seeded and chopped
1 can (2 pounds, 3 ounces) peeled plum tomatoes, drained and coarsely chopped (1½ to 2 cups)

1 teaspoon salt
1 cup whole kernel corn
2 cups refried beans (see page 238)
1¾ cups yellow cornmeal
1¾ cups cold water
4 cups boiling water
2 teaspoons salt
3 tablespoons lard or margarine
1½ cups (6 ounces) shredded Monterey Jack or Muenster

1. In a large skillet heat the oil and sauté the onion and garlic until soft. Add chili powder, cumin, and green pepper. Toss to coat onion and cook, stirring, about 2 minutes.

2. Add tomatoes and salt and cook over medium-high heat until juices have evaporated and sauce is thickened, about 15 minutes. Stir in corn and refried beans.

3. In a 3-quart saucepan combine cornmeal and cold water. Gradually stir in the boiling water. Add salt and lard and bring to a boil. Cover, reduce heat, and simmer for 30 minutes, stirring occasionally, until thickened. Preheat oven to 350°.

4. Line the bottom and sides of a 13- × 9- × 2-inch baking dish with two-thirds of the cornmeal mixture. Top with tomato-bean mixture, allowing the cornmeal to form a border around edges. Top with remaining cornmeal and spread to cover the tomato-bean mixture completely. Sprinkle with the cheese and bake at 350° for 50 minutes, or until lightly browned and set.

BEAN CROQUETTES
(Mexican)

These vegetable burgers make a focal point for an all-vegetable
Mexican combination plate.
Bake at 425° for 15 minutes.
Makes 6 servings.

3 tablespoons peanut oil
1 teaspoon ground cumin
1 tablespoon grated onion
3 tablespoons flour
¾ cup chicken broth or vegetable broth (see page 59)
½ cup (2 ounces) shredded Monterey Jack or mild Cheddar
2 cups cooked black, pinto, or pink beans, mashed

1 egg, lightly beaten
3 to 4 serrano chili peppers, seeded and finely chopped
½ teaspoon salt
1 cup cooked rice (⅓ cup raw)
¾ cup (1½ sticks) margarine
4 cups fresh bread crumbs
   Flour
1 egg, lightly beaten

1. Heat the oil in a small saucepan. Add the cumin and onion and sauté 3 to 4 minutes. Stir in the flour and cook, stirring, 2 to 3 minutes. Gradually stir in the broth and bring to a boil, stirring until mixture is thick and smooth. Remove from heat and stir in the cheese. Cool.

2. Combine the cooled sauce, beans, egg, chilies, salt, and rice in a medium-size bowl. Cover and chill 1 to 2 hours. Meanwhile melt the margarine in a large skillet and sauté the bread crumbs until lightly browned. (Unless you have a very large skillet it is best to do this in two batches.) Preheat oven to 425°.

3. Form chilled croquette mixture into flat ovals, using about 2 table-spoons of the mixture for each. Drop into flour and coat lightly. Drop into unbeaten egg, coat, and roll in bread crumbs. Place on a lightly greased cookie sheet and bake at 425° for about 15 minutes, or until crispy.

STUFFED CABBAGE
(Italian)

Trimmed and blanched large spinach, kale, Swiss chard, or mustard greens can be used in place of cabbage.
Bake at 350° for 30 minutes.
Makes 6 servings.

1 medium-size head of cabbage
¼ cup vegetable oil
1 large onion, finely chopped (1 cup)
1 clove garlic, finely chopped
1 teaspoon salt
½ teaspoon freshly ground black pepper
1 cup raw long-grain rice
2 cups water
1 package (10 ounces) frozen chopped spinach, thawed and squeezed dry
¼ teaspoon ground nutmeg

½ cup chopped celery
2 tablespoons lemon juice
1 container (15 ounces) ricotta
1 can (16 ounces) tomato sauce
1 medium-size onion, finely chopped (½ cup)
1 clove garlic, finely chopped
1 teaspoon leaf basil, crumbled
½ teaspoon leaf oregano, crumbled
2 tablespoons chopped fresh parsley
¼ teaspoon salt
¼ cup (1 ounce) freshly grated Parmesan

1. Plunge the cabbage into a large kettle of boiling salted water and simmer 8 to 10 minutes, or until the leaves can be removed without breaking.
2. Remove enough large leaves, or put 2 smaller ones together, to make 18 wrappers for cabbage rolls.
3. Meanwhile heat the oil in a medium-size saucepan and sauté the onion until tender but not browned. Add garlic and cook 1 minute. Add the salt, pepper, rice, and water. Bring to a boil, cover, and simmer 20 minutes, or until liquid has been absorbed.
4. Add the spinach, nutmeg, celery, lemon juice, and ricotta and mix well. Divide the rice mixture among the cabbage leaves and wrap up, tucking in the sides to enclose filling. Place in a double thickness of muslin and squeeze to form neat tight packages. Remove muslin and place rolls seam side down in a shallow 3-quart baking dish. Preheat oven to 350°.
5. Meanwhile heat the tomato sauce with the onion, garlic, basil, oregano, parsley, and salt. Simmer 10 minutes. Pour over cabbage rolls. Cover with aluminum foil and bake at 350° for 15 minutes. Sprinkle with the Parmesan and bake, uncovered, for 15 minutes, or until thoroughly hot.

STUFFED CABBAGE ROLLS
(Hungarian)

Cheese-flavored rice fills these cabbage rolls.
Makes 6 servings.

Sauce

2 tablespoons vegetable oil
1 large onion, finely chopped
  (1 cup)
2 cloves garlic, finely chopped
1 can (2 pounds, 3 ounces) Italian
  plum tomatoes
1 can (6 ounces) tomato paste
1 teaspoon salt
¼ teaspoon freshly ground black
  pepper
1 teaspoon leaf oregano, crumbled
1 teaspoon leaf basil, crumbled

Rolls

1 cup raw long-grain rice
2 cups water
½ teaspoon salt
1 medium-size head of green
  cabbage (1½ to 2 pounds)
2 tablespoons vegetable oil
1 large Spanish or Bermuda onion,
  thinly sliced
1 stalk celery, thinly sliced
1 teaspoon sweet paprika
  Pinch of cayenne, optional
1 egg, lightly beaten
¼ cup chopped fresh parsley
½ cup (2 ounces) shredded
  Muenster, Monterey Jack, or
  mild Cheddar

1. To make the sauce heat the oil in a heavy saucepan and sauté the onion until tender but not browned. Add the garlic and cook 1 minute.

2. Add the tomatoes, tomato paste, salt, pepper, oregano, and basil. Bring to a boil and simmer 25 minutes, or until slightly thickened.

3. In a medium saucepan place the rice, water, and salt and bring to a boil. Cover and simmer for 20 minutes, or until water is absorbed.

4. Remove the core and any damaged outside leaves from the cabbage and plunge it into a kettle of boiling water for 5 minutes, or until the leaves can be pulled off easily.

5. Meanwhile heat the oil in a skillet and sauté the onion and celery until wilted. Sprinkle with the paprika and cayenne. Mix in the cooked rice, egg, parsley, and cheese. Toss to mix. Fill each large cabbage leaf with several tablespoons of the rice filling. Roll up, tucking in the edges to make a neat roll. Place roll in a piece of cheesecloth and gradually squeeze the bundle until the roll is firm and will hold its shape when taken from the cheesecloth.

6. Place a layer of tomato sauce in a large heavy skillet or sauté pan. Add cabbage rolls as they are made. Put more sauce between rows and pour over remaining sauce. Cover, bring to a boil, and simmer 45 minutes. Serve with boiled potatoes, if you wish.

EGGPLANT PARMIGIANA
(Italian)

An old favorite brought up to date.
Bake at 350° for 20 minutes.
Makes 4 servings.

1 medium-size eggplant (1 to 1¼ pounds), peeled and cut into ⅓-inch slices
Salt
¾ cup olive or vegetable oil, approximately
1 clove garlic, finely chopped
1 large onion, finely chopped (1 cup)
2 cans (2 pounds, 3 ounces each) peeled plum tomatoes, drained and coarsely chopped

1 teaspoon leaf basil, crumbled
1 teaspoon leaf oregano, crumbled
1 teaspoon salt
½ teaspoon freshly ground black pepper
1 tablespoon flour
1 egg, lightly beaten
1½ cups (6 to 8 ounces) shredded mozzarella
½ cup (2 ounces) freshly grated Parmesan

1. Sprinkle the eggplant slices with salt and let stand 30 minutes. Meanwhile, heat 3 tablespoons of the oil in a heavy saucepan and sauté the garlic and onion until tender but not browned. Add tomatoes and cook over high heat for 15 minutes to thicken.
2. Add basil, oregano, salt, and pepper and cook over moderate heat for 10 minutes.
3. Rinse off the eggplant slices and dry on paper towels.
4. Dip slices in the flour beaten with the egg. Heat remaining oil in a heavy skillet and fry the slices in a single layer until lightly browned on both sides. Add more oil if necessary. Drain on paper towels. Preheat oven to 350°.
5. Cover the bottom of a 7- × 11-inch baking dish with 3 to 4 tablespoons tomato sauce and alternate layers of eggplant, tomato sauce, mozzarella, and Parmesan, ending with Parmesan.
6. Bake at 350° for 20 minutes, or until bubbly hot, and let stand 10 minutes before serving.

VEGETABLE MOUSSAKA
(Greek)

All the goodies in an authentic moussaka except the meat.
Bake at 350° for 45 minutes.
Makes 6 servings.

1 large eggplant (about 1½ pounds), peeled and cut into ½-inch slices
Salt
Flour
⅓ cup olive or vegetable oil, approximately
2 large onions, finely chopped (2 cups)
3 cloves garlic, finely chopped
2 carrots, diced
½ teaspoon ground cinnamon
½ teaspoon leaf oregano, crumbled
1 bay leaf, crumbled
1 teaspoon salt
½ teaspoon freshly ground black pepper
1 can (2 pounds, 3 ounces) Italian plum tomatoes
3 zucchini, sliced
¼ cup chopped fresh parsley
3 cups hot cooked rice (1 cup raw)
½ cup chopped walnuts
¼ cup (½ stick) butter or margarine
¼ cup flour
2½ cups light cream or milk
1 cup ricotta
3 eggs, lightly beaten
½ cup (2 ounces) freshly grated Parmesan

1. Sprinkle the eggplant slices with salt and set aside for 15 minutes. Rinse and pat dry on paper towels. Dust lightly with flour.
2. In a large heavy skillet heat the oil and fry the eggplant slices until tender and lightly browned. Drain on paper towels.
3. Add more oil if necessary and sauté the onions until tender but not browned. Add garlic and carrot and cook 3 minutes. Add cinnamon, oregano, bay leaf, salt, black pepper, and tomatoes. Bring to a boil and simmer 5 minutes. Add zucchini and simmer 3 minutes. Stir in the parsley. Mix the rice and nuts.
4. In a large lightly oiled baking dish or roasting pan (3- to 4-quart capacity) place a layer of eggplant, a layer of rice, and a layer of tomato sauce. Repeat until all ingredients are used. Preheat oven to 350°.
5. In a small saucepan melt the butter and blend in the flour. Cook, stirring, 2 minutes. Gradually stir in the cream, bring to a boil, and cook, stirring, 3 minutes. Remove from heat. Combine the ricotta and the eggs and stir into the sauce. Pour sauce over casserole.
6. Sprinkle with Parmesan and bake at 350° for 45 minutes, or until bubbly hot and lightly browned on top. Let stand 20 minutes before cutting into squares to serve.

IMAM BAYELDI
(Turkish Baked Eggplant)

Bake at 350° for 30 minutes.
Makes 4 servings.

2 medium-size eggplants (about 1¼ pounds each)
Salt
6 medium-size onions, thinly sliced and separated into rings
⅓ cup olive or vegetable oil, approximately
3 cloves garlic, finely chopped
1 can (2 pounds, 3 ounces) Italian plum tomatoes, drained

1 can (6 ounces) tomato paste
1 bay leaf
1 teaspoon leaf oregano, crumbled
¼ teaspoon freshly ground black pepper
½ cup (2 ounces) shredded mozzarella
2 tablespoons chopped fresh parsley

1. Peel the eggplants and cut into slices ¾ inch thick. Sprinkle both sides of each slice with salt and let stand 20 minutes.
2. Place the onion rings in a colander, sprinkle with salt, and toss to coat all sides. Set aside for about 30 minutes.
3. Meanwhile, heat 2 tablespoons of the oil in a medium-size saucepan. Sauté the garlic over low heat 1 minute. Add the tomatoes, tomato paste, bay leaf, oregano, and pepper. Bring to a boil and simmer 20 minutes.
4. Rinse off the eggplant slices and dry well with paper towels. Run water through the onions in the colander. Drain well and set aside.
5. Heat the remaining oil in a heavy skillet and sauté the eggplant slices, a few at a time, until they are golden on both sides. Using 2 skillets and more oil speeds up the process.
6. Drain the cooked eggplant on paper towels and arrange overlapping in a shallow 3-quart baking dish. Preheat oven to 350°.
7. When all the eggplant is cooked add the onions to the tomato sauce. Mix well, taste, and add salt if necessary. Pour over eggplant. Sprinkle with mozzarella and bake at 350° for 30 minutes, or until the eggplant is tender and the dish is bubbly hot. Sprinkle with parsley.

STUFFED EGGPLANT
(*Armenian*)

Bulgur is one of the many joys of Middle Eastern cooking.
Bake at 350° for 40 minutes.
Makes 4 servings.

2 large eggplants (1½ pounds each)
¼ cup olive or vegetable oil
1 large onion, finely chopped (1 cup)
2 cloves garlic, finely chopped
¼ pound mushrooms, sliced (1 cup)
1 cup bulgur (cracked wheat)
¾ cup vegetable broth (see page 59) or water

½ teaspoon salt
¼ teaspoon freshly ground black pepper
1 teaspoon leaf oregano, crumbled
½ cup chopped walnuts
2 tablespoons olive or vegetable oil
¼ cup freshly grated Parmesan

1. Cut the eggplants in half and scoop out the pulp to leave a ½-inch-thick shell. Dice the pulp. Set the shells in a shallow baking dish.
2. In a large heavy skillet heat the oil and sauté the onion until tender but not browned. Add eggplant pulp and cook until tender. Add the garlic, mushrooms, and bulgur and cook 3 minutes, stirring often. Add the broth, salt, pepper, and oregano.
3. Cover and simmer 20 minutes or until moisture has been absorbed. Add the nuts and spoon the mixture into the eggplant shells. Preheat oven to 350°.
4. Drizzle the oil over and sprinkle with Parmesan. Pour ½ cup water into the baking dish. Bake at 350° for 40 minutes, or until shell is tender and stuffing is lightly browned and very hot.

VEGETABLE-STUFFED EGGPLANT
(Indian)

An unusual stuffing with lentils, cashews, and chutney.
Bake at 350° for 1¼ hours.
Makes 6 servings.

¼ cup lentils, picked over and
　washed
2 tablespoons vegetable oil
1 large onion, finely chopped
　(1 cup)
1 clove garlic, finely chopped
3 small eggplants (¾ pound each)
　Salt
2 teaspoons curry powder
2 tablespoons flour

1¼ cups vegetable broth (see page
　59) or chicken broth
¼ cup unsalted cashews
2 tablespoons mango chutney
2 tablespoons lemon juice
1 teaspoon salt
3 tomatoes, peeled, seeded, and
　chopped
1 package (10 ounces) frozen peas

1. Cover lentils with cold water and bring to a boil. Cover and simmer 10 minutes. Drain.
2. In a large heavy skillet heat the oil and sauté the onion until tender but not browned. Add garlic and cook 1 minute.
3. Meanwhile cut the eggplants in half and scoop out pulp to leave a ½-inch-thick shell. Sprinkle shells and diced pulp with salt. Let stand 15 minutes. Preheat oven to 350°. Rinse eggplant well and dry with paper towels. Place eggplant halves, cut side down, in a shallow baking dish. Add ½ cup water and bake at 350° for 1 hour.
4. Add diced pulp to skillet and cook briefly. Sprinkle with the curry powder and flour and cook 2 minutes. Stir in the broth, lentils, cashews, chutney, lemon juice, salt, and tomatoes. Bring to a boil and cook, uncovered, until thick, about 20 minutes. Add the peas and cook 5 minutes, or until lentils and eggplant are done.
5. When eggplant halves are almost tender pour off water. Fill shells with lentil mixture and bake 15 minutes, or until very hot.

STUFFED EGGPLANT
(*Greek*)

Hearty main dish to enjoy with a salad and soup.
Bake at 350° for 40 minutes.
Makes 4 servings.

2 large eggplants (1½ pounds each)
¼ cup olive or vegetable oil
1 large onion, finely chopped
   (1 cup)
1 clove garlic, finely chopped
1 can (1 pound) peeled plum
   tomatoes
1 teaspoon salt
¼ teaspoon freshly ground black
   pepper
2 tablespoons chopped fresh
   parsley

2 tablespoons snipped fresh
   dillweed
½ teaspoon cinnamon
1½ cups fresh bread crumbs
½ cup (2 ounces) crumbled feta
   cheese
¼ cup pignoli (pine nuts), optional
¼ cup (1 ounce) freshly grated
   Parmesan

1. Cut the eggplants in half lengthwise and scoop out the pulp, leaving a
    ¼-inch-thick shell. Chop the pulp finely.
2. Heat the oil in a heavy skillet and sauté the onion until tender. Add
    the garlic and cook 1 minute. Add the tomatoes, salt, pepper,
    parsley, dill, and cinnamon.
3. Heat to boiling and add eggplant pulp. Cook, stirring occasionally,
    until eggplant is tender, about 15 minutes. Add bread crumbs, feta,
    and nuts. Mix well. Preheat oven to 350° degrees. Pile the eggplant
    mixture into eggplant skins. Sprinkle with Parmesan, place in a but-
    tered shallow baking dish, and bake at 350° for 40 minutes.

KALE PIE
(French)

We need to become more adventurous in using garden greens, and this is an excellent example of what can be done.
Bake at 450° for 15 minutes, then at 325° for 40 minutes.
Makes 6 servings.

Pastry for a one-crust 9-inch pie
1 bunch (about 1 pound) kale, tough stems removed and discarded, or Swiss chard
3 tablespoons olive or vegetable oil
1 large onion, finely chopped (1 cup)
1 clove garlic, finely chopped
1 tablespoon lemon juice
3 eggs, separated
1½ cups sour cream

2 tablespoons chopped fresh chives, or 2 teaspoons freeze-dried
1 tablespoon all-purpose flour
½ teaspoon salt
¼ teaspoon freshly ground black pepper
½ cup (2 ounces) freshly grated Parmesan
½ cup fresh soft bread crumbs

1. On a lightly floured board roll out the pastry to a 12-inch circle. Fit into a 9-inch pie plate, fold under the edge, and flute to make a stand-up edge. Chill.
2. Wash and shred the kale finely. Heat 2 tablespoons of the oil in a large heavy skillet and sauté the onion until tender but not browned. Add the garlic and the kale and cook until the kale wilts.
3. Drain well and squeeze if very moist. Place kale mixture in a large bowl and add the lemon juice. In a small bowl combine the egg yolks and sour cream. Sprinkle chives and flour over kale mixture and stir in. Preheat oven to 450°.
4. Stir in the egg mixture, salt, and pepper. Beat egg whites until stiff but not dry and fold into kale mixture. Pile into the prepared pie shell. Combine the cheese and bread crumbs and sprinkle over surface. Drizzle with remaining tablespoon oil.
5. Bake at 450° for 15 minutes, then at 325° for 40 minutes, or until filling is set and puffed. Let stand 10 minutes before cutting.

LENTIL-NUT BURGERS
(American)

Good-looking burgers that could persuade you to reject costly ground beef forever.
Makes 8 burgers.

1 cup dried lentils
½ cup raw brown rice
3 cups water
1 tablespoon salt
½ cup very finely ground walnuts
⅓ cup plain wheat germ
6 green onions, very finely chopped

1 slice firm bread, made into crumbs
½ teaspoon salt
¼ teaspoon freshly ground black pepper
¼ teaspoon leaf thyme, crumbled
Plain wheat germ
3 tablespoons vegetable oil

1. Pick over and wash the lentils and place in a medium-size saucepan with the brown rice, water, and salt. Bring to a boil, cover, and simmer for 50 minutes, or until lentils and rice are tender. Remove from heat and let stand 10 minutes.

2. With a potato masher mash the lentil-rice mixture along with remaining liquid.

3. Stir in nuts, wheat germ, green onions, bread crumbs, salt, pepper, and thyme. Shape into 8 patties and roll in wheat germ.

4. Heat the oil in a large heavy skillet and fry the patties until brown on both sides, about 10 minutes. Serve with scalloped tomatoes and broccoli.

CHILI-AND-CHEESE-STUFFED PEPPERS
(*Mexican*)

Instead of dipping in batter and deep-frying, these stuffed peppers are baked in tomato sauce.
Bake at 350° for 15 to 20 minutes.
Makes 3 or 4 servings.

6 long thin Italian-style peppers (bell peppers can be substituted)
1½ cups (6 ounces) shredded Monterey Jack or mild Cheddar
2 serrano chili peppers, seeded and finely chopped
¼ cup peanut oil
1 small onion, finely chopped (¼ cup)
4 cloves garlic, finely chopped
2 cups tomatoes, peeled, seeded, and chopped, or drained chopped canned tomatoes

¼ teaspoon ground cloves
½ teaspoon ground cinnamon
½ bay leaf, crumbled
¼ teaspoon leaf thyme, crumbled
¼ teaspoon freshly ground black pepper
1 teaspoon salt
1 teaspoon sugar
2 cups chicken broth or vegetable broth (see page 59)

1. Holding the peppers on the end of a long fork, grill over a gas flame or place under the broiler, turning often, until black and blistered. Wrap in a damp towel or place in a brown paper bag until cool enough to handle. Peel.
2. Make a slit in the side of each pepper and remove seeds and veins. Combine cheese and chili peppers and stuff each pepper with the mixture. Set aside.
3. Heat the oil in a large skillet, add onion and garlic, and sauté until limp. Add tomatoes, cloves, cinnamon, bay leaf, thyme, pepper, salt, and sugar and cook 10 minutes. Add broth and cook over medium-high heat, uncovered, until sauce has cooked down and is thick. Preheat oven to 350°.
4. Place about ¾ to 1 cup sauce in the bottom of a baking dish large enough to hold the peppers in a single layer. Arrange peppers on top of sauce and pour remaining sauce over and additional cheese, if you wish. Bake at 350° for 15 to 20 minutes, or until heated through and the cheese is melted.

POTATO AND CHEESE CURRY
(American)

It is possible to use bean curd (tofu) in place of the cheese.
Makes 4 servings.

⅓ cup butter or margarine
8 ounces farmer cheese or fresh
   mozzarella, cut into 1-inch cubes
1 large onion, finely chopped
   (1 cup)
1 clove garlic, finely chopped
1 teaspoon salt
1 teaspoon ground ginger

1 large tomato, peeled and
   chopped
2 large potatoes, peeled and diced
½ teaspoon turmeric
½ teaspoon ground cumin
½ teaspoon chili powder
1 teaspoon ground coriander

1. Heat the oil in a large heavy skillet and sauté the cheese quickly to brown. Remove and drain on paper towels.
2. In the butter remaining in skillet sauté the onion until tender but not browned. Add garlic and cook 1 minute. Sprinkle with salt and ginger and add tomato. Add 2 cups water and bring to a boil. Add potatoes, turmeric, cumin, chili powder, and coriander. Bring to a boil, cover, and simmer until potatoes are tender, about 20 minutes. Add cheese and serve over hot cooked rice, if you wish.

POTATO AND SOUR CREAM PIE
(German)

Hearty enough for a main dish. All you need to add is a spinach
and mushroom salad.
Bake at 400° for 50 minutes.
Makes 8 servings.

2 large baking potatoes
2 tablespoons butter or margarine
1 tablespoon warm milk
1 container (1 pound) small-curd
   cottage cheese
1 container (8 ounces) sour cream
¼ cup (1 ounce) shredded Swiss or
   Gruyère
2 eggs, lightly beaten

2 teaspoons salt
½ teaspoon freshly ground black
   pepper
¼ cup very finely chopped green
   onion
2 tablespoons chopped chives, or
   2 teaspoons freeze-dried
1 unbaked 10-inch pie shell

1. Bake or boil the potatoes until tender. Peel and mash in a large bowl with the butter and milk until smooth. Preheat oven to 400°.
2. Beat in the cottage cheese, sour cream, Swiss cheese, eggs, salt, pepper, green onion, and chives until smooth. Pour into pie shell and bake at 400° for 50 minutes, or until filling is puffed and golden and shell is cooked.

POTATO-STUFFED DUMPLINGS
(Russian)

Excellent with two colorful puréed vegetables such as broccoli and carrots. Serve fruit and cheese for dessert.
Makes 4 servings.

1 cup plus 2 tablespoons sifted all-purpose flour	½ teaspoon salt
¼ teaspoon salt	¼ teaspoon freshly ground black pepper
1 teaspoon vegetable oil	1 tablespoon snipped fresh dillweed
½ cup boiling water, approximately	
1½ pounds potatoes, peeled and cut into chunks	6 tablespoons (¾ stick) butter or margarine, melted
¼ cup large-curd cottage cheese	Sour cream

1. Place the flour, salt, and oil in a bowl. Using a fork gradually stir in the boiling water to make a crumbly mixture. Let cool. On a lightly floured board knead the dough until smooth and elastic. Cover with a damp towel and let rest 15 minutes.
2. Meanwhile cook the potatoes in boiling salted water to cover until tender, about 15 minutes. Drain and mash until smooth. Beat in the cheese, salt, pepper, and dill. Cool to room temperature.
3. Divide dough into 12 pieces and roll out each piece to a round about 5 inches in diameter. Keep dough and rolled pieces covered.
4. Place 1½ tablespoons potato mixture on each circle. Gather dough up and around the filling and pinch to close. Cover with a damp cloth.
5. Drop dumplings, two or three at a time, into a large kettle of boiling salted water and cook 3 minutes or until done. Remove to a warm serving dish with a slotted spoon and keep warm. Cook remaining dumplings. Pour butter over and serve with sour cream, if you wish.

SPINACH PIE
(Greek)

Spectacular but easy.
Bake at 350° for 1 hour.
Makes 10 servings.

2 packages (10 ounces each) frozen
   chopped spinach
1 cup (2 sticks) unsalted butter or
   margarine
2 bunches green onions, chopped
2 cups (8 ounces) feta cheese,
   crumbled
1 carton (8 ounces) pot or farmer
   cheese*

6 eggs, lightly beaten
¼ cup fresh bread crumbs
½ cup chopped fresh parsley
⅓ cup snipped fresh dillweed
¾ teaspoon salt
¼ teaspoon freshly ground black
   pepper
1 package (1 pound) phyllo pastry
   or strudel leaves

1.   Thaw the spinach and squeeze out as much liquid as possible. Put in a medium-size bowl.

2.   Heat 3 tablespoons of the butter in a skillet and sauté the green onions until tender but not browned. Add to the spinach.

3.   Add feta and pot cheeses, eggs, bread crumbs, parsley, dill, salt, and pepper to spinach mixture and mix well. Melt remaining butter.

4.   Unfold the phyllo dough and cover with a damp towel. Remove sheets one at a time and arrange in a buttered 13- × 9- × 2-inch baking dish. Brush each sheet with the melted butter. Repeat, fitting 6 more sheets and buttering each one.

5.   Spread spinach mixture over pastry and top with 8 more buttered sheets of pastry. Brush top with butter. Heat oven to 375°. Cut through the top layers of pastry, marking it into 10 squares.

6.   Lower oven temperature to 350° and bake 1 hour, or until golden. Let stand 10 minutes and cut into squares as marked.

*Dry curd low-fat cottage cheese can be substituted.

SPINACH PANCAKE
(German)

An unusual stacked pancake that is really tasty.
Bake at 350° for 15 minutes.
Makes 4 servings.

2 pounds loose fresh spinach, or 2 bags (10 ounces each), or 2 packages (10 ounces each) frozen chopped spinach, thawed
2 tablespoons butter or margarine
1 medium-size onion, finely chopped (½ cup)
¾ teaspoon salt
¼ teaspoon freshly ground black pepper
⅛ teaspoon ground nutmeg
¼ teaspoon leaf marjoram, crumbled

⅓ cup sour cream
2 cups sifted all-purpose flour
1 teaspoon baking soda
1 teaspoon salt
2 eggs, lightly beaten
2 cups sour milk, buttermilk, or 1 cup milk plus 1 tablespoon lemon juice
2 tablespoons vegetable oil
½ cup (2 ounces) shredded Muenster, Monterey Jack, or mild Cheddar

1. Trim and clean the fresh spinach and cook in a large kettle with just the water clinging to the leaves until wilted, about 5 minutes. Drain and squeeze dry. Squeeze the thawed frozen spinach dry.
2. Meanwhile heat the butter in a large skillet and cook the onion until tender but not browned. Stir in the spinach, salt, pepper, nutmeg, marjoram, and sour cream. Reheat gently. Keep warm.
3. Place the flour, soda, and salt in a medium-size bowl. Add the eggs and gradually beat in the sour milk to give a smooth batter. Beat well. Add the oil.
4. Heat a 6- or 7-inch crêpe pan or a large griddle and butter lightly. Pour in about ⅓ to ½ cup of batter and cook until browned on underside. Turn and brown the other side. Repeat until all batter is used; you will have 5 or 6 large thick pancakes. Preheat oven to 350°.
5. Set one pancake in the bottom of a greased deep pie plate. Spread with spinach mixture and some of the cheese. Repeat layers until all ingredients are used, ending with a pancake and remaining cheese.
6. Bake at 350° for 15 minutes, or until bubbly hot and cheese on top has melted. Cut into 4 wedges and serve with homemade tomato sauce, if you wish.

MALFATTI
(Italian Spinach Dumplings)

Light and airy, these dumplings are a great way to enjoy the
perfect combination of spinach, ricotta, and Parmesan.
Bake at 350° for 20 minutes.
Makes 4 servings.

3 tablespoons butter or margarine
1 medium-size onion, finely
  chopped (½ cup)
1 clove garlic, finely chopped
1 package (10 ounces) frozen
  chopped spinach, thawed and
  squeezed dry
1 cup ricotta
½ cup (2 ounces) freshly grated
  Parmesan
2 eggs, lightly beaten

3 tablespoons flour
½ teaspoon salt
¼ teaspoon freshly ground black
  pepper
⅛ teaspoon ground nutmeg
½ cup fresh soft bread crumbs
2 teaspoons chopped fresh basil, or
  ½ teaspoon dried
2 tablespoons butter or margarine
¼ cup (1 ounce) freshly grated
  Parmesan

1. In a medium-size heavy skillet heat the butter and sauté the onion
    until tender. Add the garlic and cook 1 minute.
2. Remove from heat and transfer to a bowl. Beat in the spinach, ricotta,
    Parmesan, eggs, flour, salt, pepper, nutmeg, bread crumbs, and
    basil. Beat to mix well. Chill 20 minutes.
3. Shape spinach mixture into ½-inch ovals, dust lightly with flour, and
    set on wax paper.
4. Poach the ovals in batches in a large kettle of simmering salted water
    for 8 to 10 minutes, stirring gently to make sure they do not stick
    together. Do not boil vigorously. Remove with a slotted spoon and
    drain on paper towels. Preheat oven to 350°.
5. Repeat until all ovals have been cooked. Melt the butter in an oven-
    proof shallow casserole and place the ovals in a single layer, turning
    once in the butter. Sprinkle with the Parmesan and bake at 350° for
    20 minutes.

TIENS
(French Spinach Pie Without a Crust)

Another classic that calls for two varieties of garden greens.
Bake at 375° for 25 minutes.
Makes 4 servings.

2 tablespoons butter or margarine
2 tablespoons vegetable oil
1 pound fresh spinach, shredded
1 pound fresh kale, Swiss chard, or mustard greens, trimmed and shredded
2 medium-size onions, finely chopped (1 cup)
2 cloves garlic, finely chopped
3 small zucchini, diced

½ cup chopped fresh basil leaves, or 1 teaspoon dried
¼ cup chopped fresh parsley
1 teaspoon salt
¼ teaspoon freshly ground black pepper
6 eggs, lightly beaten
½ cup (2 ounces) shredded Swiss
½ cup (2 ounces) freshly grated Parmesan

1. Heat the butter and oil in a large heavy kettle or Dutch oven. Add the spinach and kale, cover, and cook until wilted.
2. Remove greens to a colander or strainer and press out as much liquid as possible. Return greens to kettle. Add onions, garlic, and zucchini and cook, covered, until vegetables are crisp-tender. Drain and press out liquid again. Preheat oven to 375°.
3. In a large bowl mix the greens mixture with the basil, parsley, salt, pepper, and eggs. Mix well. Turn into an extra-deep greased 10-inch pie plate or shallow baking dish.
4. Sprinkle with the cheeses and bake at 375° for 25 minutes or until set. Allow to stand 10 minutes before cutting into wedges or squares. Or serve at room temperature.

ZUCCHINI PARMIGIANA
(Italian)

Great way to utilize some excess zucchini crop.
Bake at 375° for 25 minutes.
Makes 4 servings.

4 medium-size zucchini, sliced
¼ inch thick
2 tablespoons vegetable oil
1 medium-size onion, finely
chopped (½ cup)
1 clove garlic, finely chopped
1 can (1 pound) tomatoes
2 tablespoons tomato paste

1 tablespoon chopped fresh basil,
or ½ teaspoon leaf, crumbled
¾ teaspoon salt
¼ teaspoon freshly ground black
pepper
2 tablespoons freshly grated
Parmesan
6 ounces mozzarella, thinly sliced

1. In a medium-size heavy skillet sauté the zucchini in the oil until lightly browned, about 5 minutes. Arrange zucchini in overlapping pattern in a heatproof baking dish. Add the onion and garlic to skillet and cook 3 minutes, stirring frequently.
2. Add tomatoes, tomato paste, basil, salt, and pepper. Bring to a boil and cook, uncovered, 10 minutes. Preheat oven to 375°.
3. Stir in the Parmesan. Pour over zucchini, top with mozzarella, and bake at 375° for 25 minutes.

STUFFED ZUCCHINI
(Greek)

A good-looking addition to a buffet table.
Bake at 350° for 30 minutes.
Makes 6 servings.

6 medium-size zucchini
¼ cup olive or vegetable oil
1 large onion, chopped (1 cup)
1 clove garlic, finely chopped
1 cup chopped celery
⅓ cup raw long-grain rice
1 teaspoon salt
¼ teaspoon freshly ground black
pepper

¾ cup vegetable broth (see page 59)
or chicken broth
¾ cup fresh soft bread crumbs
⅓ cup lemon juice
¼ cup chopped walnuts
2 eggs, separated
⅓ cup freshly grated Parmesan
Vegetable broth (see page 59) or
chicken broth

1. Cut the zucchini in half lengthwise and scoop out the pulp, leaving a ¼-inch shell. Dice the pulp and reserve. Preheat oven to 350°.

2. In a medium-size heavy saucepan heat the oil and sauté the onion until tender but not browned. Add the garlic, celery, and rice and cook, stirring, until rice is translucent, about 8 minutes.
3. Add salt, pepper, and broth and bring to a boil. Cover and simmer 15 minutes. Add the diced zucchini, bread crumbs, 3 tablespoons of the lemon juice, nuts, and egg whites. Pile into zucchini shells set in a shallow baking dish.*
4. Sprinkle with grated Parmesan and bake at 350° for 30 minutes or until hot and brown.
5. In a small saucepan combine the egg yolks with remaining lemon juice and the drippings from the baking dish, made up to ¾ cup with vegetable or chicken broth or water. Heat, stirring, over low heat until mixture thickens but do not boil. Serve stuffed zucchini topped with lemon sauce.

*Extra stuffing can be put into custard cups or ramekins and baked along with the zucchini.

MIXED VEGETABLE CURRY
(Indian)

Other combinations of vegetables can be used instead of carrots, potatoes, cauliflower, beans, and peas.
Makes 4 servings.

⅓ cup vegetable oil	1 small head of cauliflower, cut into small flowerets
2 large onions, finely chopped (2 cups)	2 medium-size tomatoes, peeled, seeded, and chopped
3 cloves garlic, finely chopped	¼ pound green beans, cut into 1-inch lengths
2 bay leaves, crumbled	1 cup fresh or frozen peas
2 hot green chilies, chopped	1 teaspoon turmeric
2 carrots, diced	1½ teaspoons salt
2 medium-size potatoes, peeled and diced	1 cup water

1. In a large heavy saucepan or Dutch oven heat the oil and sauté the onion until tender but not browned. Add the garlic, bay leaves, and chilies and cook, stirring, about 5 minutes.
2. Add the carrot, potato, and cauliflower, and cook, stirring, 5 minutes.
3. Add the tomatoes and green beans and cook 5 minutes. Add the peas, turmeric, salt, and water. Bring to a boil, cover, and simmer, stirring occasionally, until vegetables are crisp-tender, about 15 minutes.

COLD VEGETABLE ROLL
(Spanish)

Serve with mayonnaise to accompany cold chicken or as part of
a cold vegetable or salad platter.
Makes 6 servings.

2 pounds red-skinned potatoes or
  other waxy boiling potatoes
  Boiling salted water
2 tablespoons butter or margarine
  Warm milk
1 teaspoon salt
¼ teaspoon freshly ground black
  pepper
3 tablespoons olive or vegetable oil
1 large onion, finely chopped
  (1 cup)

2 cloves garlic, finely chopped
½ cup diced cooked carrots
½ cup diced green pepper
½ cup cooked peas
½ cup diced well drained cooked
  zucchini
½ cup (2 ounces) finely diced
  Muenster, optional
  Mayonnaise

1. Cook the potatoes in boiling salted water until tender, about 25 minutes depending on size. Peel and place in a mixing bowl with the butter. Mash potatoes until light and fluffy, smooth and dry, adding only a minimum of warm milk. Season with salt and pepper.

2. Spread the mashed potatoes on greased wax paper to a rectangle about 9 × 12 inches. Heat the oil in a skillet and sauté the onion until tender but not browned. Add the garlic and cook 1 minute. Remove from heat.

3. Add the carrots, green pepper, peas, zucchini, and cheese. Toss to mix. Add a tablespoon or two of mayonnaise, just enough to make vegetables cling together.

4. Spread the vegetable mixture over the mashed potatoes. Roll up the mashed potatoes starting at the long side, enclosing the vegetables, and using a spatula to loosen from wax paper. Place on a platter and chill at least 1 hour.

MIDDLE EASTERN VEGETABLE KEBABS

Try to cut the vegetables into even-size pieces so that they cook
in the same length of time.
Makes 4 servings.

2 medium-size zucchini, cut into
½-inch thick slices
½ pound medium-size mushroom
caps
8 small white onions, steamed until
crisp-tender, about 15 minutes
2 medium-size green peppers,
seeded and cut into 1½-inch
squares
2 medium-size sweet red peppers,
seeded and cut into 1½-inch
cubes
1 small eggplant, cut into 1-inch
cubes and steamed 10 minutes

½ cup olive or vegetable oil
3 tablespoons lemon juice
½ teaspoon salt
¼ teaspoon freshly ground black
pepper
1 clove garlic, finely chopped
½ teaspoon oregano
3 cups hot cooked rice (1 cup raw)
½ cup chopped walnuts
⅓ cup crumbled feta cheese
¼ cup Greek olives, pitted and
sliced

1. Place the zucchini, mushrooms, onions, green and red peppers, and
   eggplant in a large glass or ceramic shallow dish. In a small bowl
   combine the oil, lemon juice, salt, pepper, garlic, and oregano. Pour
   over vegetables. Toss gently and marinate 2 to 3 hours.
2. Alternate the vegetables on 4 individual skewers and broil over charcoal or under the broiler for 5 minutes, or until vegetables are cooked
   and lightly browned. Brush with remaining marinade during cooking
   and turn frequently.
3. Meanwhile combine the rice, walnuts, feta, and olives. Serve the
   kebabs on top of the rice.

BROWN RICE AND
VEGETABLE CASSEROLE
(American)

Hearty main dish served with a chick-pea or kidney bean salad.
Bake at 400° for 20 minutes.
Makes 4 servings.

2 tablespoons vegetable oil
1 cup raw brown rice
1 medium-size onion, finely
chopped (½ cup)
2 cups vegetable broth
(see page 59)
½ teaspoon salt
¼ teaspoon leaf oregano, crumbled
3 tablespoons vegetable oil
1 large onion, finely chopped
(1 cup)
1 clove garlic, finely chopped

2 cups cauliflowerets
2 cups broccoli flowerets
1 can (6 ounces) water chestnuts,
drained and roughly chopped
1 cup raw unsalted cashews or
walnuts, toasted at 250° for 25
minutes
2 tablespoons soy sauce
½ cup sour cream
2 cups (8 ounces) shredded
Monterey Jack or mild Cheddar
¼ cup chopped fresh parsley

1. In a heavy saucepan or casserole heat the oil and sauté the brown rice and onion until rice begins to brown. Add broth, salt, and oregano. Cover and simmer 40 minutes, or until rice is tender.

2. Meanwhile heat the oil in a wok or heavy skillet and sauté the onion until tender but not browned. Add garlic, cauliflowerets, and broccoli flowerets and stir-fry 3 minutes.

3. Add the water chestnuts, cashews, soy sauce, and sour cream and mix well. Preheat oven to 400°.

4. Place the cooked brown rice in the bottom of a greased 3-quart casserole or shallow baking dish. Top with the stir-fry mixture, sprinkle with the cheese and parsley, and bake at 400° for 20 minutes.

BROWN RICE

Makes 4 servings.

1 cup raw brown rice	1 teaspoon salt
	2½ cups water

Place rice, salt, and water in a medium-size saucepan. Bring to a boil, cover, and simmer 45 minutes, or until rice is tender and water has been absorbed. If necessary, add more water.

RED BEANS AND RICE
(American)

Louisiana is the home of this classic combination, where it is likely to be spiked with hot pepper seasoning.
Makes 6 to 8 servings.

1 pound dried red kidney beans (pinto or cranberry can also be used)	2 green peppers, seeded and diced
	1 large onion, finely chopped (1 cup)
2 onions	2 cloves garlic, finely chopped
1 bay leaf	1 teaspoon leaf oregano, crumbled
½ teaspoon freshly ground black pepper	2 teaspoons salt
3 tablespoons vegetable oil	4 cups hot cooked rice (1½ cups raw)

1. Pick over and wash the beans and place in a deep kettle or Dutch oven. Cover with 2 quarts cold water and let soak in a cool place overnight.
2. Bring to a boil and add the onions, bay leaf, and pepper. Cover and simmer 1½ to 2 hours or until beans are tender. Cooking time depends on age and moisture content of beans.
3. Meanwhile heat the oil in a skillet and sauté peppers, onion, and garlic until tender but not browned. Add oregano and salt.
4. Drain excess water from beans or evaporate by boiling with cover off. Add sautéed vegetables and reheat. Serve over rice.

GREEN RICE CASSEROLE
(American)

Plain broiled, steamed, or poached fish is complemented by
the appearance and flavor of green rice; omit the cheese, if you
wish.
Bake at 350° for 45 minutes.
Makes 6 servings.

¼ cup (½ stick) butter or margarine
1 large onion, finely chopped
　(1 cup)
3 cups cooked rice (1 cup raw)
2 cups (8 ounces) shredded sharp
　Cheddar

1 cup chopped fresh parsley
½ teaspoon salt
¼ teaspoon freshly ground black
　pepper
2 eggs, lightly beaten
2 cups milk

1. In a small skillet heat the butter and sauté the onion until tender but
   not browned. Preheat oven to 350°.
2. In a greased casserole combine the rice, cheese, parsley, salt, pepper, and cooked onion mixture. Toss to mix. Combine the eggs and
   milk and pour over rice. Bake at 350° for 45 minutes, or until set.

SAFFRON RICE
(Indian)

Serving curry? Then this is the perfect rice to go with it.
Makes 4 servings.

3 tablespoons vegetable oil
1 large onion, finely chopped
　(1 cup)
1½ cups raw long-grain rice
½ teaspoon leaf saffron, or
　1 teaspoon turmeric
¼ cup boiling water
1 teaspoon salt

4 whole cloves
1 cinnamon stick, broken into 4
　pieces
4 cardamom pods, crushed
3 cups boiling water
¼ cup golden raisins
¼ cup unsalted cashews

1. In a heavy saucepan heat the oil and sauté the onion until tender but not browned. Add the rice and cook, stirring occasionally, for 5 minutes.
2. Meanwhile soak the saffron in ¼ cup boiling water. If using turmeric omit soaking.
3. Add soaked saffron, salt, cloves, cinnamon, cardamom, and 3 cups boiling water. Cover and simmer 15 minutes, or until the rice has absorbed the water. Add raisins and cook 5 minutes.
4. Serve sprinkled with the cashews.

TOMATO RISOTTO
(Italian)

Quick and easy but rewarding.
Bake at 375° for 25 minutes.
Makes 4 servings.

2 tablespoons butter or margarine	1 can (13¾ ounces) chicken broth, or 2 cups vegetable broth (see page 59)
1 medium-size onion, finely chopped (½ cup)	
1 clove garlic, finely chopped	1 teaspoon salt
1 cup raw long-grain rice	¼ teaspoon freshly ground black pepper
2 large ripe tomatoes, peeled, seeded, and chopped	½ teaspoon leaf oregano, crumbled

1. In a medium-size heavy ovenproof casserole melt the butter and sauté the onion until tender but not browned. Add the garlic and rice and cook, stirring, 5 minutes over low heat. Preheat oven to 375°.
2. Add the tomato, broth, salt, pepper, and oregano and bring to a boil. Cover and bake at 375° for 25 minutes, or until rice has absorbed the liquid.

RISOTTO WITH VEGETABLES
(Italian)

Serve risotto as a separate course, instead of a pasta dish before the main meat, fish, or poultry. Portions of everything to follow can be smaller, and the variety is exciting.
Makes 4 servings.

2 tablespoons olive or vegetable oil
1 medium-size zucchini, diced (1 cup)
¼ pound mushrooms, diced (about 1 cup)
3 to 4 green onions, sliced (about ¼ cup)
2 tablespoons butter or margarine

1 cup Aborio (imported from Italy) rice or raw long-grain rice
3½ to 4 cups (two 13¾ ounce cans) chicken broth
½ teaspoon salt
½ teaspoon freshly ground black pepper
½ teaspoon leaf marjoram, crumbled

1. Heat the oil in a medium-size heavy skillet and sauté the zucchini, mushrooms, and green onions until tender and just starting to brown, about 10 minutes. Remove from heat and set aside.
2. Heat the butter in a medium-size saucepan and add the rice. Cook, stirring, until rice starts to turn golden, but do not burn.
3. Add 1 cup chicken broth and cook, stirring, over high heat until rice absorbs the liquid. Add ½ cup more broth and cook until absorbed. Continue adding broth and cooking until rice is tender and most of broth has been used. Stir in the sautéed vegetables, salt, pepper, and marjoram.

WILD RICE AND MUSHROOMS
(American)

If you prefer rice with a nuttier, stronger flavor rinse the grain once only and proceed to step 2. Cooking time will be increased to a total of 50 to 60 minutes.
Makes 6 servings.

1 cup raw wild rice
1 can (13¾ ounces) chicken broth
½ teaspoon salt
¼ cup (½ stick) butter or margarine
1 small onion, finely chopped (½ cup)
½ pound mushrooms, sliced (2 cups)

¼ teaspoon salt
¼ teaspoon freshly ground black pepper
2 tablespoons finely chopped fresh parsley

1. Wash the rice and place in a large bowl. Cover with boiling water and let stand until lukewarm. Strain and return rice to bowl. Repeat soaking in boiling water and draining until most of the grains have opened, about four times.
2. Place rice in a large saucepan with broth and salt and bring to a boil. Cover and simmer 30 minutes, or until rice has absorbed liquid and is tender.
3. Meanwhile melt the butter in a medium-size skillet and sauté the onion until golden, about 5 minutes. Add the mushrooms and cook, stirring occasionally, until wilted, 3 minutes. Add salt, pepper, and parsley. Stir mushroom mixture into cooked rice, drained if necessary.

WILD RICE AND CARROT CASSEROLE
(American)

Wild rice is a luxury but it can be stretched by the addition of carrots and mushrooms. Great accompaniment to chicken and fish dishes.
Bake at 325° for 1 hour.
Makes 6 to 8 servings.

1½ cups raw wild rice	1 cup shredded carrots
3 cups water	¼ teaspoon freshly ground black
2 teaspoons salt	pepper
¼ cup (½ stick) butter or margarine	½ cup half-and-half
1 large onion, finely chopped	1 egg, lightly beaten
(1 cup)	
½ pound mushrooms, sliced	
(2 cups)	

1. Wash the rice very well. Combine with the water and salt in a medium-size saucepan. Bring to a boil and cook 15 minutes. Remove from heat and let stand 30 minutes.
2. In a large heavy casserole melt the butter and sauté the onion until tender but not browned. Add the mushrooms and cook, stirring, until wilted. Add carrots, pepper, and wild rice. Preheat oven to 325°.
3. Combine the half-and-half with the egg and stir into the casserole. Cover and bake at 325° for 30 minutes. Stir with fork. Cover and bake 15 minutes longer. Remove cover, fluff with a fork, and bake 15 minutes longer. Serve sprinkled with chopped parsley, if you wish.

GRITS CASSEROLE
(American)

An old-fashioned favorite that can make a grits fan out of the most skeptical.
Bake at 350° for 40 minutes and at 375° for 10 minutes.
Makes 4 servings.

5 cups water
1 cup hominy grits
2 cups (8 ounces) grated sharp Cheddar

½ cup (1 stick) butter or margarine
3 eggs, separated
1 teaspoon salt

1. Bring the water to a boil in a heavy saucepan. Gradually stir in the grits, bring to a boil, and cook, stirring, 25 minutes, or until very thick.
2. Stir in the cheese and butter. Beat the egg yolks lightly and spoon some of the hot mixture into them. Return to the bulk of grits in the saucepan. Add salt. Cool to room temperature.
3. Preheat oven to 350°. Beat the egg whites until stiff but not dry and fold into the cooled grits mixture. Spoon into a soufflé or baking dish and bake 40 minutes in a 350° oven. If at the end of this time the top is not browned turn the oven up to 375° and bake 10 minutes longer.

BULGUR WITH TOMATOES
(Armenian)

This mixture makes a delicious stuffing for poultry.
Makes 6 servings.

¼ cup (½ stick) butter or margarine
1 medium-size onion, finely chopped (½ cup)
2 cups bulgur (cracked wheat)
1 can (2 pounds, 3 ounces) Italian plum tomatoes
1½ teaspoons salt
½ teaspoon freshly ground black pepper

1 teaspoon leaf oregano, crumbled
1 teaspoon leaf basil, crumbled
1 large green pepper, seeded and diced
1 cup (4 ounces) shredded long-horn, Monterey Jack, or mild Cheddar
2 tablespoons chopped fresh parsley

1. In a large heavy skillet melt the butter and sauté the onion until tender but not browned. Add the bulgur and cook, stirring, until grain starts to brown.
2. Add tomatoes and their liquid, salt, pepper, oregano, basil, and green pepper. Bring to a boil, cover, and simmer 25 minutes, or until grain has absorbed the liquid and is tender. Stir in the cheese and parsley.

KASHA AND PEAS
(Russian)

Without the peas and green pepper this mixture makes an excellent poultry stuffing.
Makes 4 to 6 servings.

¼ cup (½ stick) butter or margarine
1 large onion, finely chopped (1 cup)
1 egg, lightly beaten
1 cup kasha (roasted buckwheat kernels)
2 cups water

1 teaspoon salt
1 cup ricotta
1 cup frozen peas
1 cup (4 ounces) shredded Cheddar
1 medium-size green pepper, seeded and cut into rings

1. Heat the butter in a cast-iron skillet and sauté the onion until tender but not browned. Mix egg and kasha and add to skillet. Cook, stirring constantly, until grains are separated.
2. Stir in the water and salt, bring to a boil, cover, and simmer 5 minutes. Remove from heat. Add the ricotta and peas and sprinkle with the Cheddar.
3. Broil 3 to 5 minutes until cheese melts. Garnish with green pepper rings.

GHIVETCH
(Bulgarian Vegetable Casserole)

Add and subtract vegetables but keep the total volume of vegetables more or less the same.
Bake at 350° for 1¾ hours.
Makes 8 to 10 servings.

¾ cup olive or vegetable oil
2 cloves garlic, finely chopped
¼ cup chopped fresh parsley
2 teaspoons leaf thyme, crumbled
¼ teaspoon crushed hot red pepper flakes
1 tablespoon salt
½ teaspoon freshly ground black pepper
3 medium-size potatoes, peeled and sliced
2 large onions, sliced
1 medium-size butternut squash, peeled and cubed

3 medium-size zucchini, sliced
2 green peppers, seeded and sliced
1 small cauliflower, cut into small flowerets
2 stalks celery, sliced
½ pound green beans, cut into 2-inch lengths
4 medium-size tomatoes, peeled and sliced
1 cup fresh or frozen peas
Salt

1. In a small bowl or screw-cap jar place the oil, garlic, parsley, thyme, red pepper flakes, salt, and pepper. Beat or shake to mix well. Preheat oven to 350°.
2. In a large heavy 6- to 8-quart casserole make layers of the vegetables as they are listed except for tomatoes and peas. Sprinkle each layer with some of the flavored oil mixture.
3. Cover very tightly and bake at 350° for 1¼ hours. Add the tomatoes and peas. Cover and bake 30 minutes, or until all the vegetables are tender. Taste and add salt, if needed. Although not traditional this mixture is great served with yogurt or sour cream.

RATATOUILLE
(French Vegetable Stew)

This recipe can easily be doubled if you wish to keep it in the refrigerator for 3 days or in the freezer up to 3 months.
Makes 6 servings.

⅓ cup olive or vegetable oil, approximately

2 medium-size onions, sliced

1 green pepper, seeded and sliced into ¼-inch strips

2 large zucchini, cut into ¼-inch slices

1 medium-size eggplant, peeled and cut into ¾-inch cubes

2 cloves garlic, finely chopped

1 teaspoon leaf basil, crumbled

1 teaspoon leaf oregano, crumbled

1 can (2 pounds, 3 ounces) plus 1 can (1 pound) peeled, well-drained, and coarsely chopped tomatoes

1½ teaspoons salt

¾ teaspoon freshly ground black pepper

1. Heat the oil in a large skillet and sauté the onion and green pepper until wilted. Remove with slotted spoon to a heavy casserole or Dutch oven. In the same skillet sauté the zucchini until barely tender, 5 minutes. Transfer to the casserole.

2. Add more oil if necessary and sauté the eggplant in 2 batches. Add to casserole. Add the garlic, basil, oregano, tomatoes, salt, and pepper to the skillet and bring to a boil, stirring to scrape up all browned bits.

3. Pour tomato mixture over vegetables and cook, uncovered, until vegetables are tender and mixture is thick, about 20 minutes. Check seasonings. Serve hot or lukewarm as an appetizer, side dish, or filling for omelets and crêpes.

VEGETABLE STEW
(French)

Lentils and leeks are the two ingredients that give this stew a
Gallic touch.
Makes 8 servings.

1 pounds (2 cups) lentils
5 cups water or vegetable broth
(see page 59)
3 tablespoons vegetable oil
2 leeks, well washed and thinly
sliced
1 clove garlic, finely chopped
2 stalks celery, thinly sliced
4 carrots, diced

4 large potatoes, diced
1 small white turnip, diced
1 can (16 ounces) peeled tomatoes,
drained
2 teaspoons salt
½ teaspoon freshly ground black
pepper
1 teaspoon leaf thyme, crumbled
1 tablespoon chopped fresh parsley

1. Pick over and wash the lentils and place in a heavy kettle or Dutch
   oven. Add the water and bring to a boil. Cover and simmer 50 minutes, or until lentils are almost tender.
2. Meanwhile heat the oil in a skillet and sauté the leeks until tender.
   Add the garlic, celery, carrots, potatoes, and turnip and sauté, stirring, over low heat 10 minutes.
3. Add the vegetables to the lentils. Add tomatoes, salt, pepper, and
   thyme and simmer 20 minutes, uncovered, or until the vegetables
   are tender. If there is excess liquid mash some of the lentils with a
   potato masher to thicken. Sprinkle with parsley.

CIAMBOTTA
(Italian Vegetable Stew)

Makes 6 servings.

⅔ cup olive or vegetable oil
2 large onions, sliced and separated
into rings
2 cloves garlic, finely chopped
6 small young zucchini, cut in half
crosswise and sliced lengthwise
4 potatoes, sliced lengthwise

2 green peppers, seeded and cut
into strips
2 teaspoons leaf oregano, crumbled
1½ teaspoons salt
½ teaspoon freshly ground black
pepper
1 bay leaf, crumbled

1. In a large heavy saucepan or Dutch oven heat the oil and cook the onion until tender but not browned.
2. Add remaining ingredients and toss to mix well. Cover and simmer, stirring every few minutes to prevent sticking, for 30 minutes, or until vegetables are cooked. Let stand 10 minutes before serving.

VEGETABLE CASSEROLE
(American)

Substitute cauliflower for broccoli, kale for spinach, leek for green onion, and add other vegetables on hand. This a highly flexible recipe.
Bake at 350° for 30 minutes.
Makes 8 servings.

3 tablespoons vegetable oil
3 carrots, diced
1 bunch green onions, sliced, including the green part
2 stalks celery, sliced
1 large green pepper, seeded and diced
2 cups small broccoli flowerets, blanched in boiling salted water 3 minutes and drained
1 cup shredded spinach
½ cup walnuts, coarsely chopped

3 eggs, lightly beaten
4 cups cooked brown rice (see page 221)
1 teaspoon salt
½ teaspoon freshly ground black pepper
1 cup (4 ounces) shredded Cheddar
½ cup (1 stick) butter or margarine, melted
2 tablespoons lemon juice
3 tablespoons chopped fresh parsley

1. In a large skillet heat the oil and sauté the carrot, green onion, celery, and green pepper until tender. Preheat oven to 350°.
2. In a large bowl combine the cooked vegetables, broccoli, spinach, walnuts, eggs, brown rice, salt, and pepper. Mix well and turn into an oiled casserole. Sprinkle with cheese. Cover and bake at 350° for 30 minutes.
3. Combine butter, lemon juice, and parsley. Pour over casserole.

LETCHO
(Hungarian Vegetable Stew)

Almost every European country has a traditional vegetable
stew, and this is one of the simplest.
Makes 6 servings.

¼ cup vegetable oil
3 large onions, sliced and separated
  into rings
2 teaspoons paprika
1 eggplant, peeled and sliced
  Salt
4 medium-size green peppers,
  seeded and cut into strips

4 tomatoes, peeled and chopped,
  or 1 can (1 pound) tomatoes
  Salt to taste
¼ teaspoon freshly ground black
  pepper

1. In a large skillet heat the oil and sauté the onions over low heat until
    tender and golden. Sprinkle with the paprika and cook, stirring, 2
    minutes.
2. Meanwhile sprinkle the eggplant with salt and let stand 15 minutes.
    Rinse, dry well, and dice.
3. Add eggplant to the skillet and cook 5 minutes, stirring frequently.
    Add green pepper, tomatoes, salt, and black pepper. Bring to a boil,
    cover, and simmer 20 minutes, or until vegetables are tender.

VEGETABLE STEW
(Spanish)

Makes 6 servings.

½ cup olive or vegetable oil
2 large onions, thinly sliced and
  separated into rings
2 cloves garlic, finely chopped
3 stalks celery, sliced
3 large sweet green peppers,
  seeded and sliced lengthwise
3 red peppers, seeded and sliced
  lengthwise
2 medium-size zucchini, sliced
2 medium-size yellow squash,
  sliced

3 cups diced cooked potato
6 large tomatoes, peeled and
  chopped, or 1 can (2 pounds,
  3 ounces) Italian plum tomatoes
1½ teaspoons salt
½ teaspoon freshly ground black
  pepper
1 can (1 pound, 4 ounces)
  garbanzos (chick-peas), drained,
  rinsed, and drained

1. In a large heavy saucepan heat the oil and sauté the onion rings over low heat until golden. Add garlic and cook, stirring, 4 minutes.
2. Add the celery and green and red peppers and cook 4 minutes, stirring occasionally. Add the zucchini and squash and cook 5 minutes.
3. Add potato, tomatoes, salt, and pepper. Bring to a boil and simmer, uncovered, until thick and stewlike, about 20 minutes.
4. Add garbanzos and reheat. Serve sprinkled with parsley, if you wish.

VEGETABLE STEW
(Rumanian)

Bake this tasty vegetable mélange alongside a roasting chicken
to make double use of the energy.
Bake at 350° for 1¾ hours.
Makes 8 to 10 servings.

¾ cup olive or vegetable oil
2 cloves garlic, finely chopped
3 tablespoons chopped fresh parsley
1 teaspoon leaf thyme, crumbled
1 teaspoon leaf sage, crumbled
¼ teaspoon crushed hot red pepper flakes
1 tablespoon salt
3 medium-size potatoes, peeled and sliced
2 large onions, sliced
1 small butternut squash, peeled and cubed

3 medium-size zucchini, sliced
2 green peppers, seeded and cut into strips
1 small cauliflower, cut into flowerets
2 stalks celery, sliced
½ pound green beans, cut into 2-inch lengths
4 tomatoes, peeled and sliced, or 1 can (1 pound) tomatoes
1 cup fresh or frozen peas
Salt and freshly ground black pepper to taste

1. In a screw-top jar or small bowl combine the oil, garlic, parsley, thyme, sage, pepper flakes, and salt. Shake or beat to mix well. Preheat oven to 350°.
2. In a 6- to 8-quart casserole layer the vegetables, starting with potatoes and ending with celery. Sprinkle each layer with the oil mixture. Cover tightly and bake at 350° for 1½ hours.
3. Add the green beans, tomatoes, and peas. Cover tightly again and bake 15 minutes, or until beans are crisp-tender and other vegetables are tender. Taste and add salt and pepper, if needed. Serve hot or warm.

CHOLENT
(Israeli Vegetable Stew)

This dish is usually made with beef early on Friday to be ready
for serving on the Sabbath with no further work involved.
Bake at 200° to 250° for 6 to 24 hours.
Makes 6 servings.

1 pound dried lima beans (about
  2½ cups)
¼ cup vegetable oil
3 large onions, finely chopped
  (3 cups)
2 cloves garlic, finely chopped
4 tomatoes, peeled, seeded, and
  chopped, or 1 can (1 pound)
  tomatoes

6 medium-size red-skinned
  potatoes, scrubbed
2 teaspoons salt
½ teaspoon freshly ground black
  pepper
¼ teaspoon ground cinnamon
¼ teaspoon ground cumin
1 bay leaf, crumbled
¼ cup pearl barley
6 cups vegetable broth (see page
  59) or water

1. Pick over the beans, wash well, and place in a large bowl with water
   to cover to a depth of 2 to 3 inches. Soak at room temperature
   overnight.
2. In a large kettle or Dutch oven heat the oil and sauté the onions until
   tender but not browned. Add the garlic and cook 1 minute. Drain the
   beans and add to the kettle with the tomatoes, potatoes, salt, pepper,
   cinnamon, cumin, bay leaf, barley and broth. Preheat oven to 200°.
3. Bring to a boil, cover *very* tightly (this is important), and bake at 200°
   to 250° a minimum of 6 hours and up to 24 hours.

VEGETABLE TIMBALES
(French)

A timbale is nothing more than a molded custard but it is an
attractive addition to any main dish.
Bake at 350° for 40 minutes.
Makes 6 servings.

2 tablespoons butter
1 small onion, finely chopped
  (¼ cup)
2 stalks celery, diced
½ green pepper, seeded and diced
¼ pound mushrooms, sliced (1 cup)
2 small zucchini, diced

4 eggs, lightly beaten
¾ cup light cream or half-and-half
½ teaspoon salt
¼ teaspoon freshly ground black
  pepper
½ teaspoon leaf thyme, crumbled

1. In a large heavy skillet melt the butter and sauté the onion until tender but not browned. Add celery, green pepper, mushrooms, and zucchini and sauté, stirring frequently, until vegetables are crisp-tender. Do not overcook. Preheat oven to 350°.
2. In a small bowl mix together the eggs, cream, salt, pepper, and thyme. Pour over the vegetables and spoon the mixture into six buttered ramekins, individual soufflé dishes, or custard cups.
3. Set the dishes in a 13- × 9- × 2-inch baking dish. Place on the oven shelf and pour boiling water in outer dish to extend two-thirds up the sides of the small dishes. Bake at 350° for 40 minutes, or until set. Serve in dishes or let stand 10 minutes, loosen around the edges with a spatula, and unmold.

COLD CURRIED VEGETABLES
(Indian)

This is a wonderful addition to a summer salad plate, salad bar, or buffet at any time of year.
Makes 6 servings.

3 tablespoons butter or margarine	1 cup diced cooked potatoes
½ tart apple, peeled, cored, and chopped	1 cup cooked cauliflowerets
½ stalk celery, finely chopped	1 cup cooked peas
1 small onion, finely chopped (¼ cup)	½ cup chopped green onions
2 tablespoons curry powder	1 cup diced cooked carrot
½ teaspoon ground coriander	1 cup cooked or canned corn kernels, drained
¼ teaspoon ground ginger	½ cup chopped green pepper
1 container (8 ounces) sour cream	½ teaspoon salt
1 container (8 ounces) plain yogurt	1 tablespoon chopped fresh mint

1. In a small skillet melt the butter and sauté the apple, celery, and onion until very tender but not browned. Sprinkle with the curry powder, coriander, and ginger and cook, stirring, 2 minutes.
2. In a large bowl combine the curry mixture, sour cream, and yogurt.
3. Add the potatoes, cauliflower, peas, green onions, carrot, corn, green pepper, salt, and mint. Toss to mix and chill well before serving.

Note: Almost any cooked cubed or diced vegetable can be used in this mélange. Mix and match according to what you have.

COLACHE
(Italian Vegetable Sauté)

An Italian version of ratatouille without eggplant but with broccoli and corn added.
Makes 6 servings.

¼ cup olive or vegetable oil
1 large onion, finely chopped (1 cup)
2 cloves garlic, finely chopped
1 green pepper, seeded and diced
1 red pepper, seeded and diced
2 medium-size zucchini, sliced
2 medium-size summer squash, sliced
2 cups broccoli flowerets
¼ pound mushrooms, sliced (1 cup)

3 large tomatoes, peeled, seeded, and chopped, or 1 can (1 pound) tomatoes, drained and chopped
2 cups corn kernels cut from the cob (about 6 ears)
1½ teaspoons leaf oregano, crumbled
1½ teaspoons leaf basil, crumbled
1½ teaspoons salt
½ teaspoon freshly ground black pepper

1. In a large skillet heat the oil and sauté the onion until tender but not browned. Add the garlic and green and red peppers and sauté, stirring, 2 minutes.
2. Add the zucchini, squash, broccoli, and mushrooms and sauté, stirring, 8 to 10 minutes. Add tomatoes and bring to a boil. Add the corn, oregano, basil, salt, and pepper. Simmer 5 minutes, stirring often. Serve over rice, if you wish.

VEGETABLE TEMPURA
(Japanese)

Makes 6 servings.

2 cups sifted all-purpose flour
1 teaspoon salt
⅛ teaspoon baking soda
1 egg yolk
2 cups ice water
Vegetable oil for frying
2 medium-size zucchini, thinly sliced

1 green pepper, seeded and cut into strips
1 large onion, sliced and separated into rings
½ pound button mushrooms
1 cup broccoli flowerets, steamed 5 minutes

1. In an electric blender combine the flour, salt, baking soda, egg yolk, and water. Blend to mix. Let stand 15 minutes.
2. Heat 3 to 4 inches of oil in a deep heavy kettle, deep-fat fryer, or electric wok until it registers 375° on a deep-fat thermometer.
3. Test batter consistency by dipping one piece of vegetable and letting excess drip off. There should be a light coating left on. Dip and fry, a few at a time, in the hot oil until golden. Drain on paper towels and keep warm in the oven heated to 250° until all are cooked.

VEGETABLES WITH GREEN SAUCE
(Italian)

The green sauce is also good over pasta or single vegetables.
Makes 8 servings.

3 medium-size zucchini, sliced, blanched in boiling salted water 2 minutes, drained, and plunged into ice water

½ pound whole green beans, steamed 5 to 8 minutes and drained

½ head of cauliflower, cut into small flowerets and steamed 5 minutes

2 pounds small new potatoes (red-skinned if available), scrubbed and cooked in boiling salted water 15 minutes or until done

2 pounds fresh peas, shelled, cooked briefly, and drained

1 stalk fennel, sliced and steamed 5 minutes

4 carrots, sliced and steamed 8 minutes

8 hard-cooked eggs, quartered

½ cup olive or vegetable oil

1 large onion, finely chopped (1 cup)

2 cloves garlic, crushed

1 cup shredded fresh spinach

½ cup chopped watercress

¼ cup chopped fresh parsley, flat Italian variety, if available

½ teaspoon salt

¼ teaspoon freshly ground black pepper

¼ cup dry vermouth

½ cup vegetable broth (see page 59) or water

1. As each vegetable is cooked, arrange it on a large deep platter and keep warm. Garnish platter with egg quarters.
2. Meanwhile heat the oil in a heavy saucepan and sauté the onion until tender but not browned. Add the garlic and cook 2 minutes. Add remaining ingredients. Stir and cook until greens are wilted.
3. Sauce may be poured over vegetables as is or it can be whirled in an electric blender or food processor, if you wish.

STIR-FRIED ASPARAGUS
(Chinese)

This is my favorite way to fix the first asparagus of the season.
Makes 6 servings.

1 bunch fresh asparagus (about
   1½ pounds)
3 tablespoons vegetable oil
3 tablespoons soy sauce
¼ teaspoon salt

1 teaspoon finely chopped fresh
   ginger root, or ¼ teaspoon
   ground
1 tablespoon toasted sesame seeds,
   optional*

1. Break woody stems from spears of asparagus and discard. Wash well.
   If stems are very fat peel with a potato peeler, Cut off tips and set
   aside. Cut stalks into 1-inch lengths on the bias.
2. In a large skillet or wok heat the oil and add the stalks. Stir-fry 5
   minutes, add tips, and stir-fry 3 minutes.
3. Add soy sauce, salt, ginger, and water chestnuts. Stir to mix. Cover
   and cook 30 seconds to 1 minute, or until stalks are crisp-tender.
   Sprinkle with sesame seeds.

*Sesame seeds can be toasted in a small skillet over medium heat while shaking
frequently to prevent burning.

REFRIED BEANS
(Mexican)

Refried beans are used as a side dish and as an ingredient in
many Mexican dishes. They are filling, delicious, and nutri-
tious.
Makes 6 to 8 servings.

1 pound dried black, pinto, or pink
   beans
4 to 6 cups water
1 medium-size onion, coarsely
   chopped (¾ cup)
2 tablespoons lard or margarine

1½ to 2 tablespoons salt
¼ cup (½ stick) lard or margarine
1 large onion, finely chopped
   (1 cup)
2 cloves garlic, finely chopped,
   optional

1. Pick over and wash the beans. Place in a large saucepan with the
   water, bring to a boil, and simmer 2 minutes. Remove from heat,
   cover, and let stand 1 hour.

2. Add coarsely chopped onion and 2 tablespoons lard. Bring to a boil, cover, and simmer 45 minutes to 1 hour, or until beans are almost tender. Add salt and cook another 30 minutes, or until beans are tender. (Salt tends to toughen beans if added early in the cooking.) Drain and reserve any extra liquid.
3. Heat the remaining lard in a large skillet, add onion, and cook until soft. Add garlic and cook 1 minute. Add beans and mash into the onion mixture with a potato masher, or the back of a spoon. Add some of the reserved bean liquid, if necessary.
4. Cook, stirring, until beans form a thick purée. Refried beans can be used immediately or refrigerated or frozen for later use.

BAKED WHITE BEANS AND VEGETABLES
(Italian)

Bake this casserole at the same time you are roasting a chicken or turkey breast.
Bake at 350° for 1½ hours.
Makes 6 servings.

6 small red-skinned potatoes, scrubbed and a band of peel removed from around the middle of each
1 medium-size eggplant, peeled and diced (about 1½ pounds)
3 medium-size zucchini, sliced
4 to 5 large tomatoes, peeled and chopped, or 1 can (2 pounds, 3 ounces) Italian plum tomatoes

2 large onions, sliced and separated into rings
¼ cup chopped fresh Italian parsley
2 cloves garlic, finely chopped
¾ cup olive or vegetable oil
1 teaspoon salt
½ teaspoon freshly ground black pepper
1 teaspoon leaf oregano, crumbled
1 teaspoon leaf basil, crumbled
1 can (1 pound, 4 ounces) white kidney or cannellini beans

1. In a large heavy heatproof casserole layer the potatoes, eggplant, zucchini, tomatoes, and onion rings. Preheat oven to 350°.
2. In a small bowl combine the parsley, garlic, oil, salt, pepper, oregano, and basil and pour over the vegetables. Bring to a boil on top of stove, cover tightly, and bake at 350° for 1 hour.
3. Add the beans, toss mixture, and bake, uncovered, 30 minutes, or until vegetables are tender and mixture is consistency of a soup-stew. Serve over rice with freshly grated Parmesan, if you wish.

TUSCAN BEANS
(Italian)

If you have fresh sage use 1 to 2 teaspoons finely chopped and taste the difference.
Makes 4 servings.

2 tablespoons olive or vegetable oil
2 cloves garlic, finely chopped
1 large tomato, peeled, seeded, drained, and chopped
¼ teaspoon leaf sage, crumbled
½ teaspoon salt
¼ teaspoon freshly ground black pepper

2 cups cooked cannellini (white kidney) beans (If canned, drain and rinse well. For dried see instructions for soaking and cooking on page 241.)

1. Heat the oil in a small skillet and sauté the garlic about 1 minute. Add tomatoes and cook 5 minutes to thicken.
2. Add sage, salt, and pepper and cook 5 minutes. Add beans and reheat.

WHITE BEANS WITH TOMATOES
(French)

Add 3 cups of diced cooked turkey or chicken to this bean dish, season to taste, and it makes a hearty one-pot supper.
Makes 8 servings.

1 pound dried white beans (2 cups)
1 large onion, peeled
3 whole cloves
2 stalks celery, cut into quarters
2 carrots, cut into quarters
1 bay leaf
2 tablespoons vegetable oil
3 tablespoons butter or margarine
1 large onion, finely chopped (1 cup)

2 cloves garlic, finely chopped
1 teaspoon leaf thyme, crumbled
3 large tomatoes, peeled, seeded, and chopped, or 1 can (2 pounds, 3 ounces) tomatoes, drained and chopped
2 tablespoons chopped fresh parsley
Salt and freshly ground black pepper to taste

1. Pick over and wash the beans and place in a bowl with cold water to extend at least 2 inches above the beans. Let stand overnight.
2. Drain the beans and place in a kettle or Dutch oven with water to cover by 1½ inches. Add the onion studded with the cloves, celery, carrot, bay leaf, and vegetable oil. Bring to a boil. Cover and simmer 50 minutes, or until beans are tender. Remove whole onion and celery and carrot pieces.
3. Meanwhile heat the butter in a skillet and sauté the chopped onion until tender but not browned. Add the garlic, thyme, tomatoes, and parsley, bring to a boil, and simmer 10 minutes.
4. Drain the beans. Add beans to tomato mixture, reheat, and add salt and pepper to taste.

NEW ENGLAND BAKED BEANS
(American)

New Englanders serve them first as a side dish, then cold as a sandwich filling, and they make a soup with leftovers. You can never make too big a pot.
Bake at 275° for 5 to 6 hours.
Makes 8 servings.

1 pound dried Navy or pea beans	1 tablespoon dry mustard
1½ teaspoons salt	3 tablespoons catsup
1 small onion, finely chopped (¼ cup)	¼ pound lean salt pork, scored (optional)
3 tablespoons molasses	1 large onion, cut in half
¼ cup maple syrup	

1. Pick over and wash the beans and soak overnight in water to cover.
2. In a large kettle bring the beans and liquid to boiling. Lower heat, cover, and simmer 45 minutes, or until the skins of the beans blow off when placed in a spoon and gently blown over. Beans should be firm-tender.
3. Drain and reserve liquid. Preheat oven to 275°. Place beans in a 3-quart bean pot or heavy casserole. Combine salt, onion, molasses, syrup, mustard, and catsup and pour over beans. Stir well to mix. Set salt pork and onion halves on top of beans and add enough reserved liquid to come within ½ inch of top layer of beans. Cover and bake in a 275° oven for 4 hours, adding more liquid as needed and stirring every hour. Uncover and bake 1 to 2 hours longer, stirring occasionally, until tender.

PUREED BROCCOLI
(American)

Add this pretty green purée to a vegetable plate for color and smooth texture.
Makes 6 to 8 servings.

 1 large bunch broccoli (about 2½ pounds)
1½ teaspoons salt
 ¼ teaspoon freshly ground black pepper

 ¼ teaspoon ground nutmeg
 ¼ cup heavy cream

1. Separate flowerets from stems of broccoli. Peel stems with potato peeler and slice or dice. Cook stems in boiling salted water for 8 minutes. Add the flowerets and continue cooking until tender, about 8 minutes longer.
2. Drain. Purée in batches in an electric blender or food processor with the salt, pepper, nutmeg, and cream until smooth. Reheat.

BRAISED RED CABBAGE
(German)

A colorful sweet-sour vegetable to add to a vegetable plate or serve as a side dish.
Makes 6 servings.

2 tablespoons butter or margarine
1 medium-size onion, finely chopped (½ cup)
1 medium-size red cabbage (about 2 pounds), shredded
3 tart apples (Granny Smiths), peeled, cored, and sliced

2 tablespoons cider vinegar
1 tablespoon brown sugar
½ cup dry red wine
1 teaspoon salt
¼ teaspoon freshly ground black pepper

1. In a large heavy skillet melt the butter and sauté the onion until tender but not browned. Add the cabbage and sauté 5 minutes, stirring frequently.
2. Add the apples and sauté 5 minutes. Sprinkle over the vinegar, sugar, wine, salt, and pepper. Cover and simmer 20 minutes. It keeps several days in the refrigerator and even improves with reheating.

CARROT CROQUETTES
(Indian)

Use either as a side dish vegetable or appetizer.
Makes about 24.

1 pound carrots, scraped and sliced
2 medium-size potatoes, peeled and cubed
1 teaspoon salt
2 teaspoons chopped fresh cilantro (Chinese parsley) or parsley
2 eggs, separated
1 small onion, finely chopped (¼ cup)
1 clove garlic, finely chopped

¼ cup whole wheat or all-purpose flour
¼ teaspoon baking powder
½ teaspoon ground cumin
2 canned jalapeño chili peppers, seeded and chopped
Salt to taste
Unflavored packaged bread crumbs
Vegetable oil for frying

1. Place the carrots and potatoes in a medium-size saucepan. Add salt and enough boiling water to barely cover. Cover and simmer 20 minutes, or until vegetables are very tender. Drain well and mash in a large bowl.
2. Add parsley, egg yolks, onion, garlic, flour, baking powder, cumin, and peppers. Mix well. Taste and add salt if needed. Refrigerate until stiff, about 2 hours.
3. Beat the egg whites until stiff but not dry and fold into carrot mixture. Form into balls. If mixture is too soft fold in 2 to 3 tablespoons bread crumbs.
4. Roll balls in bread crumbs. Pour oil into a deep heavy kettle to a 3-inch depth. Heat to 375° on a deep-fat thermometer.
5. Fry the carrot croquettes, a few at a time, in the hot oil until golden. Drain on paper towels.

CARROT LOAF
(American)

Slices on an all-vegetable plate are attractive and make the lack of meat less noticeable.
Bake at 350° for 1¼ hours.
Makes 4 servings.

2 cups crumbled soda crackers
1 cup light cream or half-and-half
2½ cups coarsely grated carrot
1 large onion, finely chopped (1 cup)
½ cup (2 ounces) shredded Monterey Jack or mild Cheddar

1 cup chopped walnuts
½ teaspoon salt
¼ teaspoon freshly ground black pepper
½ teaspoon leaf sage, crumbled
3 eggs, lightly beaten

Preheat oven to 350°. In a large bowl combine the crackers and cream. Add the remaining ingredients and mix well. Pack into a greased loaf pan or casserole and bake at 350° for 1¼ hours, or until set. Let stand 10 minutes before cutting to serve.

PAKORAS
(Indian Cauliflower Fritters)

An Indian tempura. It is always tempting to guess where a dish had its origin.
Makes about 6 servings.

1 cup sifted all-purpose flour
½ teaspoon baking powder
1½ teaspoons salt
2 teaspoons ground coriander
1½ teaspoons ground cumin
¼ teaspoon turmeric

½ teaspoon ground ginger
Pinch of cayenne, optional
1⅓ cups cold water, approximately
Vegetable oil for frying
1 medium-size cauliflower, broken into flowerets

1. Place the flour, baking powder, salt, coriander, cumin, turmeric, ginger, and cayenne into the container of an electric blender. Add 1 cup of the water and blend until smooth, adding more water to make the batter the consistency of thick pancake batter. Let stand 1 hour.

2. Heat 2 inches of oil in a heavy saucepan with straight sides until it registers 360° on a deep-fat thermometer. Dip cauliflower in batter and fry, a few at a time, until golden, turning often. Drain on paper towels and keep warm while frying the rest of the cauliflower. Sprinkle with extra salt, if you wish.

CAULIFLOWER AND CHEESE
(American)

The gentle hint of curry is the mystery ingredient that makes
this version different.
Bake at 350° for 10 minutes.
Makes 4 servings.

1 medium-size head cauliflower	1 cup (4 ounces) shredded Swiss or
3 tablespoons butter	mild Cheddar
½ teaspoon curry powder	3 tablespoons butter or margarine
3 tablespoons flour	½ cup fresh bread crumbs
1½ cups hot milk or light cream	2 to 3 tablespoons chopped fresh
3 drops liquid red pepper	chives, or 2 to 3 teaspoons
seasoning	freeze-dried
Salt to taste	

1. Break the cauliflower into flowerets. Steam for 5 minutes, or until crisp-tender. Pile in a buttered baking or au gratin dish.
2. Meanwhile melt the butter with the curry powder and cook 1 minute. Blend in the flour and cook 2 minutes. Remove from the heat and gradually stir in the milk. Cook, stirring, over medium heat until thickened and smooth, about 5 minutes.
3. Remove from the heat and stir in the liquid red pepper seasoning, salt to taste, and the cheese until the cheese melts. Pour over the cauliflower. Preheat oven to 350°.
4. Melt 3 tablespoons butter and sauté the bread crumbs until lightly browned. Sprinkle over the cauliflower and bake at 350° for 10 minutes, or until heated through. Sprinkle with chives and serve immediately.

CAULIFLOWER AND BROCCOLI WITH SESAME SEEDS
(Chinese)

Crisp-tender green and white flowerets are complemented with a hint of ginger and a sprinkle of toasted sesame seeds.
Makes 6 servings.

¼ cup vegetable oil
½ cup finely chopped green onions
2 cloves garlic, finely chopped
3 cups broccoli flowerets (about ½ bunch)
3 cups cauliflower (about ½ medium-size head)
½ cup sliced water chestnuts

3 tablespoons dry sherry
3 tablespoons soy sauce
½ teaspoon salt
1 teaspoon finely chopped fresh ginger root, or ¼ teaspoon ground
2 tablespoons toasted sesame seeds*

1. In a large skillet or wok heat the oil and stir-fry the green onion and garlic 1 minute. Add the broccoli and cauliflower and stir-fry 2 minutes.
2. Add water chestnuts, cherry, soy sauce, salt, and ginger. Stir, cover, and cook 4 minutes, stirring occasionally, until vegetables are crisp-tender. Sprinkle with sesame seeds and serve immediately.

*Sesame seeds can be toasted in a small skillet over medium heat while shaking frequently to prevent burning.

BRAISED HEARTS OF CELERY
(French)

Discover a new way with celery. It is delicious cooked alone, or mixed with other vegetables.
Makes 4 servings.

2 large hearts of celery, split lengthwise
½ cup chicken broth
2 tablespoons butter or margarine
½ teaspoon salt
¼ teaspoon freshly ground black pepper

1 tablespoon lemon juice
½ teaspoon Dijon mustard
⅛ teaspoon leaf sage, crumbled
1 tablespoon butter or margarine
1 tablespoon chopped fresh parsley

1. Place the celery heart halves, cut side down, in a large heavy skillet. Add remaining ingredients except last tablespoon butter and parsley and bring to a boil. Cover and simmer 20 minutes, or until barely tender.
2. Using a slotted spoon transfer celery to a warm platter. Cook sauce in skillet over high heat until reduced and slightly thickened. Whirl in the remaining tablespoon butter, pour over celery, and sprinkle with parsley.

ISRAELI FALAFEL

Pushcarts in New York are making this Middle Eastern favorite popular with the outdoor snacking crowds.
Makes 4 to 6 servings.

2 cups cooked dried chick-peas, or 1 can (1 pound, 4 ounces) chick-peas, drained and rinsed
⅓ cup water
1 cup fresh soft bread crumbs
½ teaspoon baking soda
2 cloves garlic, finely chopped
1 egg, lightly beaten
2 tablespoons chopped fresh parsley
¾ teaspoon salt
¼ teaspoon freshly ground black pepper
½ teaspoon turmeric
¼ teaspoon leaf marjoram, crumbled
1 tablespoon tahini (sesame paste) or olive oil
1 tablespoon flour
Flour
Vegetable oil for frying
Pita bread

1. Grind the chick-peas using the coarse blade of a meat grinder, or briefly whirl in a food processor. Do not use a blender.
2. Add remaining ingredients including tablespoon of flour but not the extra flour, oil, or bread. Mix well and form into about 20 one-inch balls. Toss in flour and fry, a few at a time, in 2 inches of oil heated to 365° in a deep heavy kettle until golden. Drain on paper towels. Serve in halves of pita bread with lettuce, chopped tomato, and more tahini, if you wish.

CORN PUDDING
(American)

Delicious with roast chicken.
Bake at 350° for 40 minutes.
Makes 4 to 6 servings.

3 tablespoons butter or margarine	1 teaspoon Worcestershire sauce
¼ cup flour	1 teaspoon Dijon mustard
1¼ cups light cream or half-and-half	2 cups fresh corn kernels, cut from
3 eggs, separated	the cob, or canned drained
¾ teaspoon salt	
¼ teaspoon freshly ground black pepper	

1. Melt the butter in a small saucepan, blend in the flour, and cook 2 minutes. Gradually stir in the cream and bring to a boil, stirring until thick. Preheat oven to 350°.
2. Stir some of the hot sauce into the egg yolks, lightly beaten. Return to the saucepan and stir in the salt, pepper, Worcestershire, mustard, and corn. Beat the egg whites until stiff but not dry and fold into the corn mixture. Turn into a greased 1½- to 2-quart baking or soufflé dish and bake at 350° for 40 minutes, or until puffed and lightly golden.

CORN AND SQUASH CASSEROLE
(Mexican)

Serve with hot tortillas.
Makes 6 servings.

¼ cup (½ stick) butter or margarine	2 jalapeño peppers (from a 4-ounce can), seeded and chopped
1 large onion, finely chopped (1 cup)	1 teaspoon salt
1 medium-size zucchini, cut into ¼-inch slices	¼ teaspoon freshly ground black pepper
1 medium-size yellow summer squash, cut into ¼-inch slices	½ teaspoon ground coriander
1 clove garlic, finely chopped	1 cup (4 ounces) shredded Monterey Jack or mild Cheddar
1 can (1 pound) tomatoes, drained	
2 cups corn kernels, cut from 4 to 6 ears, or drained canned, or frozen from a poly bag	

1. Heat the butter in a large heavy kettle or Dutch oven and sauté the onion until tender but not browned. Add the zucchini, squash, and garlic and cook, stirring frequently, for 5 to 7 minutes, or until squash is lightly browned.
2. Add tomatoes and bring to a boil. Add the corn, jalapeño peppers, salt, pepper, and coriander. Cook, uncovered, 5 minutes, or until squash is crisp-tender. Pour into a heatproof baking dish. Sprinkle with cheese and broil for 2 to 3 minutes, or until cheese melts.

SPICY GREEN BEANS
(Indian)

Plain green beans will never be as appealing after you've tried them this way.
Makes 4 servings.

¼ cup (½ stick) butter or margarine
1 teaspoon mustard seeds
1 medium-size onion, finely chopped (½ cup)
1 pound green beans, trimmed and cut diagonally into 1-inch lengths
½ small cauliflower, separated into small flowerets (about 1 cup)

1 teaspoon salt
1 teaspoon ground coriander
Pinch of cayenne
¼ teaspoon ground ginger
1 container (8 ounces) plain yogurt

1. In a large skillet heat the butter and cook mustard seeds 30 seconds, or until they start to pop. Stir in the onion and cook 2 minutes.
2. Add the beans and cauliflower and cook, stirring, about 6 minutes.
3. Stir in the salt, coriander, cayenne, and ginger. Cover and cook over low heat 10 minutes, or until beans are crisp-tender, stirring 2 or 3 times. Stir the yogurt and then stir into vegetable mixture.

GREEN BEANS PROVENCALE
(French)

Green beans will never be dull if you flavor them with traditional Provençale seasonings of garlic, tomatoes, black olives,
and thyme.
Makes 6 servings.

2 pounds whole young green
  beans, trimmed
2 tablespoons olive or vegetable oil
2 medium-size onions, thinly sliced
3 cloves garlic, finely chopped
1 can (2 pounds, 3 ounces) Italian
  plum tomatoes, drained
1 teaspoon leaf thyme, crumbled

1 teaspoon salt
½ teaspoon freshly ground black
  pepper
¼ cup chopped fresh parsley
¼ cup sliced black olives, optional
¼ cup (1 ounce) grated Gruyère or
  Swiss

1. Blanch the beans in a large kettle of boiling salted water, uncovered,
   for 5 minutes. Drain and refresh in ice water.
2. Heat the oil in a medium-size heavy skillet and sauté the onion and
   garlic until wilted, about 3 to 4 minutes. Add tomatoes and cook over
   high heat to thicken, about 10 minutes.
3. Add thyme, salt, and pepper and cook 5 minutes. Just before serving
   add beans, toss to coat, and serve sprinkled with parsley, black olives,
   and cheese.

CURRIED EGGPLANT I
(Indian)

The heat in this curry mixture comes from ginger and hot
pepper flakes—add more of both if you enjoy fiery hot food.
Makes 6 servings.

¼ cup vegetable oil
2 large onions, finely chopped
  (2 cups)
2 cloves garlic, finely chopped
1 to 2 teaspoons curry powder
1 teaspoon chopped fresh ginger
  root, or ¼ teaspoon ground
½ teaspoon turmeric
⅛ teaspoon crushed hot red pepper
  flakes, optional

4 tomatoes, peeled and chopped,
  or 1 can (1 pound) tomatoes
2 eggplants (about 1 pound each),
  peeled and cubed
1 teaspoon salt
1 cup chicken or vegetable broth
  (see page 59)
1 green pepper, seeded and diced
1 tablespoon lemon juice

1. In a large skillet heat the vegetable oil and sauté the onion until tender but not browned. Add the garlic, curry powder, ginger, turmeric, and red pepper flakes and cook, stirring, 2 minutes.
2. Add the tomatoes and bring to a boil. Stir in the eggplant, salt, and broth. Cook, uncovered, stirring often until eggplant is tender, about 25 minutes. Add green pepper and lemon juice and serve over hot cooked rice, if you wish.

CURRIED EGGPLANT II
(Indian)

Chick-peas in one form or another are an important ingredient in Indian cooking.
Makes 6 servings.

1 medium-size eggplant, peeled and cut into 1-inch cubes
Salt
2 tablespoons vegetable oil
2 large onions, thinly sliced and separated into rings
2 teaspoons curry powder
1 teaspoon ground coriander
⅛ teaspoon cayenne, optional
1 can (2 pounds, 3 ounces) Italian plum tomatoes
1 teaspoon salt
2 cans (15 ounces each) chick-peas, drained, rinsed, and drained

1. Sprinkle the eggplant with salt and let stand 10 minutes. Rinse and pat dry.
2. Heat the oil in a large heavy skillet and cook the onion until tender but not browned. Add the eggplant and cook 10 minutes.
3. Sprinkle with the curry powder, coriander, and cayenne and cook, stirring, 2 minutes. Add the tomatoes and salt and cook, uncovered, 25 minutes, or until the eggplant is tender. Stir often.
4. Stir in the chick-peas and reheat. Serve over rice.

BAKED EGGPLANT AND ZUCCHINI
(Italian)

Bake at 350° for 25 minutes.
Makes 6 servings.

1 large eggplant (about 2 pounds),
  peeled and thinly sliced
  Salt
½ cup vegetable oil, approximately
6 medium-size zucchini, thinly
  sliced
1 medium-size onion, finely
  chopped (½ cup)
6 tomatoes, peeled, seeded, and
  chopped

1 teaspoon leaf basil, crumbled
1 teaspoon leaf oregano, crumbled
½ bay leaf
¾ teaspoon salt
½ teaspoon freshly ground black
  pepper
⅓ cup freshly grated Parmesan

1. Sprinkle the eggplant slices with salt and let stand 20 minutes. Rinse and dry on paper towels. Heat half the oil in a large skillet and fry the eggplant until lightly browned.
2. Drain on paper towels. Add remaining oil and fry the zucchini slices until lightly browned. Drain on paper towels.
3. Add the onion and sauté until tender but not browned. Meanwhile place the tomatoes in a medium-size saucepan and cook, stirring occasionally, until thick. Add basil, oregano, bay leaf, salt, and pepper. Preheat oven to 350°.
4. Pour half the tomato mixture into a shallow baking dish. Top with layers of eggplant and zucchini. Pour over remaining tomato mixture, sprinkle with cheese, and bake at 350° for 25 minutes, or until vegetables are tender.

IRISH COLCANNON
(Kale or Cabbage and Mashed Potatoes)

Leftover vegetables were probably the reason for this dish being developed in the first place.
Makes 4 servings.

3 cups shredded kale or green
  cabbage
3 tablespoons butter
1 medium-size onion, finely
  chopped (½ cup)
¼ cup water

2 cups creamy mashed potatoes
  (leftovers are fine)
¾ teaspoon salt
¼ teaspoon freshly ground black
  pepper

1. Place the kale, butter, and onion in a large sauté pan or deep skillet and cook, stirring, 10 minutes, or until kale is crisp-tender. Add water, cover, and cook until kale is tender. Pour off excess liquid or dry over low heat a minute or two with cover off.
2. Stir in the mashed potatoes, salt, and pepper and reheat.

BRAISED FENNEL
WITH CHEESE SAUCE
(Italian)

Fennel is an anise-flavored crisp vegetable that should be more widely known and appreciated.
Makes 4 servings.

4 fennel bulbs
1 cup chicken broth or vegetable broth (see page 59)
2 tablespoons butter or margarine
2 tablespoons flour
½ teaspoon salt
¼ teaspoon freshly ground black pepper

⅛ teaspoon ground nutmeg
¼ cup heavy cream or half-and-half
½ cup (2 ounces) shredded Monterey Jack or mild Cheddar
½ cup (2 ounces) freshly grated Parmesan

1. Remove the feathery green fennel leaves, chop enough to make 3 tablespoons, and reserve. Halve the bulbs, remove the hard inner core, and discard.
2. Place the bulbs, cut side down, in a large heavy skillet or sauté pan. Pour in the broth. Bring to a boil, cover, and simmer until tender, about 15 minutes. Drain liquid into a measure and reserve 1 cup.
3. Transfer fennel bulbs to a warm buttered baking dish. Meanwhile melt the butter in a small saucepan, stir in the flour, salt, pepper, and nutmeg, and cook 1 minute. Gradually stir in the reserved broth. Bring to a boil, stirring until thick. Cook 2 minutes. Stir in the cream and shredded cheese, and stir to melt. Stir in the fennel leaves and pour over fennel bulbs. Sprinkle with Parmesan and glaze under the broiler until lightly browned. Serve over rice.

LENTIL AND VEGETABLE CASSEROLE
(American)

If fresh herbs are available use three times as much as the dried called for and you will be rewarded with a delightful taste treat.
Bake at 375° for 50 minutes.
Makes 8 servings.

2 cups lentils (1 pound), picked over and rinsed
1 bay leaf
1 small onion, studded with 2 whole cloves
3 tablespoons vegetable oil
2 large onions, finely chopped (2 cups)
2 cloves garlic, finely chopped
2 large carrots, diced
1 stalk celery, chopped
1 small green pepper, seeded and diced

2 small zucchini, diced
1 can (1 pound) tomatoes, drained
2 teaspoons salt
½ teaspoon freshly ground black pepper
½ teaspoon leaf marjoram, crumbled
½ teaspoon summer savory or chervil, crumbled
¼ teaspoon leaf thyme, crumbled
2 cups (8 ounces) shredded Monterey Jack or mild Cheddar

1. Place the lentils in a large saucepan and cover with water to extend 3 to 4 inches above lentils (about 2 quarts). Add bay leaf and onion with cloves and bring to a boil. Cover and simmer 40 minutes, or until lentils are tender. Drain and use cooking liquid in soup, stew, or gravy.
2. Place lentils in a 3-quart shallow baking dish. Meanwhile heat the oil in a large heavy skillet and sauté the onion until tender but not browned. Add garlic and cook 2 minutes. Preheat oven to 375°.
3. Add remaining ingredients except for cheese and bring to a boil. Pour over lentils, cover with foil, and bake at 375° for 30 minutes.
4. Uncover, sprinkle cheese over, and bake 20 minutes, or until cheese melts and browns.

DAHL
(Indian Lentil Stew)

Every traditional Indian meal includes a side dish of dahl.
Makes 6 servings.

1½ cups lentils
1 quart water
1 teaspoon salt
1 tablespoon vegetable oil
1 teaspoon mustard seeds
½ teaspoon turmeric
⅛ teaspoon cayenne

1 teaspoon ground ginger
½ teaspoon ground cumin
1 small onion, thinly sliced
2 tablespoons chopped fresh
cilantro (Chinese parsley) or flat
Italian parsley
3 tablespoons lemon juice

1. Pick over and wash the lentils and place in a saucepan with the water. Bring to a boil, cover, and simmer 45 minutes, or until tender. Add salt.
2. Meanwhile in a small heavy skillet heat the oil and sauté the mustard seeds, covered, until they start to pop. Do not let them brown.
3. Add turmeric, cayenne, ginger, cumin, and onion and cook, stirring, until onion is tender. Stir into cooked lentils. Add cilantro or parsley and lemon juice.

CURRIED LENTILS
(Indian)

Makes a pleasant side dish for Tandoori chicken.
Makes 4 servings.

2 tablespoons vegetable oil
1 large onion, finely chopped
(1 cup)
1 tablespoon curry powder
½ teaspoon ground ginger
½ teaspoon ground cumin
Dash of cayenne or to taste
1 tomato, peeled and chopped

1 teaspoon salt
1 cup lentils, picked over, washed,
and drained
2 cups vegetable broth (see page
59) or water
2 tablespoons chopped fresh
cilantro (Chinese parsley) or flat
Italian parsley

1. In a heavy saucepan heat the oil and sauté the onion until tender but not browned. Sprinkle with the curry powder, ginger, cumin, and cayenne and cook 1 minute.
2. Add the tomato, salt, lentils, and broth and bring to a boil. Cover and simmer 45 minutes, or until lentils are tender. Sprinkle with cilantro or parsley.

BRAISED LETTUCE
(French)

Learn to cook salad ingredients and enjoy a new group of taste treats. Start with Boston lettuce, then try celery (page 246). Makes 6 servings.

¼ cup (½ stick) butter or margarine
3 green onions, finely chopped
¼ pound mushrooms, sliced (1 cup)
3 heads Boston lettuce, cut into 1-inch-wide ribbons
1 teaspoon chopped fresh rosemary, or ¼ teaspoon dried

1 teaspoon salt
¼ teaspoon freshly ground black pepper
1 tablespoon chopped fresh parsley
2 tablespoons chopped fresh chives, or 2 teaspoons freeze-dried

1. In a large heavy saucepan or sauté pan heat the butter and sauté the green onions until soft. Add mushrooms and cook 3 minutes.
2. Add the lettuce and toss to coat with butter. Add rosemary, salt, and pepper and cook, covered, until the lettuce is just wilted, about 3 minutes. Add parsley and chives and toss.

CREAMED ONIONS
(American)

A holiday favorite that deserves to be made more often. Makes 4 servings.

24 small white onions, peeled
3 tablespoons butter
3 tablespoons flour
¾ teaspoon salt
¼ teaspoon freshly ground black pepper

⅛ teaspoon ground nutmeg
1½ cups milk
¼ cup heavy cream

1. Steam the onions over boiling water until firm-tender, about 15 minutes. Drain and reserve the cooking liquid.
2. Melt the butter in a medium-size saucepan. Stir in the flour, salt, pepper, and nutmeg and cook 2 minutes. Remove from the heat and gradually stir in the milk and cream.
3. Return to the heat and bring to a boil, stirring constantly. Cook until sauce is thick and smooth, about 3 minutes. Add onions and reheat.

SOUR CREAM-ONION PIE
(German)

Serve this mouth-watering dish at your next holiday meal.
Bake at 450° for 10 minutes, then at 350° for 30 minutes.
Makes 8 servings.

¼ cup (½ stick) butter or margarine
2 large Bermuda or Spanish onions, cut into thin rings (about 3 to 4 cups)
1 container (8 ounces) sour cream
⅓ cup beer
3 eggs, lightly beaten

½ teaspoon salt
¼ teaspoon freshly ground black pepper
⅛ teaspoon ground nutmeg
2 tablespoons chopped fresh parsley
1 unbaked 9-inch pie shell

1. In a large skillet heat the butter and sauté the onion rings over low heat until golden. Cool. Preheat oven to 450°.
2. Combine the sour cream, beer, eggs, salt, pepper, nutmeg, parsley, and cooled onion rings, drained from butter.
3. Bake pie shell at 450° for 10 minutes or until set. Reduce oven heat to 350°. Pour onion mixture into pie shell and bake 30 minutes, or until set.

ROESTI POTATOES
(Swiss)

A crusty top and bottom is a must for this dish.
Makes 4 servings.

2 tablespoons butter or margarine
1 medium-size onion, shredded on a coarse grater
3 medium-size baking potatoes (about 1¼ pounds)

2 tablespoons butter or margarine
2 tablespoons vegetable oil
Salt and freshly ground black pepper to taste

1. In a medium-size heavy skillet melt the butter and sauté the onion until tender but not browned. Remove and reserve.
2. Cook the potatoes in boiling water until barely tender. When cool enough to handle peel and shred.
3. Melt remaining butter and oil in same skillet and spread half the potatoes over bottom of pan. Sprinkle with salt and pepper, top with onion, and add remaining potatoes. Sprinkle with salt and pepper.
4. Reduce heat to medium and cook 10 minutes, or until bottom is nicely browned. Turn upside down onto a plate. If necessary, add more butter to skillet. Slide potato cake back into skillet and brown second side, 8 to 10 minutes.

POTATOES WITH GREEN SAUCE
(*Portuguese*)

Looks attractive served with fish and tastes even better.
Makes 6 servings.

⅓ cup olive or vegetable oil
1 large onion, finely chopped
  (1 cup)
3 cloves garlic, finely chopped
3 pounds waxy boiling potatoes,
  peeled and sliced, or if
  red-skinned, scrubbed and skins
  left on

1 cup finely shredded fresh spinach
¼ cup finely chopped fresh parsley
1½ teaspoons salt
½ teaspoon freshly ground black
  pepper

1. In a heavy saucepan heat the oil and sauté the onion until tender but
    not browned. Add the garlic and cook, stirring, 3 minutes. Add
    potato slices and enough hot water to barely cover.
2. Bring to a boil, cover, and cook slowly 15 minutes, or until potato is
    barely tender but holds its shape.
3. Add spinach, parsley, salt, and pepper and reheat. Serve in bowls
    with cooking liquid.

TWICE-BAKED POTATOES
(*American*)

Potatoes can be prepared up to the final reheating early in the
day or the day before. Store covered in the refrigerator.
Bake at 425° for 1 hour, then at 350° for 30 minutes.
Makes 6 servings.

6 large baking potatoes, scrubbed
  and pricked
½ cup hot milk
¼ cup (½ stick) butter or margarine
⅓ cup sour cream
1¼ cups (5 ounces) shredded sharp
  Cheddar

1¼ teaspoons salt
¼ teaspoon freshly ground black
  pepper
⅛ teaspoon ground nutmeg

1. Place the potatoes directly on the shelf of the oven and bake at 425°
    for 1 hour, or until soft. Cut out a hole in the top of each potato that is
    about three-quarters of the surface and big enough to allow you to
    scoop out the insides, leaving a ¼-inch-thick shell.
2. Place the hot milk and butter in a medium-size bowl and add
    scooped-out potato. Beat with an electric mixer or mash until smooth.
    Stir in the sour cream, 1 cup of the cheese, salt, pepper, and nutmeg.
3. Stuff the mixture into the potato shells, mounding, if necessary. Place
    on a baking sheet, sprinkle with remaining cheese, and bake at 350°
    for 30 minutes, or until hot through and browned on top.

GNOCCHI
(Italian Potato Dumplings)

Handled lightly these little dumplings are delightful to serve as
a first course or as a side dish.
Bake at 350° for 10 minutes.
Makes 8 to 10 servings.

6 large baking potatoes
¾ cup (1½ sticks) butter or
  margarine
3 eggs, lightly beaten
4 cups flour
2 teaspoons baking powder
1½ teaspoons salt

½ teaspoon freshly ground black
  pepper
Boiling salted water
2 cloves garlic, finely chopped
½ cup (2 ounces) freshly grated
  Parmesan

1. Scrub the potatoes and cook in boiling salted water to cover until
    tender, about 30 minutes.
2. Peel the potatoes and force through a ricer into a bowl holding ¼ cup
    of the butter. Beat in the eggs, flour, baking powder, salt, and pep-
    per. Mix to a dough and knead until smooth.
3. Shape the dough into ½-inch-diameter rolls. Cut into 1-inch pieces
    and shape into crescents. Drop, a few at a time, into a kettle of boiling
    salted water. Simmer until they rise to the surface and are cooked
    through, about 6 minutes. Preheat oven to 350°.
4. Drain the gnocchi well and place in a greased shallow baking dish.
    Melt the remaining butter in a small skillet and sauté the garlic
    briefly. Pour over gnocchi, sprinkle with cheese, and bake at 350° for
    10 minutes.

POTATO PANCAKES
(German)

Served with a choice of applesauce or lingonberries, these pancakes are a brunch-time favorite in my home.
Makes 12 to 18 pancakes, 4 servings.

3 large baking potatoes (1 to 1½ pounds)
1 medium-size onion, grated
½ teaspoon salt
¼ teaspoon freshly ground black pepper

1 tablespoon all-purpose flour
¼ teaspoon baking powder
2 eggs, separated
½ cup vegetable oil

1. Peel and grate potatoes into a sieve. With the back of a wooden spoon press out the excess moisture.
2. In a medium-size bowl combine the potato, onion, salt, pepper, flour, and baking powder. Toss to mix. Lightly beat the egg yolks and stir into potato mixture.
3. Beat the egg whites until stiff but not dry and fold into potato mixture.
4. Heat oil in a heavy skillet. Drop batter by serving spoonfuls into hot oil so that they do not touch. Cook over medium heat until golden. Turn and brown the other side. Drain on paper towels and repeat until all batter is used, keeping the cooked pancakes warm. Serve with unsweetened applesauce.

POTATOES WITH MUSTARD SAUCE
(German)

Delightful accompaniment to broiled or baked cod or roast chicken.
Bake at 375° for 20 minutes.
Makes 6 servings.

4 large waxy potatoes
¼ cup (½ stick) butter or margarine
1 small onion, finely chopped (¼ cup)
3 tablespoons all-purpose flour
1 can (13¾ ounces) chicken broth, or 2 cups vegetable broth (see page 59)
1 cup half-and-half or milk

4 tablespoons Düsseldorf mustard
½ teaspoon salt
⅛ teaspoon freshly ground black pepper
½ cup buttered soft fresh bread crumbs
¼ cup (1 ounce) freshly grated Parmesan

1. Scrub the potatoes and cook in boiling salted water to cover until barely tender, about 30 minutes. Peel potatoes and slice into a greased shallow baking dish. Preheat oven to 375°.
2. Meanwhile melt the butter and sauté the onion until tender but not browned. Blend in the flour and cook 2 minutes. Gradually stir in the broth and the half-and-half and bring to a boil, stirring. Cook 1 minute. Stir in the mustard, salt, and pepper. Pour over potatoes. Sprinkle with the crumbs and cheese and bake at 375° for 20 minutes, or until bubbly. Glaze under the broiler, if you wish.

POTATO PIE
(Irish)

Scalloped potatoes under a crust.
Bake at 350° for 1 hour.
Makes 8 servings.

3 tablespoons butter or margarine	½ teaspoon freshly ground black pepper
6 medium-size yellow onions, thinly sliced	⅓ cup flour
1 clove garlic, finely chopped	1½ cups milk
4 pounds red-skinned potatoes, peeled and thinly sliced	Pastry for a double-crust 9-inch pie
2 teaspoons salt	1 cup heavy cream

1. Heat the butter in a skillet and sauté the onion until tender but not browned. Add the garlic and cook 5 minutes.
2. Place the potato slices in a large saucepan. Cover with boiling salted water and cook 3 minutes. Drain.
3. Butter a shallow 3-quart casserole and alternate layers of onion and potato, sprinkling each layer with some of the salt and pepper. Preheat oven to 350°.
4. Place the flour in a small bowl and gradually stir in the milk. Pour over casserole. Roll out pastry to fit top of casserole. Decorate the edge and make a large round hole in the middle to allow steam to escape.
5. Brush pastry with some of the cream. Bake at 350° for 1 hour, or until pastry is golden brown. Heat cream and pour into hole. Let stand 10 minutes before serving.

MASALA POTATOES
(Indian)

I like to serve these spicy potatoes with plain roasted chicken or rock Cornish game hens.
Makes 6 servings.

6 large potatoes
¼ cup vegetable oil
1½ teaspoons mustard seeds (black if available)
1 teaspoon finely chopped fresh ginger root, or ¼ teaspoon ground
2 serrano, or mild green chilies (from a 4-ounce can), seeded and chopped

½ teaspoon ground coriander
¼ teaspoon turmeric
1 tablespoon curry powder
2 teaspoons salt
1 tablespoon lemon juice
2 tablespoons chopped fresh cilantro (Chinese parsley) or flat Italian parsley
Plain yogurt

1. Place the potatoes in a large saucepan, add boiling salted water to cover, and bring to a boil. Cover and simmer about 30 minutes, or until potatoes are tender but not soft.
2. Remove from pan, cool slightly, peel, and cut into 1-inch cubes. Set aside.
3. Meanwhile heat the oil in a large heavy skillet. Add mustard seeds. Cook over low heat until they start to pop, stirring occasionally.
4. Add the ginger, chilies, coriander, turmeric, curry powder, and salt. Cook, stirring, 1 minute. Add the potatoes and toss to coat while reheating over low heat. Sprinkle with the lemon juice and parsley. Serve with yogurt or stir yogurt into potatoes, if you wish.

STIR-FRIED SNOW PEAS
(Chinese)

This recipe also works using the new sugar snap peas.
Makes 6 servings.

1 medium-size zucchini
3 tablespoons vegetable oil
½ cup finely chopped green onions
¼ teaspoon crushed hot red pepper flakes
¼ pound mushrooms, sliced (1 cup)
½ pound fresh snow peas, tips and strings removed

1 tablespoon soy sauce
1 tablespoon cider vinegar
½ teaspoon salt
½ teaspoon sugar
1 teaspoon finely chopped fresh ginger root, or ¼ teaspoon ground

1. Cut zucchini in half lengthwise and cut into ¼-inch slices. In a large skillet or a wok heat the oil and stir-fry the green onions 2 minutes. Stir in the red pepper and cook briefly.
2. Add the zucchini and stir-fry 2 minutes. Add the mushrooms and snow peas and cook, stirring, until vegetables are crisp-tender, about 2 minutes.
3. Stir in the soy sauce, vinegar, salt, sugar, and ginger. Serve immediately.

STUFFED ACORN SQUASH
(American)

Serve with homemade tomato sauce.
Bake at 375° for 55 minutes.
Makes 4 servings.

2 medium-size acorn squash
¾ teaspoon salt
¼ teaspoon freshly ground black pepper
1 package (10 ounces) frozen chopped spinach
2 tablespoons butter or margarine
1 medium-size onion, finely chopped (½ cup)
1 clove garlic, finely chopped

¼ teaspoon ground nutmeg
1 package (3 ounces) cream cheese, softened
2 to 3 tablespoons sour cream or plain yogurt
4 tablespoons freshly grated Parmesan
2 hard-cooked eggs, shelled and chopped

1. Halve the squash and remove seeds and strings. Place, cut side down, in a shallow baking dish with ½ inch of water in the bottom. Bake at 375° for 45 minutes, or until squash is tender. Sprinkle cut side with half the salt and pepper.
2. Meanwhile cook the spinach according to package directions, drain, and squeeze dry. Heat the butter in a small skillet and sauté the onion until tender but not browned. Add the garlic and cook 1 minute.
3. Add dry spinach, nutmeg, remaining salt and pepper, and cream cheese to skillet. Mix well and heat, if necessary, to melt cream cheese. Take off heat and stir in sour cream, 2 tablespoons of the Parmesan, and the hard-cooked eggs.
4. Stuff cooked acorn squash halves with the spinach mixture. Set in heatproof baking dish. Sprinkle with remaining Parmesan and reheat at 375° for 10 minutes.

BAKED CALABAZA
(Caribbean)

An attractive purée that is subtly flavored with curry.
Bake at 350° for 1 to 1½ hours, plus 20 minutes for the finished
casserole.
Makes 6 servings.

1 small calabaza, pumpkin, or
  Hubbard squash (2 to 4 pounds)
1 green pepper, seeded and
  chopped
1 medium-size onion, finely
  chopped (½ cup)
1 clove garlic, finely chopped
3 tablespoons butter or margarine

1½ tablespoons curry powder
⅓ cup sour cream
  Salt and freshly ground black
  pepper to taste
½ cup fresh soft white bread
  crumbs
2 tablespoons butter or margarine

1. Cut the calabaza in half and scoop out the seeds. Place, cut side
   down, in ¼ inch of water in a baking dish. Bake at 350° for about 1 to
   1½ hours, or until tender, depending on size and age.
2. When cool enough to handle scoop out the pulp and mash or purée in
   an electric blender or food processor.
3. In a medium-size heavy skillet sauté the green pepper, onion, and
   garlic in the butter for 1 minute. Stir in the curry powder and cook 2
   minutes.
4. Combine the pulp with the vegetables, sour cream, salt, and pepper.
   Turn into a buttered casserole. Brown the bread crumbs in the butter
   and sprinkle over squash mixture. Bake at 350° for 20 minutes.

SWEET POTATO AND SQUASH
CASSEROLE
(American)

Bake at 400° for 15 minutes.
Makes 6 servings.

2 pounds sweet potatoes or yams,
  peeled and cut into 1-inch cubes
2 pounds butternut or acorn
  squash, peeled and cut into
  1-inch cubes
3 cups boiling salted water
¼ cup (½ stick) butter or margarine

½ teaspoon salt
¼ teaspoon ground nutmeg
¼ teaspoon freshly ground black
  pepper
½ cup chopped pecans or walnuts
2 tablespoons butter

1. Place the sweet potatoes, squash, and boiling salted water in a large saucepan. Bring to a boil, cover, and simmer 25 minutes, or until tender. Drain.
2. Place drained vegetables in the large bowl of an electric mixer. Add the butter, salt, nutmeg, and pepper and beat until smooth. Stir in the nuts and turn into a buttered 2-quart casserole. Dot with butter and bake in a 400° oven for 15 minutes.

SQUASH AND BEAN CASSEROLE
(French)

Wonderful way to perk up midwinter menus.
Bake at 350° for 40 minutes, then at 425° for 25 minutes.
Makes 8 servings.

2 tablespoons butter	¾ teaspoon salt
1 medium-size onion, finely chopped (½ cup)	¼ teaspoon freshly ground black pepper
1 clove garlic, finely chopped	½ cup vegetable broth (see page 59)
1 stalk celery, finely chopped	1 can (15 ounces) cannellini beans, drained
1 small carrot, diced	
1 small white turnip, diced	2 eggs, lightly beaten
1 medium-size butternut squash (about 1½ pounds), peeled and diced	⅓ cup heavy cream or half-and-half
	Salt and freshly ground black pepper
½ teaspoon leaf marjoram, crumbled	½ cup (2 ounces) shredded Swiss or Gruyère
½ bay leaf	

1. In a large heavy casserole heat the butter and sauté the onion until tender but not browned. Add the garlic, celery, carrot, and turnip and cook, stirring, 5 minutes longer. Preheat oven to 350°.
2. Add the squash and cook, stirring, 2 minutes.
3. Add the marjoram, bay leaf, salt, and pepper. Pour in broth, cover tightly, and bake at 350° for 40 minutes, or until vegetables are tender.
4. Add the beans to cooked mixture and purée in batches in an electric blender or food processor. Combine the eggs and cream and stir into the purée, which should be quite thick. If it is not, heat, stirring, over high heat before adding egg and cream mixture.
5. Taste and add salt and pepper, if needed. Pour into a 3-quart casserole, sprinkle with cheese, and bake at 425° for 25 minutes, or until lightly puffed and browned.

SESAME SPINACH
(Chinese)

I like this simple preparation of spinach with fish or plain broiled or roasted chicken.
Makes 6 servings.

3 tablespoons vegetable oil
4 green onions, chopped
1 tablespoon chopped fresh ginger root, or ½ teaspoon ground
1 clove garlic, finely chopped

2 pounds fresh spinach, shredded, or 2 packages (10 ounces each) frozen leaf spinach, thawed and squeezed dry
2 tablespoons soy sauce
3 tablespoons toasted sesame seeds*

1. In a wok or skillet heat the oil and sauté the green onions briefly. Add the ginger and garlic and cook 1 minute.
2. Add the spinach and stir-fry 2 minutes. Sprinkle with the soy sauce, cover, and steam 1 minute. Sprinkle with sesame seeds and serve immediately.

*Sesame seeds can be toasted in a small dry skillet over medium heat while shaking frequently to prevent burning.

RICE-STUFFED TOMATOES
(Greek)

Serve with an all-vegetable moussaka and green salad for a fabulous buffet.
Makes 6 servings.

½ cup olive or vegetable oil
3 large onions, finely chopped (3 cups)
2 cloves garlic, finely chopped
1 cup raw long-grain rice
1 teaspoon salt
½ teaspoon freshly ground black pepper
2 tablespoons snipped fresh dillweed

¼ cup chopped fresh parsley, preferably the flat Italian variety
½ cup lemon juice
2 cups water
6 ripe tomatoes
½ cup (2 ounces) crumbled feta cheese
¼ cup sliced pitted black olives

1. Heat the oil in a large heavy saucepan or Dutch oven. Sauté the onion in the oil until tender over low heat, about 10 minutes. Add the garlic and rice and cook, stirring, until rice is lightly golden.

2. Add the salt, pepper, dill, parsley, lemon juice, and water. Bring to a boil, cover, and simmer 15 minutes, or until the moisture is absorbed. Cool and chill.
3. Meanwhile cut a 1-inch slice from the top of the tomatoes and scoop out the pulp, leaving a ¼-inch-thick shell. Turn upside down to drain.
4. Strain the excess liquid from the scooped-out pulp and add the solids to the rice mixture. Add the feta and olives. Taste for seasoning and add salt and pepper if needed. Pile chilled rice mixture into tomato shells. Garnish with parsley sprigs, if you wish.

STUFFED TOMATOES
(Turkish)

Cinnamon, almonds, mint, and raisins make this rice stuffing exotic.
Bake at 350° for 20 minutes.
Makes 6 servings.

6 large beefsteak tomatoes	⅛ teaspoon freshly ground black pepper
3 tablespoons vegetable oil	
1 medium-size onion, finely chopped (½ cup)	2 cups chopped seeded cucumbers, peeled if waxed
1 clove garlic, finely chopped	½ cup chopped watercress
½ cup raw long-grain rice	2 tablespoons chopped fresh parsley
1 cup vegetable broth (see page 59) or water	¼ cup chopped blanched almonds
¼ teaspoon ground cinnamon	2 tablespoons chopped fresh mint
½ teaspoon salt	3 tablespoons golden raisins

1. Cut a 1-inch slice off the top of each tomato and scoop out the pulp, leaving a ¼-inch-thick shell. Use the pulp in a soup, stew, or sauce. Turn tomato shells upside down to drain.
2. In a medium-size heavy skillet heat the oil and sauté the onion until tender but not browned. Add the garlic and rice and cook 10 minutes, stirring often. Add broth, cinnamon, salt, and pepper. Bring to a boil, cover, and cook 15 minutes, or until rice has absorbed the liquid. Preheat oven to 350°.
3. Remove rice from heat and add the cucumber, watercress, parsley, almonds, mint, and raisins. Toss to mix. Use to stuff the tomato shells. Place in a shallow baking dish, add ½ cup hot water to dish, and bake at 350° for 20 minutes.

DILLED ZUCCHINI
(Italian)

Serve topped with a dollop of sour cream or yogurt.
Bake at 350° for 45 minutes to 1 hour.
Makes 4 servings.

2 pounds zucchini, sliced ¼ inch
  thick
1 bunch green onions, chopped,
  including green part
3 tablespoons snipped fresh
  dillweed
¼ cup (½ stick) butter, melted

⅓ cup freshly grated Parmesan
¼ cup water or chicken or vegetable
  broth (see page 59)
1 teaspoon salt
¼ teaspoon freshly ground black
  pepper

In a large bowl combine all the ingredients. Toss to mix and turn into a
greased casserole. Cover and bake at 350° until tender, about 45 minutes
to 1 hour.

Salads

MACARONI SALAD
(American)

Fine addition to any picnic, salad bar, or buffet. Add a couple of cans of drained tuna fish for a luncheon main dish to serve six.
Makes 10 servings.

1 pound small shell macaroni, cooked according to package directions and drained
1 cup mayonnaise or salad dressing
1 container (8 ounces) plain yogurt
¾ cup milk
2 teaspoons salt
½ teaspoon freshly ground black pepper

2 tablespoons chopped fresh chives, or 2 teaspoons freeze-dried
2 cups sliced celery
1 green pepper, seeded and diced
1 medium-size red onion, thinly sliced and separated into rings

1. In a large bowl combine all the ingredients. Toss and chill.
2. Serve in a lettuce-lined bowl, if you wish.

CAESAR SALAD
(Mexican)

There has been a lot of controversy on exactly where and how Caesar salad was created but it does not affect the enjoyment of the end product.
Makes 6 servings.

¼ cup olive or vegetable oil
2 cloves garlic, crushed
2 cups small bread cubes (crouton size)
3 tablespoons lemon juice
8 flat anchovy fillets, finely chopped or mashed
½ teaspoon salt
¼ teaspoon freshly ground black pepper

¼ teaspoon dry mustard
½ teaspoon Worcestershire sauce
3 quarts torn romaine lettuce leaves
1 egg, coddled, or cooked 1 minute
½ cup (2 ounces) freshly grated Parmesan

1. Place the oil in a cup and add the garlic. Let stand at room temperature overnight. Remove and discard the garlic.
2. Heat oil in a skillet and cook the bread cubes until golden and crisp, stirring often. Drain on paper towels.
3. Mash the anchovies with the lemon juice in the bottom of a large salad bowl. Add the salt, pepper, mustard, and Worcestershire.
4. Add the greens and mix. Break the egg over and mix again. Sprinkle with the cheese and reserved garlic croutons.

MOLDED DILL SALAD
(Italian)

In general, I do not like gelatin salads but this proves to be the exception—it is delicious and an attractive addition to a summer buffet.
Makes 8 servings.

1 envelope unflavored gelatin
½ cup cold water
8 hard-cooked eggs, coarsely chopped
1 bunch green onions, chopped, including the green part
1 cucumber, halved, seeded, and diced
1 small zucchini, diced
½ green pepper, seeded and diced
⅓ cup chopped fresh parsley
1 clove garlic, finely chopped
2 cups mayonnaise
2 teaspoons Dijon mustard
1 tablespoon snipped fresh dillweed
1½ teaspoons salt
¼ teaspoon freshly ground black pepper
Lettuce leaves

1. Sprinkle the gelatin over the cold water and let soak 5 minutes. Heat the mixture until gelatin dissolves.
2. In a large bowl combine the eggs, green onions, cucumber, zucchini, green pepper, and parsley.
3. In a small bowl combine the garlic, mayonnaise, mustard, dill, salt, pepper, and dissolved gelatin. Mix well. Stir into the egg mixture and turn into an oiled one-quart mold. Chill several hours or overnight. Turn out onto a bed of lettuce leaves.

FIESTA SALAD
(Mexican)

This salad can be served instead of a dessert after a Mexican combination plate of, say, Swiss-style Enchiladas (page 176), Bean Croquettes (page 198), and Chili-and-Cheese-Stuffed Peppers (page 209).
Makes 8 servings.

⅓ cup red wine vinegar
⅓ cup vegetable oil
3 tablespoons sugar
½ teaspoon salt
6 cups shredded romaine, leaf, or iceberg lettuce
1 can (1 pound) tiny beets, drained
2 ripe bananas, sliced

2 navel oranges, peeled and sliced
½ fresh pineapple, peeled, cored, and cut into chunks
1 avocado, peeled, pitted, and sliced
½ cup dry-roasted peanuts
2 limes, cut into wedges

1. In a screw-cap jar combine the vinegar, oil, sugar, and salt and shake until sugar is dissolved.
2. Arrange the lettuce on a platter. Top with the beets, bananas, orange slices, pineapple, and avocado to make an attractive pattern.
3. Pour over the dressing, sprinkle with the peanuts, and garnish with lime wedges. Serve immediately.

GREEK SALAD WITH FETA AND OLIVES

Serve this salad with Moussaka (see page 202) for a satisfying and delicious meal.
Makes 8 servings.

2 red onions, thinly sliced and separated into rings
2 tablespoons wine vinegar
1 teaspoon salt
1 head of romaine, shredded
3 large tomatoes, peeled and chopped
1 cucumber, peeled, if waxed, seeded and chopped
1 green pepper, seeded and diced
2 stalks celery with leaves, diced
1 bunch radishes, sliced

½ cup oil-cured black olives
2 cups (8 ounces) crumbled feta cheese
2 tablespoons wine vinegar
2 tablespoons lemon juice
1 tablespoon Dijon mustard
½ teaspoon sugar
1 cup olive or vegetable oil
½ teaspoon salt
¼ teaspoon freshly ground black pepper

1. Place the onion rings and vinegar in a glass or wooden bowl. Sprinkle with the salt, toss to coat, and using your hands, work the onion, vinegar, and salt together for several minutes. Let stand 20 minutes.
2. Add the romaine, tomatoes, cucumber, green pepper, celery, radishes, olives, and feta to the onion rings. Toss to mix.
3. In a small bowl or screw-cap jar beat together or shake the vinegar, lemon juice, mustard, sugar, oil, salt, and pepper.
4. Pour over the salad and toss. Serve immediately.

MIXED MARINATED VEGETABLES
(Italian)

You've seen those big glass jars of exquisitely arranged marinated vegetables in Italian delis; here's a similar mélange to enjoy.
Makes 6 servings.

¼ pound green beans, trimmed and cut into 1-inch lengths
¼ pound wax beans, trimmed and cut into 1-inch lengths
¼ pound mushrooms, sliced (1 cup)
1 small cucumber, peeled if waxed, halved, seeded, and diced
1 stalk celery, sliced
1 small green pepper, seeded and sliced

1 small red onion, sliced
2 cups cooked dried chick-peas, or 1 can (1 pound, 4 ounces) chick-peas, rinsed and drained
½ cup olive or vegetable oil
½ cup red wine vinegar
1 clove garlic
½ teaspoon salt
¼ teaspoon freshly ground black pepper
1 teaspoon Italian herbs

1. Steam the green and wax beans over boiling water for 8 minutes. Drain and plunge into ice water.
2. Drain beans and put into a medium-size bowl with the mushrooms, cucumber, celery, green pepper, onion, and chick-peas.
3. In a screw-cap jar or bottle combine the oil, vinegar, garlic, salt, pepper, and Italian herbs. Shake to mix. Pour over vegetables, toss, and chill 2 to 6 hours.

LEBANESE VEGETABLE SALAD

Fresh mint is the important ingredient in this unusual spinach
salad.
Makes 6 servings.

3 medium-size carrots, shredded
2 small zucchini, cut into julienne
   strips
1 stalk celery, thinly sliced
¼ pound mushrooms, sliced (1 cup)
2 to 3 cups spinach leaves (one
   10-ounce bag, well trimmed)
½ cup red onion rings
1 cup finely chopped fresh parsley
¼ cup finely chopped fresh mint

½ cup olive or vegetable oil
¼ cup lemon juice
¼ teaspoon salt
⅛ teaspoon freshly ground black
   pepper
1 clove garlic, crushed
1 hard-cooked egg, shelled and
   sliced
2 tomatoes, cut into wedges

1. In a large salad bowl combine the carrot, zucchini, celery, mushrooms, spinach, onion, parsley, and mint.
2. In a screw-top jar or bottle combine the oil, lemon juice, salt, pepper,
   and garlic. Shake to mix well.
3. Just before serving shake dressing, discard garlic, and pour over
   vegetables. Toss and garnish with egg and tomato.

TABBOULEH
(Armenian Grain Salad)

This is one dish that should not be attempted if fresh mint is
unavailable. Great to take on a picnic.
Makes 8 servings.

1 cup bulgur (cracked wheat)
2 cups boiling water
½ teaspoon salt
1 bunch green onions, finely
   chopped
2 cucumbers, peeled, halved,
   seeded, and sliced
1 large green pepper, seeded and
   diced
1 stalk celery, finely diced

1 cup chopped fresh parsley
   (Italian flat variety, if available)
1 cup chopped fresh mint (mix
   several varieties, if available)
3 tomatoes, peeled and chopped
½ cup olive or vegetable oil
½ cup lemon juice
1½ to 2 teaspoons salt
¼ teaspoon freshly ground black
   pepper

1. Place the bulgur in a medium-size bowl. Pour boiling water over and stir in the salt. Let stand 15 minutes, drain, and squeeze dry.
2. In a plastic or crockery container combine the soaked bulgur with all the ingredients except the oil, lemon juice, salt, and pepper.
3. Mix the oil, lemon juice, salt, and pepper together and pour over the salad. Toss to mix, cover, and chill overnight. Check salad for seasoning before serving.

VEGETABLE SALAD
WITH HERBED DRESSING
(American)

Raw vegetables are so attractive and delicious to eat that it is always difficult to choose which ones to include. Make up your own selection for the piquant herb dressing.
Makes 8 servings.

2 medium-size zucchini, grated coarsely or cut into julienne strips
1 green pepper, seeded and diced
1 red pepper, seeded and diced
1 cup tiny broccoli flowerets
1 cup tiny cauliflowerets
2 carrots, cut into julienne strips
1 bunch radishes, thinly sliced
Boston lettuce leaves

Dressing

1 tablespoon Dijon mustard
¼ cup red wine vinegar
1 egg
6 green onions, sliced
1 clove garlic
½ teaspoon salt
¼ teaspoon freshly ground black pepper
1 teaspoon Italian herbs
1 cup vegetable oil
1 tablespoon finely chopped fresh parsley (Italian flat variety, if available)

1. Combine the zucchini, green and red peppers, broccoli, cauliflower, carrots, and radishes in a large bowl.
2. For the dressing put all the ingredients except the oil and parsley in the container of an electric blender or food processor. Whirl to mix thoroughly. With the blender still running gradually add the oil, a drop at a time, through the cover until mixture thickens. Toward the end the oil can be added a little quicker once the emulsion has been formed. Stir in the parsley.
3. Toss vegetables with dressing and arrange in a lettuce-lined salad bowl. Or you can arrange the vegetables in concentric circles on a lettuce-lined round platter and serve the dressing separately.

MEXICAN SALAD

Serve with eggs (Huevos Rancheros, page 158) for brunch.
Makes 8 servings.

1 large avocado, peeled, pitted, and diced
3 tomatoes, peeled, seeded, and chopped
1 cucumber, peeled, seeded, and diced
3 stalks celery, diced
1 large red onion, sliced and separated into rings
1 green pepper, seeded and diced
1 red pepper, seeded and diced
1 bunch radishes, sliced
1 cup young fresh peas or thawed frozen

2 tablespoons chopped fresh cilantro (Chinese parsley) or flat Italian parsley
¼ cup white wine vinegar
¾ cup olive or vegetable oil
1 clove garlic, finely chopped
1 teaspoon salt
2 jalapeño peppers (from a 4-ounce can), seeded and chopped
6 cups shredded iceberg lettuce
2 cups broken corn chips or fried tortillas

1. In a large bowl combine the avocado, tomatoes, cucumber, celery, onion, green and red peppers, radishes, peas, and cilantro. Toss lightly.
2. In a small bowl or screw-cap jar combine the vinegar, oil, garlic, salt, and jalapeño peppers and beat or shake to mix.
3. Pour dressing over vegetables and toss gently. Arrange lettuce on a large platter, top with vegetables, and garnish with chips. Serve immediately.

BEET AND ONION SALAD
(Swedish)

This is a must on a buffet or smorgasbord table.
Makes 8 servings.

2 bunches fresh beets (8 to 10)
2 sweet Spanish or Bermuda onions
¾ cup white wine vinegar

2 tablespoons sugar
2 tablespoons snipped fresh dillweed

1. Cut off the leaves of the beets, leaving 1 to 2 inches of stem. Use leaves in a salad or sauté and serve as cooked greens. Place beets in a saucepan and cover with boiling salted water. Cover and simmer 30 to 45 minutes, or until tender. Drain and cool.
2. When beets are cool rub off the skins and slice into a serving bowl. Slice the onions, separate into rings, and add to beets. Combine the vinegar, sugar, and dill and shake or beat until sugar has dissolved. Pour over beets.
3. Cover and chill several hours or overnight.

BEAN SALAD
(American)

This is a great salad to take to a picnic provided you keep it cold until it is served. In fact, I often carry the dressing in an insulated container and toss it at the picnic.
Makes 6 servings.

1 cup dried kidney, pinto, or cranberry beans, or chick-peas (½ pound)
5 cups water
1 medium-size carrot, diced (1 cup)
1 stalk celery with leaves, diced (about 1 cup)
1 small zucchini, diced (about 1 cup)
1 cup (about 4 ounces) diced Muenster

½ cup mayonnaise
¼ cup sour cream or plain yogurt
2 tablespoons finely chopped green onion
1 tablespoon Dijon mustard
½ teaspoon salt
¼ teaspoon freshly ground black pepper
3 cups broken raw spinach leaves or leaf romaine or Bibb lettuce

1. Pick over and wash the beans or peas. Place in a bowl, cover with the water, and let stand overnight. Transfer to a kettle or Dutch oven and bring to a boil. Cover and simmer 50 minutes, or until beans are tender but not mushy.
2. Drain beans and chill. Combine chilled beans with the carrot, celery, zucchini, and cheese.
3. Meanwhile combine the mayonnaise, sour cream, onion, mustard, salt, and pepper in a screw-top jar or small bowl. Shake or whisk to mix.
4. Place the spinach or lettuce in a large salad bowl. Top with bean mixture. Pour over dressing, toss to mix, and serve immediately.

DILLED CARROT AND ZUCCHINI SALAD
(*American*)

A couple of colorful vegetables, shredded and tossed with a simple dressing, is the kind of salad that complements a dinner meal.
Makes 6 servings.

3 medium-size carrots, coarsely grated or shredded
3 medium-size zucchini, coarsely grated or shredded
¼ cup finely chopped red onion
½ cup olive or vegetable oil
2 tablespoons lemon juice

½ teaspoon salt
¼ teaspoon freshly ground black pepper
2 tablespoons snipped fresh dillweed
Lettuce leaves

1. In a medium-size bowl combine the carrots, zucchini, and red onion. Put the oil, lemon juice, salt, pepper, and dill in a screw-cap jar and shake to blend.
2. Pour dressing over vegetables and toss to mix. Check the seasoning. Chill 2 to 4 hours and serve in lettuce cups.

CELERIAC REMOULADE
(*French Celery Root*)

Celery root is not in every market but it is well worth seeking out, growing, or asking a friend to pick up from the big city. Makes a great first course, if you prefer.
Makes 6 servings.

2 egg yolks
2 tablespoons Dijon mustard
3 tablespoons lemon juice
⅛ teaspoon liquid red pepper seasoning
1 teaspoon salt
¼ teaspoon freshly ground black pepper

1 cup olive or vegetable oil
2 teaspoons grated onion
3 medium-size celery roots, peeled and shredded coarsely or cut into very fine julienne strips

1. Place the egg yolks, mustard, 1 tablespoon of the lemon juice, liquid red pepper seasoning, salt, and pepper into the container of an electric blender or a small bowl.
2. Whirl or beat until smooth and while whirling or beating vigorously add the oil drop by drop until mixture thickens into a mayonnaise consistency. The oil can be added a little more quickly toward the end.
3. Beat in the grated onion and remaining lemon juice and use the sauce to moisten the celeriac. Chill well.

CHICK-PEAS VINAIGRETTE
(French)

Whether you call them chick-peas, garbanzos, or cecci, they are international. Cheese is added here to make a heartier salad to go with soup, sandwich, or light main course.
Makes 6 servings.

2 cans (20 ounces each) chick-peas, drained and rinsed
1 large red onion, thinly sliced and separated into rings
1 cup (4 ounces) tiny cubes Gruyère or Swiss
⅔ cup olive or vegetable oil
¼ cup red wine vinegar
1 clove garlic, crushed
¼ teaspoon salt
⅛ teaspoon freshly ground black pepper
¼ cup finely chopped fresh chives, or 4 teaspoons freeze-dried
¼ cup chopped fresh parsley
1 hard-cooked egg
2 tablespoons drained capers, optional

1. Place the chick-peas, onion rings, and cheese in a medium-size bowl.
2. In a screw-cap jar combine the oil, vinegar, garlic, salt, pepper, chives, parsley, chopped white of the egg, and the capers. Shake to mix.
3. Pour enough of the dressing over the salad to coat when tossed. Cover and chill several hours. Serve in lettuce-lined bowl with finely sieved egg yolk as a garnish.

CHICK-PEA AND RICE SALAD
(Italian)

Serve a hearty soup first, this salad with crusty garlic bread for
the main course, and add cheese and fresh fruit for dessert.
Makes 6 servings.

¾ cup olive or vegetable oil
¼ cup red wine vinegar
2 tablespoons lemon juice
½ teaspoon salt
¼ teaspoon freshly ground black
  pepper
1 clove garlic, crushed
¼ teaspoon crushed hot red pepper
  flakes
4 cups cold cooked rice (1¼ cups
  raw)
1 can (1 pound, 4 ounces)
  chick-peas, drained

1 large green pepper, seeded and
  chopped
2 stalks celery, chopped
1 pint cherry tomatoes, halved
1 can (15 ounces) pitted black
  olives, sliced
3 tablespoons chopped fresh
  parsley
2 hard-cooked eggs, sliced,
  optional

1. In a screw-cap jar or a small bowl combine the oil, vinegar, lemon
   juice, salt, pepper, garlic, and red pepper flakes. Shake or beat to
   blend.
2. In a salad serving bowl combine the rice, chick-peas, green pepper,
   celery, tomatoes, olives, and parsley. Toss. Add dressing to moisten
   and chill several hours. Garnish with egg slices, if you wish.

COLESLAW
(American)

Old-fashioned boiled dressing makes the kind of coleslaw I
prefer.
Makes 8 servings.

2 tablespoons flour
1½ tablespoons sugar
1 teaspoon salt
1 teaspoon dry mustard
⅛ teaspoon cayenne
1 egg, lightly beaten
¾ cup milk
2 tablespoons butter or margarine

¼ cup cider vinegar
1 medium-size head of cabbage,
  shredded (about 6 cups)
1 small green pepper, seeded and
  chopped
1 small red pepper, seeded and
  chopped
1 teaspoon salt

1. In the top of a double boiler combine the flour, sugar, salt, mustard, and cayenne. Mix the egg with the milk and stir into the dry ingredients in the double boiler.
2. Cook over simmering water until mixture thickens. Stir in butter and vinegar. Cool.
3. In a large salad bowl combine the cabbage, green and red peppers, and salt. Pour in enough of the cooled dressing to coat. Toss and chill.

CORN SALAD
(*American*)

In an all-vegetarian meal it is sometimes necessary to boost the protein content through the addition of dairy foods, and here is a fine suggestion.
Makes 6 servings.

2 cups corn kernels, cut from about 3 cobs, or drained canned, or frozen
1 container (1 pound) small-curd cottage cheese
1 small green pepper, seeded and diced
1 small red pepper, seeded and diced
1 tablespoon chopped fresh chives, or 1 teaspoon freeze-dried
1 tablespoon chopped fresh parsley
1 teaspoon salt
¼ teaspoon freshly ground black pepper
Lettuce cups

1. Steam the fresh or frozen corn kernels over boiling salted water for 3 minutes. Drain and cool.
2. In a large bowl combine the corn, cottage cheese, green and red peppers, chives, parsley, salt, and pepper. Chill and serve in lettuce cups.

SU-NO-MO-NO
(Japanese Cucumber and Radish Salad)

Crisp and pungent, this combination of raw vegetables can accompany main dishes from many cuisines.
Makes 4 servings.

2 cucumbers	2 tablespoons sesame seeds
1 stalk celery	½ cup lemon juice
2 white radishes	1 teaspoon soy sauce
1 tablespoon salt	

1. Peel cucumbers, if waxed. Otherwise score skins with a fork. Cut in half, remove seeds, and cut into julienne strips.
2. Slice celery and radishes diagonally. Place cucumber, celery, and radishes in a bowl and sprinkle with the salt. Toss to mix and let stand 2 hours. Meanwhile toast the sesame seeds in a small dry skillet over low heat, shaking frequently, until golden. Cool.
3. Squeeze the water out of the vegetables, a handful at a time, and place them in a colander. Rinse with cold water and squeeze out extra water. Place in serving bowl.
4. Add lemon juice and soy sauce. Sprinkle with sesame seeds.

CUCUMBERS IN SOUR CREAM
(Swedish)

Excellent with poached salmon.
Makes 6 servings.

¾ cup sour cream or plain yogurt
1 tablespoon lemon juice
1 teaspoon sugar
1 teaspoon salt
¼ teaspoon freshly ground black
 pepper
2 tablespoons snipped fresh
 dillweed

3 medium-size cucumbers, peeled
 if waxed or tough, halved, seeds
 removed, and thinly sliced
1 red onion, thinly sliced and
 separated into rings

1. In a small bowl combine the sour cream, lemon juice, sugar, salt, pepper, and dill.
2. Place the cucumbers and onion rings in a medium-size bowl and add the sour cream dressing. Toss to coat, cover, and chill at least 2 hours.

EGGPLANT RAITA
(Indian)

Serve as an accompaniment to curry or as a salad.
Bake at 325° for 20 minutes.
Makes 4 to 6 servings.

1 medium-size eggplant (about 1½
 pounds)
2 tablespoons vegetable oil
1 medium-size onion, finely
 chopped (½ cup)
1 to 2 teaspoons curry powder

⅛ teaspoon chili powder
2 teaspoons lemon juice
1 teaspoon salt
2 containers (8 ounces each) plain
 yogurt

1. Prick the eggplant, place directly on oven rack, and bake in an oven preheated to 325° for 20 minutes or until soft.
2. Meanwhile heat the oil in a small skillet and sauté the onion until soft but not browned. Sprinkle with curry powder and chili powder and cook, stirring, 1 minute.
3. Cut the eggplant in half and scoop the pulp into a medium-size bowl. Add the onion mixture, lemon juice, salt, and yogurt. Chill several hours.

LENTIL SALAD
(French)

It is amazing how many cuisines around the world use lentils extensively. They do not have to be soaked like most dried pulses and they absorb flavors from dressings and sauces quickly.
Makes 6 servings.

1½ cups lentils
 3 cups water
 1 bay leaf
 1 onion, peeled and studded with 2 whole cloves
 ¾ teaspoon salt
 ⅓ cup olive or vegetable oil
 2 tablespoons lemon juice
 ⅛ teaspoon dry mustard
 1 small clove garlic, finely chopped
 ½ teaspoon Worcestershire sauce
 2 drops liquid red pepper seasoning

 ⅛ teaspoon freshly ground black pepper
 2 tablespoons chopped fresh chives, or 2 teaspoons freeze-dried
 2 tablespoons chopped fresh parsley
 1 small red onion, sliced and separated into rings
 2 hard-cooked eggs, shelled and sliced

1. Pick over and wash the lentils and place in a heavy kettle or Dutch oven. Add water, bay leaf, and onion and bring to a boil. Cover and simmer 35 minutes, or until lentils are barely tender.
2. Drain off excess liquid and remove and discard the bay leaf and onion. Add the salt. In a small bowl or screw-top jar combine the oil, lemon juice, mustard, garlic, Worcestershire, red pepper seasoning, and pepper.
3. Pour dressing over hot lentils and stir in the chives. Cover and chill overnight or several hours.
4. Stir in the parsley. Arrange in a lettuce-lined bowl and garnish with onion rings and egg slices.

LIMA BEAN SALAD
(Finnish)

Mustard, dill, and anchovies do marvelous things for lima
beans in this salad, which I like to serve with fish.
Makes 8 servings.

1 container (8 ounces) sour cream
1 tablespoon lemon juice
2 teaspoons Düsseldorf mustard
½ teaspoon salt
⅛ teaspoon freshly ground black
pepper
2 tablespoons snipped fresh
dillweed

3 cups cooked fresh fava beans, or
2 packages (10 ounces each)
frozen baby lima beans, cooked
according to package directions
and cooled
3 flat anchovy fillets, chopped
Lettuce leaves

In a medium-size bowl combine the sour cream, lemon juice, mustard,
salt, pepper, and dill. Add the cooled cooked beans and anchovies. Chill
well before serving on a bed of lettuce.

MUSHROOM SALAD
(French)

Raw mushrooms in a mustard dressing is food fit for a king or a
joy for anyone.
Makes 6 servings.

3 tablespoons lemon juice
⅓ cup Dijon mustard
½ teaspoon salt
¼ teaspoon freshly ground black
pepper

¼ teaspoon leaf thyme, crumbled
½ cup olive or vegetable oil
1 pound mushrooms, sliced
(4 cups)
Boston lettuce cups

1. In a small bowl put the lemon juice, mustard, salt, pepper, and
   thyme. With a whisk beat in the oil slowly until the mixture thickens.
2. Add the mushrooms, toss, and chill. Serve in lettuce cups.

HOT POTATO AND ONION SALAD
(Spanish)

Delicious with hot or cold chicken.
Bake at 425° for 1 hour.
Makes 6 servings.

6 Idaho (baking) potatoes,
  scrubbed
6 Spanish or Bermuda onions,
  skins left on
½ cup olive or vegetable oil

1 clove garlic, crushed
2 tablespoons red wine vinegar
1½ teaspoons salt
½ teaspoon freshly ground black
  pepper

1. Bake the potatoes and onions at 425° directly on the oven shelf until
    tender, about 1 hour. Remove onions if they cook more quickly.
2. Meanwhile mix oil, garlic, vinegar, salt, and pepper in a screw-cap
    jar.
3. Skin and slice or chop onions into a serving bowl. Peel potatoes and
    slice or dice into the bowl with the onions. Remove garlic from dress-
    ing and pour dressing over hot vegetables. Toss and serve.

GERMAN POTATO SALAD

Sweet-and-sour ingredients, beer, and sour cream make this
warm salad hearty winter fare.
Makes 4 servings.

2 pounds red-skinned or new
  potatoes, scrubbed
3 tablespoons butter or margarine
1 large onion, chopped (1 cup)
2 tablespoons vinegar
¼ teaspoon dry mustard
½ teaspoon salt
¼ teaspoon freshly ground black
  pepper

1 teaspoon sugar
½ cup beer or broth
1 large green pepper, seeded and
  diced
1 cup peeled diced cucumber
1 container (8 ounces) sour cream
  or plain yogurt

1. Cook the potatoes in boiling salted water to cover until barely tender,
    about 20 minutes, depending on size. Drain and slice into a
    medium-size bowl.
2. Meanwhile heat the butter in a skillet and sauté the onion until
    tender but not browned. Add the vinegar, mustard, salt, pepper,
    sugar, and broth. Stir and heat. Pour over hot potato slices and toss to
    coat. Add the green pepper and cucumber and stir in the sour cream.
    Serve while still warm.

POTATO SALAD
(American)

The secret of a good potato salad lies in the marinating liquid poured over the hot cooked potatoes.
Makes 8 servings.

2 tablespoons lemon juice
1 tablespoon Worcestershire sauce
¼ teaspoon liquid red pepper seasoning
⅓ cup olive or vegetable oil
1 clove garlic, finely chopped
¼ teaspoon salt
⅛ teaspoon freshly ground black pepper
6 cups cubed hot cooked potatoes
6 hard-cooked eggs
1 container (8 ounces) sour cream

½ cup mayonnaise
⅓ cup chopped green onions, including the green part
3 tablespoons chopped fresh parsley
3 tablespoons chopped dill pickle
1 red pepper, seeded and diced
1½ tablespoons Dijon mustard
1½ teaspoons salt
¼ teaspoon freshly ground black pepper
1½ cups chopped celery

1. In a small bowl or screw-top jar combine the lemon juice, Worcestershire, red pepper seasoning, oil, garlic, salt, and pepper. Whisk or shake to mix and pour over hot potatoes. Toss to mix. Cover and chill.
2. Chop 4 of the eggs. In a medium-size bowl combine the sour cream, mayonnaise, green onion, parsley, dill pickle, red pepper, mustard, salt, and pepper.
3. Stir sour cream mixture into chilled potatoes along with chopped eggs and celery. Slice or quarter remaining eggs for a garnish.

DAIKON SALAD
(Japanese White Radish Salad)

Makes 6 servings.

1 teaspoon grated fresh ginger root, or ¼ teaspoon ground
1 green onion, finely chopped, including the green part
2 tablespoons sesame seeds, toasted in a small dry skillet over low heat, cooled, and ground in a coffee mill or blender
¼ cup rice vinegar or white wine vinegar

1 tablespoon sugar
2 tablespoons soy sauce
¼ teaspoon salt
1 large (about 1 pound) white radish (daikon), coarsely grated
Watercress, shredded lettuce, or spinach leaves

1. In a small bowl combine the ginger, green onion, ground sesame seeds, vinegar, sugar, soy sauce, and salt. Beat until smooth.
2. Add the radish and toss to coat. Arrange on watercress or lettuce.

SAUERKRAUT SALAD
(German)

Goes together in a jiffy the night before; just the answer for the busy working person.
Makes 6 servings.

1 can (29 ounces) sauerkraut, drained, rinsed, and drained
1 small onion, finely chopped (¼ cup)
2 medium-size red-skinned apples, cored and diced

2 stalks celery, diced
1 green pepper, seeded and diced
1 sweet red pepper, seeded and diced
½ cup sugar

Combine all the ingredients in a glass or pottery bowl, cover, and chill overnight.

WILTED SPINACH SALAD
(American)

An unusual hot salad that is a welcome addition to any simple
chicken dish.
Makes 4 servings.

3 tablespoons vegetable oil
½ cup finely chopped green onion
1 clove garlic, finely chopped
¼ pound button mushrooms
1 pound fresh spinach, trimmed,
washed, and drained

1 tablespoon lemon juice
¾ teaspoon salt
Pinch of ground nutmeg

1. In a large skillet or wok heat the oil and stir-fry the green onion until
   wilted, about 1 minute. Add the garlic and mushrooms and stir-fry 3
   minutes.
2. Add the spinach and stir-fry until wilted, about 2 minutes. Stir in the
   lemon juice, salt, and nutmeg.

ZUCCHINI RAITA
(Indian)

An excellent accompaniment to all of the curries in the fish,
chicken, and vegetable sections.
Makes 4 servings.

2 containers (8 ounces each) plain
yogurt
¼ cup finely chopped green onion

1 teaspoon ground cumin
1 teaspoon salt
4 small zucchini, finely grated

Combine all the ingredients and chill well before serving as an accompaniment to curry or as a salad on lettuce leaves.

ZUCCHINI SALAD
(American)

Yogurt dressings are tangy yet creamy and have fewer calories than those made with sour cream.
Makes 6 servings.

2 medium-size zucchini, cut into julienne strips or coarsely shredded
¼ pound mushrooms, thinly sliced (1 cup)
¼ cup finely chopped red onion
½ cup finely chopped celery heart with leaves
¼ cup finely chopped fresh parsley
1 small red pepper, seeded and finely diced

¼ cup olive or vegetable oil
2 tablespoons lemon juice
½ cup plain yogurt
½ teaspoon salt
¼ teaspoon freshly ground black pepper
Lettuce leaves
¼ cup alfalfa sprouts

1. Combine the zucchini, mushrooms, onion, celery, parsley, and red pepper in a medium-size bowl.
2. In a small bowl whisk together the oil, lemon juice, yogurt, salt, and pepper. Pour over vegetables and chill 2 to 3 hours.
3. Serve in lettuce cups or in a lettuce-lined salad bowl, topped with alfalfa sprouts.

Bibliography

Adam, Catherine. *Nutritive Values of American Foods in Common Units.* Washington, D.C.: USDA Agricultural Handbook No. 456, 1975.

Beard, James. *Beard on Bread.* New York: Alfred A. Knopf, 1973.

Bogert, Lotta Jean, George M. Briggs, and Doritt Calloway. *Nutrition and Physical Fitness,* 9th Edition. Philadelphia: W. B. Saunders Company, 1973.

Brooks, Karen. *The Forget About Meat Cookbook.* Emmaus, Pa.: Rodale Press, 1974.

Brown, Edward Espe. *The Tassajara Bread Book.* Berkeley, Calif.: Shambhala Publications, Inc., 1970.

_____. *Tassajara Cooking.* Berkeley, Calif.: Shambhala Publications, Inc., 1973.

Clayton, Bernard. *The Breads of France.* Indianapolis: Bobbs-Merrill, 1978.

_____. *The Complete Book of Breads.* New York: Simon & Schuster, 1973.

Ewald, Ellen Buchman. *Recipes for a Small Planet.* New York: Ballantine Books, 1973.

Hooker, Alan. *Vegetarian Gourmet.* San Francisco: 101 Productions, 1970.

Jordan, Julie. *Wings of Life.* Trumansburg, N.Y.: The Crossing Press, 1976.

Lappé, Francis Moore. *Diet for a Small Planet,* 2nd Edition. New York: Ballantine Books, 1975.

London, Mel. *Bread Winners.* Emmaus, Pa.: Rodale Press, 1979.

Mayer, Jean. *A Diet for Living.* New York: McKay, 1975.

Robertson, Laurel, Carol Flinders, and Bronwen Godfrey. *Laurel's Kitchen.* Berkeley, Calif.: Nilgiri Press, 1976. New York: Bantam Books, 6th Printing, 1978.

Seranne, Ann. *Good Food Without Meat.* New York: William Morrow, 1973.

Thomas, Anna. *The Vegetarian Epicure.* New York: Borzoi Book, Alfred A. Knopf, 1972.

_____. *The Vegetarian Epicure Book II.* New York: Borzoi Book, Alfred A. Knopf, 1978.

Watt, Bernice K., and Annabel L. Merrill. *Handbook No. 8: Composition of Foods: Raw, Processed, Prepared.* Washington, D.C.: USDA, 1964.

Metric Conversion Tables

TEMPERATURES

Fahrenheit°/Celsius°	(Actual Celsius°)	Fahrenheit°/Celsius°	(Actual Celsius°)
−5°F/−20°C	(−20.6°C)	180°F/82°C	(82.2°C)
32°F/0°C	(0°C)	190°F/88°C	(87.8°C)
37°F/3°C	(2.8°C)	200°F/95°C	(93.3°C)
50°F/10°C	(10°C)	205°F/96°C	(96.1°C)
60°F/16°C	(15.6°C)	212°F/100°C	(100°C)
70°F/21°C	(21.1°C)	225°F/110°C	(107.2°C)
75°F/24°C	(23.9°C)	228°F/109°C	(108.9°C)
80°F/27°C	(26.7°C)	238°F/115°C	(114.4°C)
85°F/29°C	(29.4°C)	250°F/120°C	(121.1°C)
100°F/38°C	(37.8°C)	275°F/135°C	(135°C)
105°F/41°C	(40.6°C)	285°F/140°C	(140.6°C)
110°F/43°C	(43.3°C)	300°F/150°C	(148.9°C)
115°F/46°C	(46.1°C)	325°F/165°C	(162.8°C)
120°F/49°C	(48.9°C)	350°F/180°C	(176.7°C)
125°F/52°C	(51.7°C)	375°F/190°C	(190.6°C)
130°F/54°C	(54.4°C)	400°F/205°C	(204.4°C)
135°F/57°C	(57.2°C)	425°F/220°C	(218.3°C)
140°F/60°C	(60°C)	450°F/230°C	(232.2°C)
150°F/66°C	(65.6°C)	475°F/245°C	(246.1°C)
160°F/71°C	(71.1°C)	500°F/260°C	(260°C)
165°F/74°C	(73.9°C)	525°F/275°C	(273.9°C)
170°F/77°C	(76.7°C)	550°F/290°C	(287.8°C)

POUNDS TO GRAMS AND KILOGRAMS

Pounds	Convenient Equivalent	Actual Weight
¼ lb	115 g	(113.4 g)
½ lb	225 g	(226.8 g)
¾ lb	340 g	(340.2 g)
1 lb	450 g	(453.6 g)
1¼ lb	565 g	(566.99 g)
1½ lb	675 g	(680.4 g)
1¾ lb	800 g	(794 g)
2 lb	900 g	(908 g)
2½ lb	1125 g; 1¼ kg	(1134 g)
3 lb	1350 g	(1360 g)
3½ lb	1500 g; 1½ kg	(1588 g)
4 lb	1800 g	(1814 g)
4½ lb	2 kg	(2041 g)
5 lb	2¼ kg	(2268 g)
5½ lb	2½ kg	(2495 g)
6 lb	2¾ kg	(2727 g)
7 lb	3¼ kg	(3175 g)
8 lb	3½ kg	(3629 g)
9 lb	4 kg	(4028 g)
10 lb	4½ kg	(4536 g)
12 lb	5½ kg	(5443 g)
14 lb	6¼ kg	(6350 g)
15 lb	6¾ kg	(6804 g)
16 lb	7¼ kg	(7258 g)
18 lb	8 kg	(8165 g)
20 lb	9 kg	(9072 g)
25 lb	11¼ kg	(11,340 g)

OUNCES TO GRAMS

Ounces	Convenient Equivalent	Actual Weight
1 oz	30 g	(28.35 g)
2 oz	60 g	(56.7 g)
3 oz	85 g	(85.05 g)
4 oz	115 g	(113.4 g)
5 oz	140 g	(141.8 g)
6 oz	180 g	(170.1 g)
8 oz	225 g	(226.8 g)

Ounces	Convenient Equivalent	Actual Weight
9 oz	250 g	(255.2 g)
10 oz	285 g	(283.5 g)
12 oz	340 g	(340.2 g)
14 oz	400 g	(396.9 g)
16 oz	450 g	(453.6 g)
20 oz	560 g	(566.99 g)
24 oz	675 g	(680.4 g)

LIQUID MEASURE CONVERSIONS

Cups and Spoons	Liquid Ounces	Approximate Metric Term	Approximate Centiliters	Actual Milliliters
1 tsp	¹/₆ oz	1 tsp	½ cL	5 mL
1 Tb	½ oz	1 Tb	1½ cL	15 mL
¼ c; 4 Tb	2 oz	½ dL; 4 Tb	6 cL	59 mL
⅓ c; 5 Tb	2⅔ oz	¾ dL; 5 Tb	8 cL	79 mL
½ c	4 oz	1 dL	12 cL	119 mL
⅔ c	5⅓ oz	1½ dL	15 cL	157 mL
¾ c	6 oz	1¾ dL	18 cL	178 mL
1 c	8 oz	¼ L	24 cL	237 mL
1¼ c	10 oz	3 dL	30 cL	296 mL
1⅓ c	10⅔ oz	3¼ dL	33 cL	325 mL
1½ c	12 oz	3½ dL	35 cL	355 mL
1⅔ c	13⅓ oz	3¾ dL	39 cL	385 mL
1¾ c	14 oz	4 dL	41 cL	414 mL
2 c; 1 pt	16 oz	½ L	47 cL	473 mL
2½ c	20 oz	6 dL	60 cL	592 mL
3 c	24 oz	¾ L	70 cL	710 mL
3½ c	28 oz	⁴/₅ L; 8 dL	83 cL	829 mL
4 c; 1 qt	32 oz	1 L	95 cL	946 mL
5 c	40 oz	1¼ L	113 cL	1134 mL
6 c; 1½ qt	48 oz	1½ L	142 cL	1420 mL
8 c; 2 qt	64 oz	2 L	190 cL	1893 mL
10 c; 2½ qt	80 oz	2½ L	235 cL	2366 mL
12 c; 3 qt	96 oz	2¾ L	284 cL	2839 mL
4 qt	128 oz	3¾ L	375 cL	3785 mL
5 qt		4¾ L		
6 qt		5½ L (or 6 L)		
8 qt		7½ L (or 8 L)		

INCHES TO CENTIMETERS

Inches ("in")	Centimeters ("cm") (Nearest equivalent)
1/16 in	¼ cm
1/8 in	½ cm
3/16 in	"less than ¼ in/¾ cm"
¼ in	¾ in
3/8 in	1 cm
½ in	1½ in
5/8 in	1½ cm
¾ in	2 cm
1 in	2½ cm
1½ in	4 cm
2 in	5 cm
2½ in	6½ cm
3 in	8 cm
3½ in	9 cm
4 in	10 cm
5 in	13 cm
6 in	15 cm
7 in	18 cm
8 in	20 cm
9 in	23 cm
10 in	25 cm
12 in	30 cm
14 in	35 cm
15 in	38½ cm
16 in	40 cm
18 in	45 cm
20 in	50 cm
24 in	60 cm
30 in	75 cm

Index

COPY 1